Preparing Company Plans
A Workbook for Effective Corporate Planning

Preparing Company Plans

A Workbook for Effective Corporate Planning

HARRY JONES

A Gower Press Workbook

First published in Great Britain by Gower Press Limited, Epping, Essex, 1974

ISBN 0 7161 0198 X

Typeset by Amos Typesetters, Hockley, Essex, and printed in Great Britain at the
University Printing House, Cambridge

Contents

Foreword by Hugh Parker, Managing Director—UK, McKinsey & Company, Inc.   **xi**

Acknowledgements   **xiii**

1	**Introduction**	**1**
1.1	What is corporate planning?	3
1.2	Practical objects of the workbook	4
1.3	Who should see and read this workbook?	5
1.4	How to use this book	6
2	**Planning as a Function of Corporate Management**	**7**
2.1	Corporate planning as a management tool	9
2.2	Development and status of corporate planning	10
2.3	The role of the chief executive	11
2.4	The role of the corporate planner	13
2.5	How to introduce corporate planning to a company	14
2.6	How to develop corporate planning	15
3	**Corporate Planning Systems and Organization**	**19**
3.1	The basic model for all organizations	21
3.2	Kinds of plans	30
3.3	Planning levels	35
3.4	Planning periods	38
3.5	Organizing the corporate planning department	41
3.6	Job specifications in planning	46
4	**Practical Phases of Planning**	**49**
4.1	General remarks on the practical phases of planning	51
4.2	Basic corporate objectives, guidelines and policies	53
4.3	Information base	56
4.4	Opportunities, objectives and strategies	93
4.5	Action programmes	109

4.6 Budgets   111
4.7 Planning letters   115
4.8 Schedules in the annual planning cycle   117

5   Format and Presentation of Plans   161
5.1 General remarks   163
5.2 Parts of a plan   167
5.3 Unit plans   175
5.4 Coordination of unit plans and approvals   201

6   Monitoring and Control   207
6.1 General remarks   209
6.2 Format of control reports   210
6.3 Preparation and presentation of control reports   212
6.4 Variances   213
6.5 Frequency of reporting   214

Appendices
I   Standard Forms for Planning and Control Purposes   217
II   Technological Forecasting   245
III   Relationship between Annual Rate of Increase and Cumulative
       Increase over a Number of Years   249

Bibliography   251

Index   253

Illustrations

2.1   The role of the chief executive   12
3.1   Key factors in planning   22
3.2   Basic planning model for all organizations   23
3.3   Enlargement of Figure 3.2 showing contents of information base and of the long range outlook   24
3.4   Relationship of corporate development to the process of integrated management planning in the basic model for all organizations   28
3.5   Kinds of plans in a basic type of organization   32
3.6   Kinds of plans in a multi-divisional, multi-functional type of organization   32
3.7   Kinds of plans in a multi-divisional, multi-functional and multi-regional type of organization   33
3.8   Scheme of planning levels   36
3.9   Approaches to planning periods vary with different interests   39
3.10   Organization of corporate planning departments   42
3.11   Terms of reference for the corporate planner   44
3.12   Responsibilities of integrated management planner   47
3.13   Responsibilities of head of corporate development   47
4.1   Basic objectives, guidelines and policies   121
4.2   Information base: international indicators—check list for assumptions   123
4.3   Information base: actual changes in the principal national indicators as a basis for planning assumptions   124
4.4   Information base: actual changes in cost indicators as a basis for planning assumptions   125
4.5   Information base: actual changes in some major industry output indicators as a basis for planning assumptions   126
4.6   Information base: check list of general external indicators   127
4.7   Public sources of information on general external indicators   129
4.8   Information base: recent changes, planning assumptions and forecasts   130
4.9   Information base: sales of product groups to a sub-market (plastic materials to electric cable industry)   131
4.10   Information base: profitability of sales of product groups to a sub-market   132

4.11 Information base on: (1) land resources; (2) land uses; (3) buildings and capacity resources in production   133
4.12 Information base on production capacity analysis (using illustrative data)   135
4.13 Information base on personnel prepared for use at corporate level   136
4.14 Information base: check list on financial resources   137
4.15 Information base: strengths and weaknesses shown by financial ratios   138
4.16 Information base: strengths and weaknesses in research and development activities   139
4.17 Information base: strengths and weaknesses in production activities   140
4.18 Information base: strengths and weaknesses of product line   141
4.19 Information base: strengths and weaknesses in marketing activities   142
4.20 Information base: competitor analysis—prepared for hypothetical firm in manufacturing industry   143
4.21 Information base: summary profile of own and other party businesses: semi-quantitative comparison for acquisition study: illustrated for a market oriented activity   144
4.22 Information base: portrait of a business (text is approximate and for illustration only)   145
4.23 Who prepares which information base (including forecasts) and makes specific assumptions   146
4.24 Illustrations of business opportunities derived from the analysis of information bases   148
4.25 'What business are we in' and 'Opportunities for growth' (using illustrations for three cases)   150
4.26 Basic approaches to objectives   151
4.27 Scheme of profit objectives for the first cycle of planning (contributions from different units)   152
4.28 Strategy—outline courses of action   153
4.29 Standard format for action programmes   154
4.30 Essential contents of a planning letter   155
4.31 Planning letter number 1   156
4.32 Schedule of events in the annual planning cycle   158
4.33 Network scheme of events in the annual planning cycle (showing one business division only)   159
6.1 Summary control report (covering quarterly reports and new information)   211

APPENDIX I

Table of standard forms for planning and control purposes   218
Planning form P-1: summary of operating statement   221
Planning form B-1: operating statement   222
Planning form B-1-Q: operating statement for quarters in year 1   224
Control form C-1: operating statement   226
Planning form P-2: summary of sales   227
Planning form B-2: sales planning   228
Planning form B-2-1/5: sales planning for sub-markets   229
Planning form B-2-Q: sales planning for quarters in year 1   230
Control form C-2: sales   231
Planning form P-3: summary of assets   232
Planning form B-3-FA: fixed assets   233
Planning form B-3-CA: current assets   234
Planning form P-4: summary of capital expenditure projects   235
Planning form B-4: capital expenditure projects   236
Planning form B-4-Q: capital expenditure projects for quarters in year 1   237

Control form C-4: capital expenditure projects   238
Planning form P-5: summary of sources and use of funds   239
Planning form P-6: summary of balance sheet   240
Planning form P-7: summary of use of production capacity   241
Planning form B-7: production planning   242
Planning form B-8: personnel   243

Appendix II

The four elements of a comprehensive technological forecast and the methods
which contribute to them   246
Procedure for the initial deployment of technological forecasting in a firm   247
Further procedures for the updating of technological forecasting in corporate
planning   248

Appendix III

Relationship between annual rate of increase and cumulative increase over a
number of years   250

Foreword

Harry Jones, whom I have known for some ten years, has paid me the great compliment of inviting me to contribute a foreword to his new book on corporate planning, and it is with great pleasure that I do so. Having read this excellent book, on a subject that has been in some danger of being over-publicized and to some extent over-sold, I think there are three main points to be made in introducing it to all thoughtful readers.

First, Mr Jones has been an operating manager, and his corporate planning practices and precepts are therefore based on first-hand experience of the day-to-day realities of planning within a profitable enterprise. For some time there has been a real and growing danger that topics like corporate planning have become 'something learned at business school', and there is a possibility that its genuine relevance to real management problems could become lost in a welter of PhD theses. The author, I am glad to say, with his strong practical background, refutes the view that this is an esoteric field that the average manager need not worry about.

Second, the author's former company Geigy (or Ciba-Geigy as it is now) is a multi-national organization in every sense of that term, and the author has been faced with making corporate planning work in this more than usually difficult setting. I do not suggest for a moment that the typical company is faced, like Ciba-Geigy, with planning for five different product groups in fifteen or more countries where at least ten different languages are spoken. But if corporate planning of this kind can work for Ciba-Geigy, then this should be reassuring for executives faced with perhaps less complex corporate situations.

Finally, as the author explains, this is a *workbook* (as the title clearly reflects), a 'what do we do on Monday morning?' guide, and in no way an academic treatise—and in my personal view all the more useful for this action-oriented theme.

So by way of conclusion, I warmly recommend it both to senior executives and to students of management practice generally, who should not think that Mr Jones' advice is applicable only to the chemical industry. What he is saying—with some modifications, of course—can equally be applied to ship-building, confectionery manufacture, the transport industry and companies in many other industries. I sincerely hope and expect that all practising managers who read his book will benefit from his excellent advice.

Hugh Parker
Managing Director—UK
McKinsey & Company, Inc

Acknowledgements

It was only in the mid-1960s when corporate planning started to become a highly organized framework for management, that one realized how relatively amateurish had been our previous business methods and philosophy. Nevertheless, many of the basic principles had, tacitly or under other names, or even under no names at all, been used to varying degrees and on a less formal basis. We had, we hoped, followed the formula of 'applied common sense' which is applicable to so many management techniques but which are now more systematically and calculatingly applied.

For my earlier experiences and practical opportunities to develop corporate planning as an overall management method, I am grateful—not only to the management of the former company of J. R. Geigy SA, but to all my working colleagues and advisers. Amongst the latter I number my many friends and fellow members of the Society for Long Range Planning against whose wits and experience it was always a pleasure to engage in discussion and debate. I have learned much from them since the founding meetings of 1966.

My sincere thanks are again gladly given to the Basle management of the Geigy concern (now Ciba-Geigy SA) for their earlier agreement to the contribution of 'Integrated Management Planning in Geigy' to the book entitled *Case Studies in Corporate Planning* produced by the Society for Long Range Planning in which will be found the origin of the basic methodology which I have tried to develop and adapt in the present book for wider and more general application.

Further, and on a more personal basis, I wish to record my pleasure in working experiences with old colleagues—E. Zangger, C. Eugster, A. Bodmer and P. Schatzli in Basle, T. W. Parton, now in Canada, and, nearer home, J. Grigor, A. Kemp, K. M. Townsend and H. D. Brearley. The last named have been particularly helpful in updating some of the specialized sectors on technology forecasting, networks, financial resources and industry appraisals respectively.

In addition, the interest of other friends—Kenneth Holden and J. A. Morgan of Williams and Glyn's Bank, Maurice Holgate and his working colleagues of the Refuge

Assurance Co. Ltd, and Robert Kerr of the NW Gas Board—has been highly appreciated by me. Of my many friends in 'the Society', I must mention Robert Perrin, Peter Baynes, Basil Denning and Bernard Taylor who have always been helpful and ready to discuss planning.

I am particularly grateful to Hugh Parker of the McKinsey organization—one of my original mentors in the subject—for appraising my manuscript and providing such a delightful and succinct foreword by way of introduction.

In spite of all the foregoing, I should make it clear that the book is not intended to convey any idea of the basic policy or the ambitions of any of these persons or their organizations, but that the main theme we all have in common is our approach to the quality of our future businesses through the instrument of corporate planning.

H.J.

SECTION 1

Introduction

1.1   What is corporate planning?   3
1.2   Practical objects of the workbook   4
1.3   Who should see and read this workbook?   5
1.4   How to use this book   6

SECTION 1

Introduction

1.1 WHAT IS CORPORATE PLANNING?

Corporate planning is the systematic development of action programmes aimed at reaching agreed business objectives by a process of analysing, evaluating and selecting from among the opportunities which are foreseen.

It is not forecasting, though forecasting is a necessary part of the whole procedure, since planning is concerned with future affairs.

In practice, business objectives are of two types. The first are basic corporate objectives, which indicate the general intentions and ambitions of the concern. They are usually established together with formal statements of policy which are meant here as the attitudes or the manner in which the firm approaches business, environmental, social, national and similar questions.

The second type of objectives are the more specific operational goals which emerge only after searching appraisals have been carried out of such features as:

1   The past performance of the company in relation to the world of business in which it operated.
2   Forecasts of the general environmental and business conditions in which it intends to operate.
3   The key factors for success in the areas of operation.
4   Its strengths and weaknesses.

It is from the portrait of the future, oriented to the particular interests of the firm, that the business opportunities facing it can be seen. The extent to which they can be exploited leads to specific operational objectives. They are proposed against the background of the strengths and weaknesses, in terms of its resources and abilities of all kinds, and the key factors for success, in terms of the characteristics of the business and its markets.

Once specific business objectives have been agreed, there follows the selection of strategies to be adopted for their achievement, after which come the positive working

3

steps—the action programmes needed to give effect to the agreed strategy. Budgets which quantify the planned objectives are the logical completion of the plan. They are also yardsticks for the monitoring and control of performance by the corporate management. Throughout these procedures, problems as well as opportunities will arise and must be countered; at the same time possibilities for the creation of opportunities through the company's own initiative must be at the forefront of everyone's thinking.

Since the concept of long range planning entered the world of business (in the 1950s in the USA and in the 1960s in the UK) attitudes and practices have developed.

At first, people spoke of planning for growth. Usually they meant growth in size of activity as measured by sales income but this soon yielded to the object of growth in profits. Then, with more precision, followed the conception of profits in relation to the resources used and, more recently, that of earnings per share. Planning for stability or growth with security were hardly ever mentioned though the latter was no doubt implied.

Long range planning was originally conceived as a special tool for top management in which growth was too often sought by the machinery of increasing market shares, by acquisition, merger or diversification. Nowadays planning reaches much further down the organizational levels of a company.

Concurrent with these ideas was the concept of *management by objectives*: how to set goals for one's employees to aim at. This was regarded more as a tool for the operating echelons of business. It was initiated at more personal levels, stemming less from the strategic interests of the company as a whole.

In many misguided cases, corporate planning was used as an auxiliary service located in the headquarters of a firm, usually attached to or overridden by an existing department such as finance. Here it was more of a specialist activity, working in comparative isolation and not being involved in the coordination and integration of the total of the firm's activities.

Corporate planning is now taken as an amalgam of all these sorts of activities, the sequence of long range planning and management by objectives being complementary. It has become a well recognized method for the total management of a concern, for its operation starts with the chief executive and reaches down to the heads of its divisional and functional organization and their departments.

1.2 PRACTICAL OBJECTS OF THE WORKBOOK

A company must order its affairs by well-planned procedures, and the object of this workbook is to provide step-by-step guidance for a working approach to the activities which comprise corporate planning.

The key features of this book are an overall method of management, the personal involvement of the chief executive as well as all other managers, and the place and role of the corporate planner in the organization. The exercise of leadership, organization, delegation and control will be made clear.

Planning, in spite of abundant literature and a spate of instructional seminars, is not as well understood or practised as is generally thought. There is no doubt that the reasons lie with top management. In some cases management have not been persuaded of its value or are misguidedly afraid of its usurping their entrepreneurial inclinations or their powers. In other cases, when it has been adopted, they fail to give leadership and support by not participating.

The book is intended to help towards the introduction and deployment of planning as an overall method of company management. It is intended to illustrate the principles and the justification for its use. The stepwise approach to its introduction and establishment should facilitate its deployment in practice; the illustrations should help would-be planners and, it is hoped, contribute to the better practice of planning where it is already used as a management system. It is also hoped that it will arouse sufficient interest and enthusiasm among corporate executives to motivate them to cooperate, to make good plans and to achieve them.

The procedures followed stress the importance of sound information and sound forecasting as the stages from which real business opportunities can be identified. Without these, worthwhile objectives cannot be set, nor can good decisions be made on strategy and action programmes.

Other important objectives are:

1 The systematizing of the procedures whenever practicable (this is very much in the interests of communications across the firm and makes possible the integration of sub-plans).
2 The stress on responsibility of cost centre heads, and commitments to the plans they make.

The purpose of the book is not to 'sell' corporate planning, nor to deal directly with its philosophy. These may well appear, but the intention is to provide a guide to the adoption of corporate planning and its practice as a systematic working procedure, oriented to efficient company working as measured by sound financial yardsticks.

1.3   WHO SHOULD SEE AND READ THIS WORKBOOK?

In the first case the book should be read by at least two people, the chief executive and the corporate planner, or whoever is the staff man delegated to this function.

The broad outlines should be familiar to the chief executive, in order that he will be updated as to the management philosophy inherent in the approach and as to the sort of system which he will authorize his organization to adopt. This is especially important if corporate planning is to be introduced to his company for a first cycle of operation. In other cases, it will be an indication to him of changes in approach and emphasis which are likely to modify and extend already organized planning procedures.

The chief executive particularly needs to be familiar with the positive role which he himself must plan in its practical working, as outlined in Section 2.3 (The role of the chief executive).

It goes without saying that the book, as a basic working manual, should be read, marked, learned and inwardly digested by the corporate planner himself. Again, this is especially the case if corporate planning is being introduced for the first time. The corporate planner should be the fount of information, advice and counsel on planning as a management discipline and in turn should use the book as his authority in this respect at least until the company's own experience prevails. Otherwise, the book should serve the planner as a source of ideas and procedures by which he can develop an existing system.

Next, the book should be familiar to all other corporate executives—certainly to those, and their immediate aides, who have to plan on behalf of their departmental activities, or to participate in one phase or another of overall planning. This particularly applies to Sections 4 and 5 which deal with the practical phases of planning and the format and presentation of plans.

The corporate planner could well produce a circulation list on which sections of the book of special interest to various divisional or functional heads were noted. Until a concern can produce its own planning manual, oriented to its own special interests, a copy of the workbook should always be available to those who have planning to do.

Twenty-seven action palnning test lists are provided in the workbook. They are intended as checklists to verify concepts described and to be a reminder of who should respond, and when.

1.4 HOW TO USE THIS BOOK

Apart from its use as a preliminary reader as suggested in Section 1.3, the workbook should serve as a guidance manual for the first and subsequent cycles of planning.

It should be a basis of in-house talks and discussions among the firm's executives, to ensure familiarity with the principles of planning and the intentions of top management regarding its introduction to the firm. Under these conditions the receipt and purpose of the *planning letter* from the chief executive (Section 4.7), which initiates the formal planning process each year, will readily be understood, as will the types of response that it will call for.

It is a book of working instructions on when, who and how a company and its units carry out the various requirements of the planning system. According to whether a first or a later cycle of planning is involved, selections should be made from the numerous forms, check lists and questionnaires and then adapted to the kind of business interests of the firm.

It can be a source of ideas for modifying or extending an existing planning system, and a source of procedures or models on the basis of which a company planning manual can be prepared. This is a task for the corporate planner after the first or second year's working. In practice some experience is necessary before an official company manual, properly slanted to the characteristics of the firm, can be prepared. For this reason the workbook contains the idea of a two-stage approach to the adoption of planning as proposed in Sections 2.2 and 3.1.6.

A corporate planning manual will be considerably briefer than the workbook, being more limited to the instructions and the formalized working procedures which form the basis of the company's own agreed system. It will not need to provide the reasoning for planning nor will it discuss other approaches in the way that choices of method are described in Section 4 of the workbook, which deals with the practical phases of planning. It must however contain the forms and charts which are the basis of the agreed procedures that the company has decided to adopt.

SECTION 2

Planning as a Function of Corporate Management

2.1   Corporate planning as a managemen tool   9
2.2   Development and status of corporate planning   10
2.3   The role of the chief executive   11
2.4   The role of the corporate planner   13
2.5   How to introduce corporate planning to a company   14
2.6   How to develop corporate planning   15

SECTION 2

Planning as a Function of Corporate Management

2.1 CORPORATE PLANNING AS A MANAGEMENT TOOL

Corporate planning is no more than a logical and commonsense method of running a business, though in most cases its formal adoption means a new way of life for its executives. It is comprehensive; it encompasses all corporate activities and management disciplines.

It requires the acceptance of a more formal, factual and disciplined way of running a firm's business than will have been customary. A means is provided whereby management can do things in anticipation of changes which are forecast and, more importantly, make things happen rather than simply be forced to react to pressures when they arise from the environment.

The chief executive becomes personally involved and it becomes his way of running the company. It enables him to exercise leadership and provides a formula for delegating responsibility and authority without losing control and direction. Coordination of the elements of the business is ensured so that parochialism is not allowed to override any other interest.

It help to avoid 'management by crisis' and, because most activities are agreed in advance, it permits 'management by exception'. Key personnel are obliged to accept responsibility for the planned results in their areas of working, as measured by their contribution to profits.

The unfolding of the working procedures and, indirectly, the management philosophy involved in the later parts of the workbook should serve to demonstrate the key elements as well as the detailed tasks and responsibilities in the operation of corporate planning. Many of them will not be new, but their deployment in the sequences called for will be new to many concerns. Also new will be the advantages of the searching analyses of opportunities and resources which are needed before decisions on objectives and strategies are taken.

Corporate planning is not a substitute for management; it is a tool for management to use in the direction of a business towards specified ends.

2.2 DEVELOPMENT AND STATUS OF CORPORATE PLANNING

In Section 1.1 it was explained that long range planning has developed rapidly since it first took shape in business in the US in the 1950s. It gained wide acceptance as a system of management which was then regarded as a special tool in the quest for growth, firstly by the volume of corporate activity, then by profits in which sustained growth became the keynote. It was regarded as a tool of top management in dealing with wider issues than everyday operations.

The simultaneous emergence of management by objectives from other levels of working has no doubt contributed towards the merging of the two sorts of activities, so that corporate planning now concerns all levels inside the concern as well as relations with the outside world and the manner in which events are shaping.

In many earlier cases the corporate planner did not himself become involved in planning as a cooperative task with the departments of the firm. On the contrary he often carried out planning on their behalf eventually producing a total company plan in which the real actors rarely participated. Now however, more logically and with experience, it is rightly the operating managers who undertake the practice of planning themselves. Under these conditions the corporate planner plays the role of organizing and maintaining the system of planning for management purposes; he coordinates and challenges the planning work of his colleagues and later effects the integration of all the unit plans, thus developing a balanced company plan. In this he himself has ceased to be an operational planner and is able to direct more of his efforts to the higher level strategic objectives of the company.

This turnabout of events is not surprising and more will be said about it in Section 3.1.6 when the dichotomy to integrated management planning and corporate development will be presented as the latest outcome in the conception and practice of corporate planning, especially in the long-term approach and in larger organizations.

In this account of developments the corporate planner worked on strategic issues at higher levels, then carried out planning for departmental heads, often in isolation from them. Later, formal planning responsibilities were correctly assigned to the key managers, the original planner being then responsible for the coordination of unit plans and their integration into the corporate plan.

.These procedures we now regard as integrated management planning. Under these conditions the corporate planner is able to return to the wider strategic opportunities and issues which confront the company, an activity frequently described as corporate development. This is well justified because planning has become an accepted way of life within the operating units of the firm. The operators have become competent and by this time usually enthusiastic and motivated.

Furthermore, in the case of larger organizations the role of the corporate planner has been reflected in the appointment of divisional planners, thus completing the hierarchical type of relationship between the two levels of this functional activity, the first being at the headquarters of the firm and the others in operating divisions and in functional areas. Such departmental planners are more concerned with integrated management planning and less with longer-ranging issues, while it is otherwise in the case of the corporate planner at the company headquarters.

The location of the office of corporate planning in the organization of a company is a primary indicator of the status of the activity and shows the extent to which the firm has embraced the practice of planning as a management method. Although planning is the prime responsibility of the chief executive, in practice he needs aid from a staff man, the corporate planner; and he is a man of many parts, a systems man, a coordinator, a proposer and a challenger of objectives, an arm of the chief executive.

In a soundly organized business the corporate planner is either a staff officer attached to the office of the chief executive or he has a place along with the other functional heads of the organization. In either case he has no responsibility for decision making but is an important adviser and counsellor to all who produce plans in the organization. Characteristic job specifications are given in Section 3.6.

The location of the office of the corporate planner is shown more clearly in Section 3.2 where various kinds of organizational relationships and the kinds of plans that arise in consequence are set out.

Some people now believe that the corporate planner should begin to participate in decision-taking processes himself. There is little doubt that he has considerable influence but he does not have responsibility. This remains with the head of the concern or those in its business units to whom it has been delegated. A corporate planner who increasingly participates in operational decisions is beginning to supplant the chief executive or his managers, and undermines the whole concept of corporate planning as a functional activity.

Out of these various developments, in companies of size which have practised planning for several annual cycles, the dichotomy into the two parts already mentioned—integrated management planning and corporate development—begins to be practicable. In all other cases the corporate planner continues to be a man of many parts charged not only with the role of management planning as described, but also for the 'futures' thinking on behalf of the top management.

2.3 THE ROLE OF THE CHIEF EXECUTIVE

It is important to repeat that the chief executive has an indispensable part to play in the working of the corporate planning process. Conversely, the process provides him with the most practical method of exercising his direction and control of the affairs of the company.

Figure 2.1 lists the formal planning activities in which he is involved as distinct from his general accomplishments as a leader, an organizer and a controller. Through them he is the main source of motivation to his staff.

The check list of the formal duties of the chief executive is a minimum. Even so it serves to emphasize the high degree of his involvement in the total planning process. He is the only legitimate father of a corporate planner and, as a good parent, he does not abandon his offspring and the charter he has given to it.

The quotation of 'chief executive and his managers' in various parts of the book describes most cases of real life in business and industry. In larger organizations, however, the role of the chief executive may be sub-divided on the lines of the hierarchical relevance tree. In such cases the chief executive can also mean the person who heads up and is responsible for a number of units. It is immaterial for the present purpose whether these units are actual subsidiary companies of a holding company, or are large self-contained operating divisions in a concern having a central corporate headquarters.

Under these various conditions, the top level office of chief executive (which in special cases might even be shared) stands in relation to the heads of groups or such large units

1   Authorize the adoption of corporate planning as the basis for his direction of the company's affairs; for example, the procedure of the workbook, or that which otherwise might be portrayed in a company planning manual.

2   Make it clear that he intends to give full weight and authority to the inauguration and deployment of corporate planning in his organization.

3   Agree and make known the responsibilities of the corporate planner as detailed in the manual.

4   Lead discussions among his higher colleagues aimed at conclusions on:
       basic corporate objectives, guidelines and policy,
       proposed objectives for the heads of corporate units, and
       proposed corporate assumptions.

5   Prepare the final version of annual planning letters on the basis of drafts from his corporate planner.

6   Inaugurate the official annual planning cycle by the issue of the appropriate planning letters and the items which will accompany them (the foregoing items in 5 and 6 are dealt with in detail in Section 4.7).

7   Join in dialogues at appropriate stages of the planning cycle, especially at the stages of the review of preliminary and final plans.

8   Formally approve unit plans after their integration.

9   Finalize the corporate plan, as drafted by the corporate planner with the cooperation, if necessary, of other functional heads such as that of finance.

10   Participate in, and, if so desired, lead the periodic review meetings with company units, at which progress against plans is presented.

11   Authorize justified variations from plans.

12   Present corporate plans and summaries of unit plans to the board and periodically present reports on progress against plans.

13   Participate in the analysis, evaluation and selection of strategies concerning the longer-range problems and opportunities confronting the firm as a whole; make decisions thereon. (These matters arise from 'Corporate development' activities – see Section 3. 1.6)

Figure 2.1   The role of the chief executive

or companies which are mentioned, as do the heads of groups to the managers of their own particular units.

These matters of organization are clarified further in the section on kinds of plans (Section 3.2) which will be found to be related to organizational structures.

2.4 THE ROLE OF THE CORPORATE PLANNER

The corporate planner has to ensure that good plans are made—a responsibility which is an extension of that of the chief executive.

To achieve this he has to:

1   Prepare a system of planning which is agreed as appropriate to the style and organization of the firm. For this purpose the workbook is intended to assist and serve as a model. A description of the planning system is the first of the contents of the company manual which together with the schedules, check lists and standard instructions serves as a reference book for all who prepare plans. Such a guide ensures uniformity of approach and production of departmental plans, especially action programmes and budgets, so that coordination between them, and their integration to the corporate plan, can be systematically achieved.

2   Ensure that the manual is updated, pages being replaced or new sections added as occasion demands. It is also a task of the planner to ensure that the procedures depicted in the manual are thoroughly understood in the company.

3   Act formally on behalf of the chief executive at all the key stages in the planning cycle. In this sense he is the draftsman of all the schedules and documents which, after agreement, are formally circulated to initiate the various phases of the timetable, the main elements of which are:

    information base
    planning leter no. 1
    production of preliminary plans
    review of preliminary plans
    planning letter no. 2
    review of final plans
    consolidation and production of corporate plan.

4   Assist the chief executive in the proposal of objectives for the company as a whole and for each of the operating divisions and functions; agreed objectives are embodied in planning letter no. 1. Also, assist in the challenging of plans, especially the strategies contained in them at the review stages during the planning cycle.

5   Assist others to develop their plans. He should be available at all times to help clarify instructions and, by advice and suggestions, help in the production of good plans. He coordinates planning activities between the various units of the firm.

6   Finally during the planning cycle, integrate unit plans in building up the overall company plan. This work is not merely collecting and summarizing unit plans, but involves the sifting and the reconciliation of their chief features so that a portrait of the major opportunities, objectives and strategies emerge which, in budget form, support the total profit plan.

7   Afterwards, during the period of the operation of the plan, organize suitable means of monitoring and controlling actual progress against plans at agreed intervals.

The job of the corporate planner is a staff or functional role. He makes no decisions on operational matters but can participate in the approaches to them. The role is fundamentally one of organizing for planning then contributing to the making of good plans by guidance, challenge and motivation.

The formal job specification is shown in Section 3.6.

2.5 HOW TO INTRODUCE CORPORATE PLANNING TO A COMPANY

Six key stages are called for:

1 The decision to adopt corporate planning in a concern is that of the chief executive, and it should have the unstinted approval of his board. Likewise, it is his responsibility to initiate events to ensure its launching and to make clear that his full weight and support are behind it. The chief executive should acquire, directly or indirectly, sufficient knowledge of the procedures to appreciate its value and utility. He may reach the decision to introduce planning after learning or hearing about it at seminars or from his friends in other organizations, or he may be persuaded by members of his board or by representatives of consultant organizations.

2 Following a positive decision, he has to *organize steps for the actual deployment of the system*. At this stage he has two possibilities:

> use outside assistance by way of consultants, for the introduction and for, say, the first annual cycle of planning and its first year of operation, or
> go it alone.

3 In both cases the *appointment of a corporate planner* is necessary to serve as a focal point for the services to be provided and to ensure continuity of the activity. The corporate planner would stand as the company specialist in planning methods and procedures. The appointment of a corporate planner would be from one of two sources:

> an outsider with the appropriate experience and qualifications, or
> an insider, drawn from the existing staff of the firm who had been given training at outside seminars.

The details of the job specifications and the qualifications for a corporate planner are described in other parts of the workbook (Section 3.6).

It would not be unreasonable to 'go it alone'; indeed enabling this to be done is one of the objects of this workbook. As in swimming, the first plunge is a matter of trepidation but is a practical way of learning and making progress.

4 The next steps to be taken within the company and which should follow the initial decision as quickly as possible are to:

> *inform* the senior managers and their departmental heads of the intentions
> *give the rationale,* the purpose and expected benefits
> *provide a general description* of the proposed procedures (the corporate planner makes this contribution)
> *indicate the roles* of the expected participants, and
> *afford adequate time for discussion* with the chief executive, the corporate planner designate, or any consultant or third party representative of experience in corporate planning.

Steps such as these are best taken at a company meeting, preferably out of working hours and away from business premises. The occasion is ideal for a weekend company seminar at which the chief executive would be the leader, supported by the consultant and the newly appointed planner.

If outside consultants are not to be involved to deal with the technicalities, it would be both advisable and beneficial to have present some experienced outsider, preferably a senior person from a friendly concern which is already experienced in corporate planning. This goes far to assist the acceptance of the new system and to deal with questions. It would also allay suspicions that the changes are going to be detrimental to the freedom of the managers. During the introductory in-house discussions the workbook may be presented by the corporate planner as a working guide, and circulated either as a whole or in parts suitably chosen for specific business heads.

5 A second meeting should be held soon after the first at which the corporate planner himself is deputed by the chief executive to be leader. A *series of meetings should be arranged, with each of the divisions or departments of the firm*. On these occasions the planner would deal in detail with the working procedures, and the sequence of activities which will be called for. He would describe the features of the information base, and the critical stages of planning represented by the issue of planning letters, the preparation of preliminary and final plans, and how events in practice will be followed up. On these occasions the head of the working unit involved would stand in to add the sort of authority that the chief executive provided at the introductory meeting described in step 4 above. If consultants were retained, they would provide much of the substance of such meetings.

During these events it will be realized that the desired depth and thoroughness that planning calls for are hardly likely to be achieved during the first annual cycle of events. The feedback in subsequent years will go far to make later cycles more effective.

Thus many of the essential stages of the system will be treated only in a preliminary, superficial way. The participants may not be sufficiently practised in meeting the demands on them, especially in respect of such information as in economic and business assessments or in analysing for key factors for success and strengths and weaknesses, in the appraisal of new projects, and in the coordination of activities between departments previously accustomed to work independently—'on their own initiative', as they would say, but 'parochially', as others might say. Some remarks in the following Section 2.6 on the development of corporate planning deal with the question of management education and training in the subject of corporate planning.

Nevertheless, the principles of the system of corporate planning will be put over and mental attitudes will be adjusted so that planning will start to become accepted as a new way of life in the firm.

6 The prime object at this stage is to *launch the first cycle* of operations, the first formal act of which is the issue of planning letters by the chief executive as outlined later in Section 4 which deals with the practical phases of planning.

2.6 HOW TO DEVELOP CORPORATE PLANNING

The first cycle of planning will be an experiment, albeit a serious and chastening one, not only in the formalities of the procedures but in developing the mental attitudes of the participants.

The depth and thoroughness of the efforts will certainly be capable of improvement. Attempts to meet the basic needs of the system will show gaps in the organization and its resources and in the knowledge and abilities of the executives. The appearance of such defects must not be allowed to delay the production of the first plan. In most cases defects can be seen as opportunities or problems to be rectified in the second cycle of planning.

Once the first plan has been produced—a task which will occupy some months—and during the first year of the plan, the corporate planner and his senior colleagues immediately begin reviewing their first year's experience of the system and adapting the schedules and check lists so that information bases appropriate to the particular interests of their company can be laid out. The chief executive and top management can go further to crystallize the basic objectives of the firm; likewise those in charge of the various departments involved in planning can rethink their positions.

It is good practice at this stage, and later at annual intervals, to conduct a management meeting at which the experience gained in the introductory and other cycles is reviewed and at which ideas for improvements in the system are agreed. At the same time the degree of response of the participants, and their ability to plan and conform to plans, will become clearer.

Accordingly the next steps in the development of the planning process are:

1 Improvements in the system, tailoring it to the particular interests of the firm and its kind of organization.
2 Improvements in the actual conduct of the work in the phases of planning, inter-divisional liaison, dialogues and timetables.
3 Improvements in the content of plans—their quality, brevity and shrewdness in concentrating on key factors.
4 The need for any special planning studies which may involve outside agencies.

Item 4 is part of the need to improve the information base and the forecasting which is an intrinsic part of it.

Efforts such as these should be continuous but eventually a system appropriate to the firm will be evolved and the company's planning manual and the documentation which arises will reflect these improvements; better information bases will be built up, forecasts in all areas will become more realistic and reliable, key factors will come into sharper focus, better decisions on strategy will be taken, motivation will improve and, overall, better plans will be prepared.

After the experience of the first cycle of planning, it may be realized that some redirection of the company's management training programme will be called for. Existing schedules for training could be replaced by planning seminars of the type presented by the Society for Long Range Planning, the business schools and various agencies. Attendance, even at one-day courses, by each of the managers who have to produce a plan would be invaluable to this end. Such procedures should be continued at later times as part of the programme for management development at other levels.

In subsequent cycles of planning, ideas will also start to develop concerning the dichotomy of the approach to planning, described more fully in Section 3.1.6. This recognizes that there may be a need to separate the working parts of planning from the wider issues which confront the firm. These are described as integrated management planning, which is the everyday tool of management and which will have been achieved in practice after two or three cycles, and 'futures planning' which deals with broader issues and is designated as corporate development. In the smaller concern this sub-division of approach is a development of the job of the corporate planner himself while at the other extreme in the larger organizations typified by Figures 3.6 and 3.7 it may even justify a dual appointment. The way these questions can be dealt with is suggested in Section 3.1.

ACTION PLANNING TEST LIST 1   Sections 1 and 2

QUESTIONS	RESPONSE BY	TIMING OF ACTION ARISING
1 Is the basic purpose of corporate planning understood by all to be the secure growth of profitability? Does management realize that corporate planning is a method of running a company and not a substitute for good management? Is it realized that all levels of management are involved, that all departments are interdependent and that all executives will be required to plan? If not, what action will be taken to ensure these understandings?	All management All management All management Chief executive	

2 Is it clear that:
  (a) the appointment of a corporate planner is in no way a substitute for the planning responsibilities of others?
  (b) the position is a functional one only, but
  (c) the planner will meet executives as an equal in the operation of planning as a tool of managment?
If not, what action will be taken to ensure a correct understanding of the position?
	All management
	
	Chief executive	

3 Is the chief executive prepared to play his part as outlined in Figure 2.1, and thus function as an organizer, leader and controller?	Chief executive	
4 Is it realized that more than one cycle of planning will be needed to deploy the system on a rewarding basis, so that the sooner it is started the better?	Chief executive	

5 Does the chief executive propose to introduce corporate planning to his company:
  (a) using an external adviser, or
  (b) using existing corporate resources?
In any event, outline the practical stages called for, on a definite timetable
	Chief executive	

6 From where will the appointment of the corporate planner be made?	Chief executive	
7 How will the corporate planner ensure that the appropriate parts of the workbook are familiar to the executives of the firm?	Corporate planner	
8 When will the firm's own corporate planning manual be prepared?	Corporate planner	

SECTION 3

Corporate Planning
Systems and Organization

3.1	The basic model for all organizations	21
	3.1.1 Basic objectives, guidelines and policies	22
	3.1.2 Information base and assumptions	24
	3.1.3 Opportunities, objectives and strategies	25
	3.1.4 Action programmes	26
	3.1.5 Budgets and control	26
	3.1.6 Integrated management planning and corporate development	27
3.2	Kinds of plans	30
	3.2.1 Plans of the organization	31
	3.2.2 Plans for different periods of time	33
	3.2.3 Preliminary and final plans	35
	3.2.4 Contingency plans	35
3.3	Planning levels	35
3.4	Planning periods	38
3.5	Organizing the corporate planning department	41
3.6	Job specifications in planning	46

SECTION 3

Corporate Planning Systems and Organization

3.1 THE BASIC MODEL FOR ALL ORGANIZATIONS

The methodology of planning is basically the same regardless of the sort of activity involved. The same elements in the same sequence appear in planning for small and large businesses, in urban and rural development, in local, regional and national affairs and indeed in war.

Figure 3.1 shows the common denominators in planning as a decision-making process as spelled out on the one hand by US and UK authorities in the military field and as spelled out on the other by Perrin in a simple version for corporate planning.

Probably the entrepreneur, albeit unconsciously, treads his way through the same essential phases before issuing his snap decision.

For the purpose of this workbook, the model of planning phases shown in Figure 3.2 portrays a more positive sequence of events. It provides the essential phases as a method of corporate management in that control and up-dating elements are included. The following brief comments on the separate phases of the model, as shown by the boxes in Figure 3.2, will serve as a prelude to the further treatment of them in Section 4, where detailed working methods for each of them are prescribed.

The sequence of the stages of planning which lead to the basic model used in this workbook (Figure 3.2) is born of an initial desire to accomplish something. This is followed by the question of how, but before this can properly be answered the operator must take stock of the facts of the situation, restating exactly what he wishes to accomplish, what he has to do the work with (is it enough?), exactly when and where the activities will be, who will help or hinder, what will be the timetable and so on.

These readily identifiable steps are also those propounded by the earliest of planners, the military pundits in history. They wisely paid regard to the maintenance and security of their existing position and resources pending offensive action. This aspect is reflected in corporate planning and by a 'company doctor' in treating an ailing company.

MILITARY		CORPORATE LONG RANGE PLANNING
US Department of Defense	UK Ministry of Defence	
Commander's estimate of situation:	Operational order:	
1 Mission overall tasks and multiple tasks	1 Situation: (a) enemy force (b) friendly force	1 Where we want to go
2 Situation and courses of action: (a) determination of all facts bearing on the situation (b) determination of problems (c) determination of alternative solutions	2 Mission	2 Where we are now
3 Analysis of opposing courses of action: (a) problems (b) strengths and weaknesses	3 Execution: (a) general outline (b) grouping and tasks (c) coordinating instructions	3 What we have to do
4 Comparison of own courses of action	4 Administration and logistics 5 Command and signal	4 How are we progressing?

(H. F. R. Perrin, *Focus the Future*, Management Publications, London, 1971)

Figure 3.1   Key factors in planning.
The common denominators in military decision making and the simplified version of the phases of corporate planning

3.1.1   Basic objectives, guidelines and policies

The initial stage is one of generalities, given quantitatively if possible, but otherwise couched in narrative terms. The board of a company, or its chief executive, should state what sort of company top management wishes it to be, what standards it wishes to attain (security and growth as measured by some criterion or other), the means and types of methods it will use, the areas in which it will be active, its style of management and the image it wishes to cultivate. It should give general guidance on such things as policy, how the management should order its affairs and its attitude to major issues.

Ideally these criteria should be set down before more precise and more specific

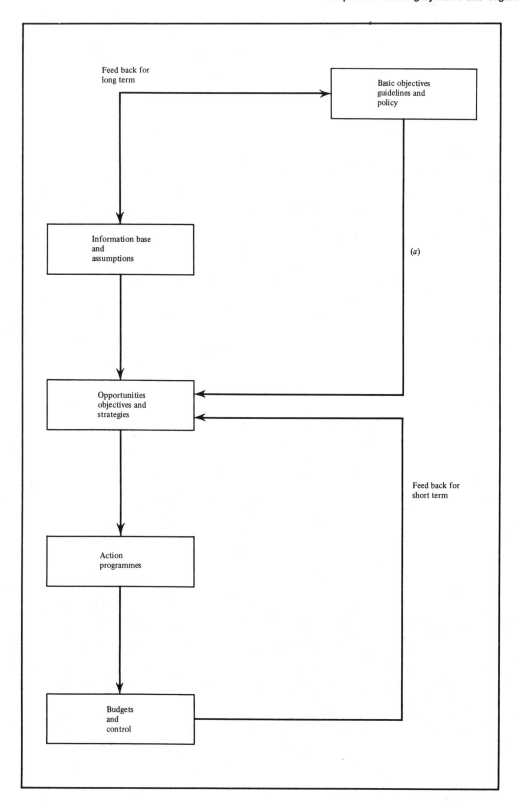

Figure 3.2   Basic planning model for all organizations

business objectives are defined. Further details on basic objectives, guidlines and policies are provided in Section 4.2.

3.1.2 Information base and assumptions

From the stage of basic objectives one might proceed directly to the setting of more specific objectives, provided adequate information were already available for decision making—the route of (a) in Figure 3.2. But sufficient data is rarely available for this to occur. It is preferable first to take stock of the expected future conditions of business and the resources of the firm in order to be able to frame realistic objectives. Such stocktaking comprises the phase of information base.

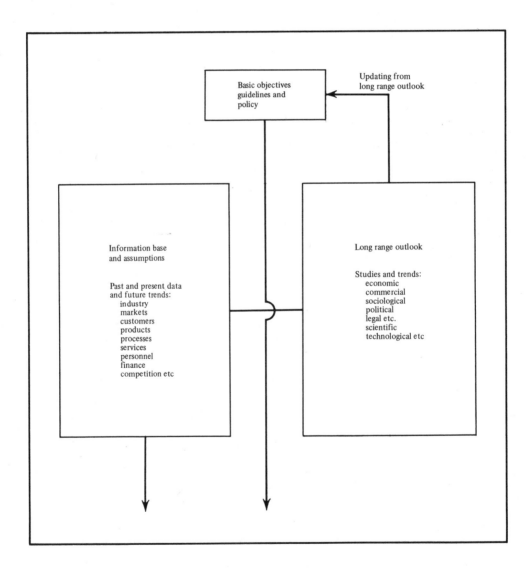

Figure 3.3 Enlargement of Figure 3.2 showing contents of information base and of the long range outlook

Preliminary indications of the working of this stage are shown in Figure 3.3 which is a detail enlargement of Figure 3.2, and which introduces the idea of a wider, long range outlook as part of the information base. More precise procedures for the building up of the bank of information as a formal process are outlined in Section 4.2.

The critical features of the information bases of all kinds are reviews of past and present business conditions which, after attempts to identify influences for change and innovation, are followed by forecasts of how they are expected to rank in the future; that is, they must be followed by assessments of trends into the time period for which planning will be undertaken. Forecasting of all sorts therefore becomes an intrinsic part of the development of an information base.

In practice the findings in the information base, especially the long range outlook, are often significant enough to justify a revision of the basic objectives of a company. Such a feedback is an important part of the planning process.

In spite of the gathering of information and the forecasts which have been made, there are usually items which are almost impossible to assess reliably. They generally arise in the economic sphere, particularly from government (political) action. Monetary, fiscal and legal matters are examples of things which cannot reliably be forecast. Assumptions about them are therefore made on the best possible basis. Such corporate assumptions are used equally by all the departments of the firm, thus ensuring that budgetary calculations are on a uniform basis and that financial deviations which occur in practice can be explained and accounted for.

3.1.3 Opportunities, objectives and strategies

Within the foregoing portrait of the business future, opportunities should be identified. These are business possibilities, measurable openings for growth by sales and such as production efficiency, and naturally for profit. They utilize fully all the firm's resources, present and potential, and call for the overcoming of threats and problems in various domains.

Within the foreseen opportunities, specific objectives for the firm and its departments can be formulated on a realistic basis. That is, they will be within practical bounds, not impossible of attainment provided the forecasts and assumptions remain valid. They will be designed within the basic objectives of the company whose impact is indicated by the route (a) of Figure 3.2.

Objectives at this stage should begin by specifying profit levels and growth rates for the company as a whole and the contributions from individual divisions. They could also include the entry of the company to new markets or the retirement from old ones. Certain objectives could emerge which might be more appropriate for the departments of a concern; guidance on this is given later in this section.

In general, quantified opportunities are regarded as the limit of 'what could be' while objectives are precisely what that firm wishes to achieve within these limits. It is pointless for a firm to start its planning by setting objectives which may prove to be impossible because they are beyond the levels of opportunity as revealed by the information base.

This is the reasoning for the sequence of phases given in the basic model and for the need for a good information base before setting the objectives.

The next stage of planning is how the specified objectives are to be attained. This is the phase of strategy, the working methods to be employed. In some cases there may be no choice but to continue with little or no change, but more usually—and more desirably—there will be alternatives which need evaluation so that decisions can be taken as to which path is the most likely to be successful consistent with a given degree of economic effort. Thus strategy is a process of identifying alternative means of reaching objectives, evaluating them and then making decisions. It is dealt with further in Section 4.4.4.

An example of decision making for strategy at the corporate level would be the allocation of resources to a research department for innovation projects as an alternative to licensing and royalty payment. Such a corporate strategy becomes an objective at the next lower level of management. This hierarchical conception of planning levels is an important facet of corporate planning as treated in this workbook and is explained as a practical procedure in Section 3.3.

3.1.4 Action programmes

So far we have dealt with what was assumed to be possible (opportunities), what a firm wishes to attain with them (objectives) and how it decided to reach them (strategy). We next need to itemize the working detail of the strategy selected. This is the action programme.

Action programmes are among the most important working documents of the formal planning process since they do more than recall the objectives and the strategies; they state who is responsible for the work in practice, what he or they have to do and when, how the results of the effort will be measured, especially the profit impact, and the costs of the operation. Action programmes, as detailed in Setcions 4.5 and 5.2.4, contain sufficient numerical data to enable the control function to be exercised weekly, monthly or at other intervals. They are also a well recognized part of the management procedure known as management by objectives, but in the sequence of the phases in this workbook they are integrated with all the elements of the corporate planning process, having their roots in the basic objectives of the firm.

3.1.5 Budgets and control

The last box in the basic planning model of Figure 3.2 contains a summary of the firm's planned activities in terms of figures, the budget. The budgets for finance, sales, production, personnel and so on are all collected and, after integration, form the basis of the company budget. Budgets serve for comparison and for control during the currency of the plan. It is imperative that they are based on well-documented versions of the earlier phases of planning.

The budget is not the plan; it is a consequence of the planned activities and affords a numerical portrayal of intentions which are the objectives and resource allocations of the firm. Budgets are largely in financial terms, but not exclusively so. They are concerned with numbers in respect of such matters as percentages of markets, growth rates, personnel enlistment and wastage, volume of sales and so on. Naturally the financial sections are coordinated with the firm's accounting procedures but they must always be a reflection of planning activities; they must not pre-empt them. Indeed, the development of budgets as a phase of corporate planning may actually displace many of the firm's previous accounting processes, certainly those at the working levels of divisions and functions.

Budgets are dealt with in more detail in Section 4.6, while cooperation between the planning and finance departments is reviewed in Section 5.2.6.

The stage of control in the last box of the model is applied at suitable working intervals during the currency of the year for which planning has taken place, usually the first of say five. According to the sort of detail involved, the control function may be applied weekly, monthly or quarterly. Such items as sales, stocks, creditors and debtors, production and the like, may call for more frequent comparison against the budget than such items as balance sheets, capital expenditure progress, training programmes and research results. Apart from straight numerical comparisons, control is also effected against the non-numerate items in action programmes. It is a principle of control that the next higher authority in the hierarchical level of responsibility exercises this function, not simply by comparing with the budget but by enquiring into the management action that was involved in the execution of the plans.

These procedures are described further in Section 6 (Monitoring and control) where the principle of dealing with variances is involved, variances here being regarded as part of the system of management by exception.

3.1.6 Integrated management planning and corporate development

The remarks in Sections 3.1.1 to 3.1.5 deal with the fundamental phases of the basic process of corporate planning. Ideally they should all be covered in the first cycle of a company's planning effort but experience shows that this is impractical in all but the simplest of businesses. As was explained in Section 2.5, which dealt with the introduction of corporate planning as a way of management, it is desirable to start the practical procedures as soon as top management have elected to adopt the system. Under these conditions there is rarely sufficient time and data available to make many of the studies that are required, and to make these in sufficient depth. Additionally, skills and planning resources may be called for which are simply not immediately available within the existing repertoire of the planning staff or, indeed, of the management as a whole. Many call for deeper and more time-consuming efforts than a few weeks would allow. A sound information base is built up only after continuous efforts over more than one annual cycle of planning, while some subjects may call for consultation with outsiders.

The recognition of these facts lies at the basis of Section 2.2 which deals with the status of corporate planning and with the recommended schemes for procedures in the first and subsequent cycles of planning in a company as advised in Sections 2.5 and 2.6. The first cycle of planning in most firms is of an experimental character, and is refined and improved as subsequent cycles operate. It is invariably based on limited information, and takes on the nature of a learning process. As the system develops in most companies of size, it becomes clear that the head of the corporate planning department has two key lines of responsibility, the first being the deployment of planning as an *integrated management system* in which the participants progressively improve the quality of their planning, while the second takes on more and more the organizing of special corporate studies, especially those arising from the longer and wider outlooks, and from a deeper analysis of the company's posture. The second of these key lines is now termed *corporate development*.

Figure 3.4 shows the relationship of corporate development to the process of integrated management planning within the basic model for all organizations.

Fundamentally the longer-range outlook taken by corporate development is a gathering of wider information, especially about long-term trends, longer than those of the typical one to five year planning periods. The trends deal not only with the current business interests of the firm but with areas beyond those normally investigated and certainly beyond those encompassed by line and functional managements. Advisedly, these areas include wider surveys of industry which lead to merger and acquisition planning and surveys of the whole framework in which the firm operates (economic,

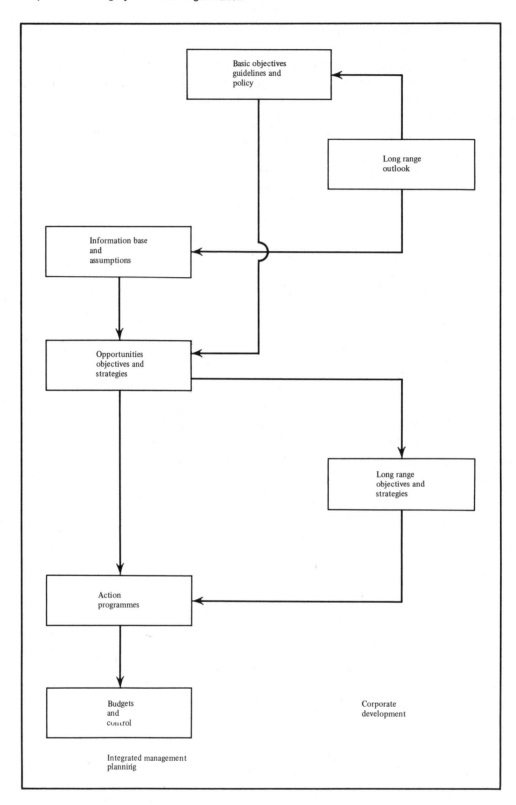

Figure 3.4 Relationship of corporate development to the process of integrated management planning in the basic model for all organizations

ACTION PLANNING TEST LIST 2   **Section 3.1**

QUESTIONS	RESPONSE BY	TIMING OF ACTION ARISING
1 Specify the basic stages in the planning of military and business operations. Are there any differences?	Chief executive and corporate planner	
2 Were any of the following elements of the planning system *not* successfully presented at the inaugural meeting of the chief executive mentioned in the text: (*a*) basic corporate objectives, guidelines and policy (*b*) information base, assumptions and forecasts (*c*) opportunities, objectives, strategy and action programmes, and (*d*) budgets and control? If so, how will they be represented?	Corporate planner	
3 Explain the practical and conceptual differences between: (*a*) integrated management planning, and (*b*) corporate development, but state in what ways they are both basic features of corporate planning When, and under what circumstances, do you anticipate the introduction of these features in your particular organization?	Chief executive and corporate planner	

sociological, technological and so on), rising to assessments at national and international levels. Such studies contribute to an enrichment of the information base and of the opportunities for the firm through the formulation of long range objectives fed into the system as shown.

3.2 KINDS OF PLANS

The numbers and kinds of plans called for depend in the first instance upon the nature of the organization involved.

The examples quoted throughout this workbook generally relate to an organization concerned with the production of materials sold on an industrial scale. It has research and development departments (R & D), production units and business or marketing activities. There may be a plurality of these units if the firm is multi-divisional or has regional selling organizations. In addition it has departments which are described as functional, being concerned with finance, personnel and management services, and others of a general administrative nature according to the size of the company and its policy regarding organizational structures.

Other concerns will have different sorts of key departments. Thus financial businesses such as banking, insurance and hire purchase will have key departments concerned with earning the income of the firm and which may be regarded as equivalent to a sales or marketing department. An insurance firm may have divisions responsible for policies in various areas (industrial, life, motor, shipping) and functional departments for corporate finance, investment, personnel and other services. Similarly, a banking organization will have operationing divisions such as domestic banking (probably organized on a regional basis), investment, trustee and other money-earning advisory or service activities, and at the same time will have functional departments for personnel, corporate finance, management services and the like. Companies engaged in retailing will have analogous structures which show the operating divisions as the income earning units, and the customary functional units providing a coordinating and company-wide service to all the operations of the company, such as purchasing and personnel. All the key units of the concern are required to prepare plans which in any case are of two types, preliminary plans and final plans. The distinction between the two sorts of plans is explained in Section 3.2.2. In certain cases, contingency plans may be called for.

For the purpose of this workbook, a business is defined as a divisional activity which essentially involves marketing. Marketing varies in that it may be the marketing of services or of products, the latter being either product or use oriented. A business includes all those activities associated with marketing such as promotion, market research, service to customers, distribution, sales and so on. In the case of larger vertically organized businesses, there may be included such functions as their own production, R & D, finance and administration; furthermore, a business division having more than one unit for marketing may find it advantageous to recognize this as a 'sub-business' in itself. In this workbook, these are frequently referred to as 'departments' and rank as level 3 in the hierarchy of planning.

Before planning can properly be implemented in a company, a clear picture of the organization must be available. Charts which show the corporate and divisional structures are a standard feature of all plans. The corporate planner should seek to ensure that such charts are prepared, that they are approved by the chief executive and are well understood by all concerned.

In certain cases it may happen that an executive in an organization 'wears two hats' and is responsible for two areas of activity. He will therefore be responsible for the production of two kinds of plans.

3.2.1 Plans of the organization

According to the sort of company structure in being, there can be the following:

1 business or divisional plans
2 functional plans
3 regional (geographic) plans
4 group plans (groups of businesses or companies)
5 corporate or headquarters plans.

Figure 3.5 shows the simplest type of corporate structure, a mono-divisional and probably a mono-product/market type which will call for a corporate plan and departmental plans, such as R & D, production, marketing, finance and administration and others, in the actual case shown. Figure 3.6 shows a larger concern which can be described as a multi-divisional, multi-product/market type which will call for:

1 a corporate plan
2 business plans (four, in the actual case shown)
3 functional plans, such as R & D, production, finance and administration, purchasing, personnel, etc.

Figure 3.7 shows the multi-divisional, multi-product/market, and multi-regional or multi-national type. This is at the extreme end of the organizational scale and contains a multiplicity of hierarchical relationships based on the first type in Figure 3.5 and developed in Figure 3.6. Such organizations call for:

1 business division plans
2 functional plans
3 corporate plans
4 regional plans
5 group business division plans
6 group functional plans
7 group headquarters plans.

Between these types there may be many variations, the key theme being the separation of corporate activities into:

1 Operating or line units having a business activity. They are profit centres with the responsibility of earning income by the sale of products or services. Their heads report to the chief executive.
2 Other units described as functional, usually located at the company or group head-quarters. Their duty to each of the operating units in the firm is the provision of specialist services in accordance with the basic corporate concepts and policy. Their responsibilities are at corporate level only, their heads reporting directly to the chief executive as shown in Figure 3.6. Functional units may be regarded as cost centres, working efficiently within agreed maximum costs.

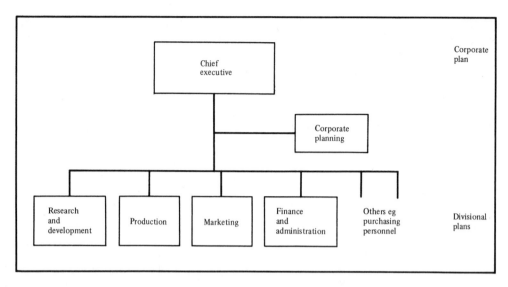

Figure 3.5   Kinds of plans in a basic type of organization

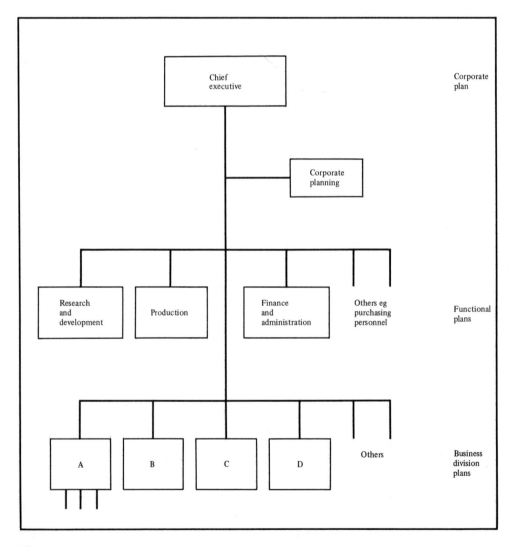

Figure 3.6   Kinds of plans in a multi-divisional, multi-functional type of organization

3   Groups of business units, or in some cases groups of subsidiary companies, which in the final analysis are to be regarded as profit centres.

In depicting the various sorts of organizational structures, the location of the office of the corporate planner is shown as a staff function, attached to the office of the chief executive and reporting directly to him as explained further in Section 3.4.

The participants in the planning work of the company are all the heads of the units shown in these figures, whether they are called managers, directors or executives. The unit plans for their areas of responsibility arise as a consequence of objectives received from the next higher level above them. In turn they feed back and when integrated form the plan of that level. This is the corporate level in the organizations typified in Figures 3.5 and 3.6, and the regional and group plans in Figure 3.7.

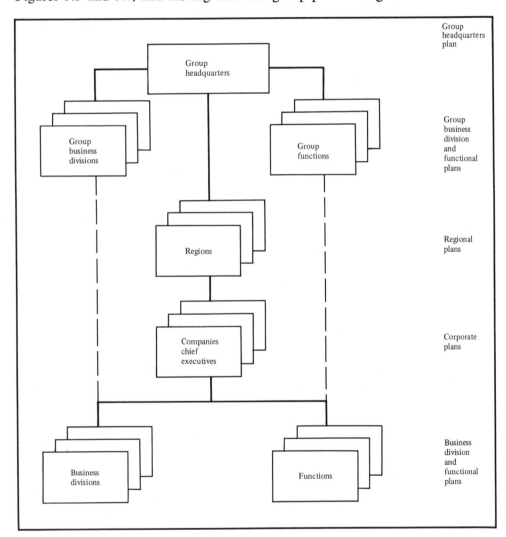

Figure 3.7   Kinds of plans in a multi-divisional, multi-functional and multi-regional type of organization

3.2.2   Plans for different periods of time

The problem of short, medium and long range plans is dealt with in Section 3.4 but in essence is covered by the now customary production each year of a five-year plan in

ACTION PLANNING TEST LIST 3 Section 3.2

QUESTIONS	RESPONSE BY	TIMING OF ACTION ARISING
1 Produce a three-level chart of the organization of your company, showing 'top management', business divisions and functions, and sub-units of the last two. Which of Figures 3.5, 3.6 and 3.7 does it most resemble?	Corporate planner	
2 Which alternative will you adopt for the location of the corporate planner on the chart of organization: (*a*) as a staff office attached to that of the chief executive, or (*b*) as a functional unit, alongside others? Why?	Chief executive	
3 Specify how short, medium and long range plans are handled in the concept of integrated management planning and corporate development	Corporate planner	
4 Why are preliminary plans always called for in each planning cycle?	All management	
5 Under what conditions are contingency plans prepared?	All management	

which the first year's activities are given in working detail. Long range plans are often the product of the special studies, for example, of the sector of corporate development; according to the model of Figure 3.4 they have their input to the annual five year plan whenever action is justified.

3.2.3 Preliminary and final plans

The annual five-year plans are separated into preliminary and final plans, regarded in practice as preliminary and final editions. These separations occur during the practical phases of the annual planning process since the preliminary editions of the plans of the various units are integrated to determine the extent of progress towards the overall corporate objectives. They afford an opportunity for dialogue between the various levels and divisions of management and serve as a feedback stage, which in real life may be repeated informally until agreement is reached. After this point, final plans are worked up and contain greater detail, especially for the first year in respect of action programmes and budgets. The timetable for the phasing of these two sorts of plans is dealt with in Section 4.8.

3.2.4 Contingency plans

Dialogues on the preliminary plans often enable a better choice of strategies to be made, especially if information is limited and if the assumptions are not of high probability. In such cases alternative strategies may be developed as the basis of contingency plans, to be brought forward as occasion demands.

Contingency plans are justified when there are significant though not high probabilities of new outlooks and assumptions on events coming to pass.

3.3 PLANNING LEVELS

In the preceding Section 3.2, plans were distinguished according to their kind of origin. Now we introduce a working conception which arises from the hierarchical nature of the organization starting from the chief executive and flowing downwards through other executives and managers, to departmental levels, wherever these are involved in planning.

In practice we recognize three levels for this purpose:

1 corporate level
2 business division and functional levels
3 sub-units of business division and functional levels.

The recognition of these levels enables planning as a responsibility of management to be put into practice by a scheme of levels of opportunities, objectives and strategies.

The scheme of planning levels is illustrated by Figure 3.8. It is based on a situation in which a company has several opportunities, each of which may be regarded as suitable for one or other of its business divisions. On this basis a company may conclude that the first opportunity at its level justifies an objective also at its level 1. An example of this could be a chemical concern, with an existing pharmaceutical business. At the corporate level 1, there is foreseen an opportunity in the industry of veterinary chemicals and its objective would be to gain $x\%$ of a given market. Its choice of strategy

—and it might have several—is to nominate this as an objective for its pharmaceutical business as at level 2. This objective is then taken by the business which in turn develops its level-2 strategies. These strategies in turn are named as objectives for its own sub-units (such as R & D or marketing) becoming objectives at their level 3.

The final plan of the pharmaceutical business would contain a section dealing with this particular objective briefly outlining the strategies it proposes to employ through its various departmental resources. It would also include a list of the action programmes involving these resources. A further example of these procedures is given in Section 4.4.4 as a case study on strategies. In this case the initial corporate objective is again that of increasing profitability and considers several strategies given out as level-2 objectives.

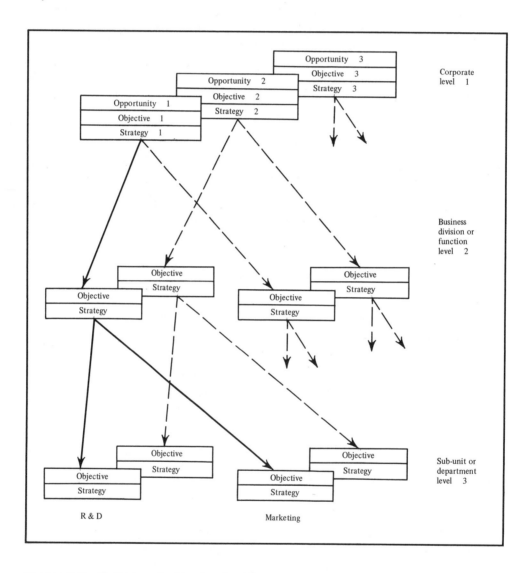

Figure 3.8   Scheme of planning levels

Such procedures are followed at the corporate level 1 for all its key opportunities and are directed to most of its units. Directions such as these are an essential feature of planning letters which, as outlined in Section 4.7, are the instruments by which a chief executive delegates responsibilities to his divisional managers. Compliance with

ACTION PLANNING TEST LIST 4

QUESTIONS	RESPONSE BY	TIMING OF ACTION ARISING
1 Develop the chart of organization prepared in answer to question 1 of section 3.2, by producing separate charts for each of the business divisions and functions, showing the names of the heads of the unit and its sub-units. Assign planning levels to each one	Corporate planner	
2 How will understanding be ensured that a strategy from level 1 becomes an objective at level 2, and so on? (Figure 3.8)	Corporate planner	

this procedure is an important feature of corporate planning as a means whereby any higher management keeps the reins of the business in its own hands while still delegating agreed responsibilities to the heads of its operating units. The flow back of lower-level strategies and their action programmes enables the corporate planner to produce the corporate plan in a systematic fashion, not diluted with detail and concentrating on the key elements of the objectives and strategies of the company as initiated at top management level.

3.4 PLANNING PERIODS

By periods we mean here the time in years ahead for which planning is undertaken, thus:

1 short range plans for one year
2 medium range plans up to five years
3 long range plans beyond five years, often as far ahead as 10 and 20 years.

It is for this variety of planning periods that the general title of long range planning has lost its specificity; planning can be for any viable period.

The choice of a planning period in given circumstances is influenced by the subject and the purpose involved. Thus basic objectives may endure almost without limit, more specific objectives may stand for five years or more, while action programmes in planning systems are set up for one year only.

Examples of topics which call for widely differing planning periods are shown in Figure 3.9.

In all events, the greater the time period, the less the degree of precision which is justified. Much depends on how far ahead one can reliably foresee while progress through repeating annual cycles of planning will permit greater precision to appear as time passes. In addition, different elements of a company's business call for varying times of commitment and involvement. The chief criteria which determine the duration of a planning period are:

1 The time needed to arrive at decisions.
2 The lead time required to implement decisions.
3 The period over which decisions, so implemented, can have an impact, that is, the life cycles of products and processes, and hence the time over which investment recoveries and profits can be foreseen.

For practical purposes a basic five-year plan, updated annually, offers the best compromise. Only the first year of such a plan calls for action programmes and detailed budgets; in other words whatever planning period is ultimately involved, only the action which is called for in the relative present is specified and taken in corporate planning. The opportunity for updated action in the year following occurs in the next cycle, when further consideration and precision can be applied.

These considerations apply also to the output of long range studies from the side of corporate development, that is, according to whether the action is required in the current planning period or in later years.

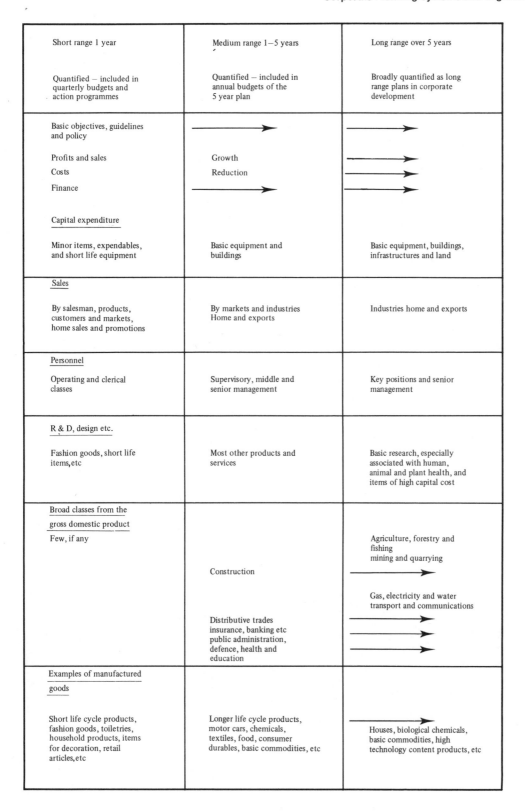

Short range 1 year	Medium range 1–5 years	Long range over 5 years
Quantified – included in quarterly budgets and action programmes	Quantified – included in annual budgets of the 5 year plan	Broadly quantified as long range plans in corporate development
Basic objectives, guidelines and policy	⟶	⟶
Profits and sales	Growth	⟶
Costs	Reduction	⟶
Finance	⟶	⟶
Capital expenditure		
Minor items, expendables, and short life equipment	Basic equipment and buildings	Basic equipment, buildings, infrastructures and land
Sales		
By salesman, products, customers and markets, home sales and promotions	By markets and industries Home and exports	Industries home and exports
Personnel		
Operating and clerical classes	Supervisory, middle and senior management	Key positions and senior management
R & D, design etc.		
Fashion goods, short life items, etc	Most other products and services	Basic research, especially associated with human, animal and plant health, and items of high capital cost
Broad classes from the gross domestic product Few, if any		Agriculture, forestry and fishing mining and quarrying ⟶
	Construction	
		Gas, electricity and water transport and communications ⟶
	Distributive trades insurance, banking etc public administration, defence, health and education	⟶ ⟶
Examples of manufactured goods		
Short life cycle products, fashion goods, toiletries, household products, items for decoration, retail articles, etc	Longer life cycle products, motor cars, chemicals, textiles, food, consumer durables, basic commodities, etc	⟶ Houses, biological chemicals, basic commodities, high technology content products, etc

Figure 3.9 Approaches to planning periods vary with different interests

ACTION PLANNING TEST LIST 5

QUESTIONS	RESPONSE BY	TIMING OF ACTION ARISING
1 What governs the 'time horizon' with respect to the period for which planning needs to be undertaken?	Corporate planner	
2 State how a five year plan can be laid out to cater for the long, medium and short range objectives.	Corporate planner	

3.5 ORGANIZING THE CORPORATE PLANNING DEPARTMENT

The appointment of a corporate planner and the approval of his job specification is the responsibility of the chief executive. As indicated in Section 3.2 the office is a staff one, located within the top management, the incumbent reporting directly to the chief executive.

In the case of small- to medium-sized concerns of the types shown in Figure 3.5, and possibly some in Figure 3.6, their size being roughly indicated by a sales income of up to £10 million and with employees numbering up to 1000, the department of corporate planning need only comprise the incumbent and his secretary.

At the other end of the scale, the central planning department of a large organization (Figure 3.7), perhaps of international status and activity, being already responsible for a system of integrated management planning and corporate development, may well need five to ten persons with the customary office support.

In these organizations there will also be planning officers located in each of the main businesses or subsidiary companies. The central planning office has a functional relationship to such planning officers whose prime responsibility is the conduct of the integrated management planning system within their immediate areas. Such local officers stand in relation to the heads of the businesses or subsidiary companies as the central planner does to the group chief executive.

This style of organization is preferred to that in which the central staff carries planners each having special responsibilities for one or more lower level units.

Between the cases shown in Figures 3.5 to 3.7, there are many stages according to the extent to which planning has developed, and to the size and complexity of the whole organization.

Nevertheless, the formal work of the planner in dealing with the preparation of the manual and its up-dating, the drafting of schedules and documentation during the phases of planning and monitoring, the liaison and coordination needed and the final integration of plans, can be a full-time occupation, leaving little or no time for special studies and investigations, to say nothing of the objective discussions he should have with the chief executives. After the first cycle or two of planning, the former activities will have become more systematically organized when the planner can turn more to the basic and longer-ranging issues which confront the firm and which may ultimately form the basis of corporate development. Prior to this stage the separation of the work within the department may justify the appointment of the first assistant to the planner, to take over the more routine aspects of integrated management planning, thus leaving the senior person the opportunity to engage in the special work of corporate development.

Organizational developments beyond this stage involve the head of the department having two assistants, the first as already mentioned and the second charged to assist in the corporate development affairs. Over and above the necessary secretarial facilities, other departmental 'legs' may eventually be justified. By this is meant specialist assistants for, say, operational research, economics, finance, market research and technological forecasting. In order to avoid empire building (Parkinson's Law!) the criteria for such additions would be for special studies and projects:

1 which affect the concern as a whole and are not the obvious responsibility of the head of a given unit elsewhere in the firm, and

2 for which there is no existing company or management service available, or if such exists, is already fully engaged.

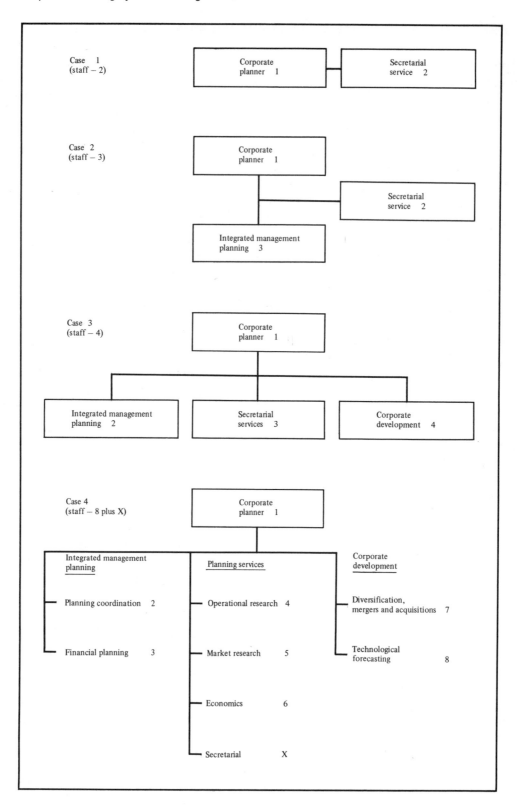

Figure 3.10   Organization of corporate planning departments

ACTION PLANNING TEST LIST 6 **Section 3.5**

QUESTIONS	RESPONSE BY	TIMING OF ACTION ARISING
1 Foreshadow the conditions under which the office of the corporate planner should be extended from the Case 1 of Figure 3.10	Chief executive	
2 What sort of organization calls for divisional planners, what would be their particular role and their relationship to the corporate planner?	Chief executive	
3 Which of the 'legs' to the position of the corporate planner shown in parts of Figure 3.10, appear to be necessary in view of the present organization and resources of the firm?	Chief executive	

Basic function

To ensure that plans which portray growth and prosperity are made at all levels.

Organizational relationships

1 Reports to   chief executive.
2 Supervises   staff assistants.
3 Other contacts   corporate executives, heads of business divisions and functions, and
                      through them, the appropriate members of their staffs.

Activities and responsibilities

Methodology

1   Prepare an agreed planning system, appropriate to the organization and the interests of
    the firm, in which the participation of the heads of key departments is specified.
2   Ensure that the planning system and the roles of the participants are known and
    understood through their presentation in a corporate planning manual which embraces
    detailed formats, instructions and timetables for the annual cycles of planning, and for
    the monitoring and control of activities.
3   Continuously revise and update the manual so that it always reflects the planning needs
    of the company and developments in planning techniques.

Formal activities

As a staff executive, act on behalf of the chief executive at all the key stages of planning, and
assist:
4   In the preparation of his planning letters.
5   In the coordination and integration of unit plans.
6   In the preparation of the corporate plan.
7   In the control procedures for reporting on progress against plans.

Functional activities

8   Participate in the determination of basic corporate objectives, guidelines and policy.
9   Propose basic economic and general assumptions.
10 Propose specific business objectives, firstly at corporate level and at level 2 for business
    divisions and functions.
11 Assist the chief executive and others in the identification and selection of strategies to
    achieve the objectives.
12 Participate in the challenge of unit plans and ensure they are consistent with the overall
    objectives of the company.
13 Through liaison between executives, ensure coordination between the plans of different
    units.
14 Integrate unit plans in the preparation of the corporate plan.
15 Assist and advise all executives in the preparation and presentation of their plans.
16 Organize and participate in periodic reporting and reviews of progress against plans.

Figure 3.11   Terms of reference for the corporate planner

Specific functional activities

17 Prepare the information base for the company as a whole, particularly concerning political, economic, sociological, legal, fiscal and monetary matters; also in respect of general trends in business, industry and markets.

18 Identify corporate opportunities for the growth of profitability in the context of external trends, especially in technology, competition developments, and diversification expansion goals. In this he will recognize internal improvement opportunities in the light of its strengths and weaknesses and its resources.

19 Propose objectives and strategies to exploit the growth opportunities in (18).

20 Keep abreast of developments in management techniques which are of assistance in planning.

Limits of authority

1 As a staff officer, the corporate planner has only direct operating responsibility over the members of his own staff.

2 As a member of the top management, he participates in major company decision making regarding the company's long-run future.

3 As a member of the top management, he keeps the chief executive and his colleagues continuously informed concerning external developments which affect the company's objectives, strategies and policy.

Criteria for measuring performance

1 The appropriateness of the planning system to the organization and interests of the firm.

2 The extent to which management techniques are deployed to advantage in planning.

3 The objectivity and thoroughness of his functional activities.

4 The extent to which the methodology and his presentation of it, motivates his colleagues.

5 The respect and confidence that is displayed in him, and the degree to which his advice and cooperation is sought and used.

Fig. 3.11 cont.

Figure 3.10 depicts the departmental organizations, showing the simplest and most extreme cases together with examples of intermediate stages, of which there are of course many variations according to the demand for planning activities and the complexities of the parent organization.

3.6 JOB SPECIFICATIONS IN PLANNING

By this term is meant the terms of reference, position description, the delineation of responsibility and authority, and position in relation to the next higher authority and other levels in the organization, all with reference to the corporate planner.

In earlier parts of this workbook the general characteristics of the work and role of the planner have been mentioned (Sections 2.4 and 3.4) and here it remains to spell out the formal details of the job specification.

Typical terms of reference for the job of corporate planner are given in Figure 3.11, while Figures 3.12 and 3.13 summarize the division of activities as and when the dichotomy of planning into integrated management planning and corporate development begins to take effect as the organization grows. The summaries are adaptable to the stepwise progression of the organization as shown in Figure 3.10, though differences between the extreme cases of 1 to 4 will occur according to the nature and the size of the organization of the company.

There is no need to offer specifications for the 'legs' to the departmental organization, the planning services of case 4 in Figure 3.10, other than to suggest that such personnel (operational research, finance and so on) should have mature qualifications in their particular disciplines and be able to apply these skills and abilities in support of the department in general, and in support of projects under consideration by it as special studies.

In respect of the behavioural characteristics, the following are the more abstract requirements of a corporate planner. They would apply in the selection of suitable incumbents and in job evaluation for the purpose of determining renumeration on one or other of the now well-known scales of assessment:

1 His know-how should comprise a broad understanding of the major functions of a business and their interrelationships, based on experience and professional knowledge of management disciplines.
2 His problem solving abilities should not only be adaptive but creative in approach, showing capabilities of independent and objective thinking.
3 His responsibilities are limited and not directly measurable by financial yardsticks though the need for persuasion and the motivation of others is considerable.

Responsible for the maintenance and development of the system of corporate planning evolved by the head of corporate planning.

Administrates the planning system, ensuring its understanding and procedures.

Is responsible for the formal activities in the practical stages of planning outlined in items 4–7 in Figure 3.11 as well as the liaison between planning executives to ensure the coordination of unit plans.

Integrates unit plans in the preparation of the corporate plan and acts as adviser to all involved.

Reports to the corporate planner and has no authority outside his own staff.

Figure 3.12 Responsibilities of integrated management planner

Responsible for the provision of assistance to the corporate planner, and thus to the chief executive, in the preparation of long-term objectives and policies, strategies and programmes.

Carries out special studies on company-wide interests and problems.

Has the objects of studying diversification for growth, of analysing major changes in industry and business and generally acting as the 'futures' man of the company.

Coordinates the preparation of long range objectives, strategies and programmes as developed in the company and which take effect through the procedures of integrated management planning.

Serves as assistant to the corporate planner in the review of plans which reflect the long-term objectives adopted. Has no authority outside his own staff.

Figure 3.13   Responsibilities of head of corporate development

ACTION PLANNING TEST LIST 7 Section 3.6

QUESTIONS	RESPONSE BY	TIMING OF ACTION ARISING
1 What are the four essential characteristics of the job of the corporate planner, with reference to the data in Figure 3.11?	Chief executive	
2 How is the working performance of the corporate planner measured?	Chief executive	
3 Indicate the difference in the jobs of the assistants to the corporate planner in respect of: (*a*) integrated management planning, and, (*b*) corporate development	Chief executive and corporate planner	

SECTION 4

Practical Phases
of Planning

4.1	General remarks on the practical phases of planning	51
4.2	Basic corporate objectives, guidelines and policies	53
4.3	Information base	56
	4.3.1 General remarks	56
	4.3.2 General external events—economic, industrial production, fiscal and monetary, sociological and political indicators at international and national levels	58
	4.3.3 Industry, markets, and own performance of products or services	63
	4.3.4 Resources	66
	4.3.5 Technology	74
	4.3.6 Key factors for success	77
	4.3.7 Strengths and weaknesses	81
	4.3.8 Competitor analysis	83
	4.3.9 Portrait of a business	86
	4.3.10 Assumptions and their levels	88
	4.3.11 Who produces which information base, forecasts and assumptions	91
4.4	Opportunities, objectives and strategies	93
	4.4.1 General remarks	93
	4.4.2 Opportunities	95
	4.4.3 Objectives	97
	4.4.4 Strategies	**102**
4.5	Action programmes	109
4.6	Budgets	111
4.7	Planning letters	115
4.8	Schedules in the annual planning cycle	117

SECTION 4

Practical Phases
of Planning

4.1 GENERAL REMARKS ON THE PRACTICAL PHASES OF PLANNING

The key steps in the planning process described in Section 4 of the workbook are outlined in the basic model in Figure 3.2. In it, the sequence of operations, formally starting with the basic objectives and policy of the firm, consists fundamentally of steps calling for information and assumptions, opportunities, objectives and strategies, action programmes and budgets.

Stage 1 of the practical sequence of operations (information base) has an output which also serves as a feedback to the basic corporate objectives and, according to its nature, may influence them. In fact the progressive adaptation of the objectives of a firm is one of the salient features of corporate planning.

Basic objectives are liable to amendment according to the evolution of the information base and forecasts of the environment in which the firm is to work. The full picture of the future conditions of business will not be available until a sound information base has been built up. This is rarely the case when planning is introduced, and good planners place a high value on information, its continual updating, and sound forecasting.

Since planning is a continuous process, any description of the individual steps must assume an arbitrary starting point. It is assumed in the workbook that the concern is already established and is in business, but that it is about to adopt corporate planning for the first time. There will therefore already be some information available, on which the other phases of planning can proceed. Most firms ought at least to have information on their markets and competitors, and on the status of their own products or services in relation to them. Even so we need to be clear about what sort of planning activities can reasonably take place in a first cycle of planning, and those which must take place, if not in the first one, certainly in later cycles.

It will be repeatedly stressed in this workbook that it is better to start planning immediately a formal decision has been taken, even though really good planning will only come about with experience. To try to introduce all the facets of a sophisticated

ACTION PLANNING TEST LIST 8

QUESTION	RESPONSE BY	TIMING OF ACTION ARISING

1   After studying the whole of Section 4, on the Practical Phases of Planning, decide
    (a)   which items can be dealt with in sufficient depth for use in the first cycle of planning, and
    (b)   which call for further work in preparation for their use in subsequent cycles
	Corporate planner	

planning system in the first cycle may prove to be a frustrating experience; such a course will certainly be disappointing and probably lead to loss of interest by all concerned. The full deployment of a sophisticated planning scheme is usually too much to be achieved in a single year.

The treatment of the following sub-sections is effected in the light of this dual approach as between the first and other later annual cycles of planning. The be allowed to develop with time. Many sections of the information base will certainly not be immediately realizable and, in place of positive information, which is not available on account of lack of time or expertise, assumptions or approximations concerning them will need to be made. (Section 4.3.10 deals more formally with assumptions.)

The treatment of the following sub-sections is effected in the light of this dual approach as between the first and other later annual cycles of planning. The essential stages in the first cycle will be emphasized. Likewise suggestions are given as to which items may be deferred for incorporation in later cycles of planning when familiarization and expertise have been acquired.

In summary, since planning is a continuing process, its introduction does not have to await the complete build-up of an information base or dogmatic ideas on basic objectives. It can proceed in stages, the first being largely experimental but which constitutes an important learning process. Benefits, improvements and adaptations will go on from one cycle to another. In practice most organizations find that at least two cycles of annual planning effort are needed before it is felt that planning begins to take good shape and to show its value. It then becomes a working way of life for those involved.

4.2 BASIC CORPORATE OBJECTIVES, GUIDELINES AND POLICIES

Although the citation of the objectives of a company are a legal requirement in its memorandum and articles of association, they are usually so vague or widespread as to be almost useless as a starting point for planning.

Accordingly a better definition is needed in line with the first of the boxes shown in Figures 3.2, 3.3 and 3.4 which describe the total planning system. This is a task for the chief executive and the corporate planner, aided by senior colleagues. Their proposals should be approved by the board if its members do not actually participate.

The *basic objectives* of a firm are the lines of business it wishes to pursue and the extent to which it will participate in them. Thus the basic objectives may be to engage in automobile manufacture or in the chemical industry. It may be thought desirable to go further and specify which sorts of automobiles, or which sector of the chemical industry. Better still, it should attempt to define its area of proposed activity by a *functional* approach. This means defining the line of business as transportation (rather than as automobiles), then of people or goods, and only later specifying the particular sort of vehicles in mind.

These are qualitative functional approaches to corporate objectives. Their value lies in the fact that they are not product oriented but are more service oriented—a change in outlook which is tremendously valuable in planning since they help to answer the question: 'What business are we in?

Figure 4.25 in Section 4.4.2 illustrates several cases of this sort of thinking in that the products and processes of the organization and the services it ultimately renders to the customer are each viewed systematically as a means of determining areas for growth or, conversely, to identify possible threats to the business.

Once the functional objective of a business has been defined, at corporate or divisional level, the other objectives of which products and which processes to adopt in support of the functional objective follow more naturally. So also do the quantitative aspects of sales and market shares, profits and ultimately profits in relation to the resources used.

A serious approach to the question of what business are we in, and an answer, is a valuable starting point for growth planning, especially in determining the direction of growth by diversification from existing internal skills and know-how.

It is arguable whether the basic objective of a firm is the earning of profits on a reliable and growing scale, or simply the engagement in an activity. This is a chicken-and-egg situation but for the working approach in planning we take the qualitative objective first and then clothe it with dimensions, especially profitability, since this is the obvious and universally accepted yardstick for measuring how well it engages in its affairs and how efficiently it performs in pursuance of its functional objectives. No company is formed with the intention of faring badly. Even at this stage it is implicit that a basic objective of the firm is to safeguard the shareholders' interests and indeed to enhance them over as long a time as possible.

Hence basic objectives start by being qualitative, that is, descriptive in nature. They may be expanded to include certain dimensions but rarely include that of time. By comparison we shall see that in Section 4.4 specific or operational objectives are more fully defined; there they become more precise, and include the dimensions of quantity (scale of operations measured by some yardstick or other) and of time, (the period in years for their achievement).

By *guidelines and policies* is meant the style of management, its attitude to public issues, the image it wishes to cultivate and the degree to which it will go further than the requirements of the law and moral constraints. These include its attitude to social and environmental factors, to its personnel for job satisfaction, loyalty and safety, to its suppliers and, of course, to its shareholders. It should provide statements on how the management should order its affairs and the general methods by which it seeks to prosecute its business. In this sense it shows its responsibilities and recognizes the constraints under which it operates. It may also define its wishes to maintain its independence in respect of its finance such as shareholdings and borrowings.

Often a manager puts forward what to him is a serious suggestion, only to be told by the top management: 'Oh, but we don't do things like that' or 'But we don't believe in bonus systems'.

Hence, for working purposes in planning it is helpful for the key items to be set down in a formal manner, not only to communicate them to the senior people but to ensure that top management have actually thought about them and crystallized their attitude to its overriding principles and values. It is only these that confer unity and effective continuity upon the direction of a concern.

Nevertheless, there are two very practical points to add:

1 In the first cycle of planning, not too much will be achieved in these respects. It will invariably be found that many things cannot be stated explicitly or put down in writing. Indeed at this stage they may well be left open to evolve more gradually.
2 The philosophy of the firm must be adaptive, that is it must be flexible and capable of variation according to the manner in which events, both external and internal, materialize.

Accordingly, the first cycle of planning will afford an opportunity to put down provisional conceptions which in later cycles can give way to crystallized ideas, born of

ACTION PLANNING TEST LIST 9

QUESTIONS	RESPONSE BY	TIMING OF ACTION ARISING
1 On which of the topics listed in Figure 4.1 do positive corporate attitudes already exist? Record them for confirmation by the chief executive	Corporate planner and chief executive	
2 Organize dialogues within top management, on the topics on which *no* attitudes or criteria are yet available Decide which topics have a primary impact on the firm's business, whether other topics demand recognition and reach (*a*) positive answers or, (*b*) provisional answers, to be resolved before the second cycle of planning commences	Corporate planner and chief executive	
3 Ensure that the outcome from items 1 and 2 are made known to all executives by a formal note	Corporate planner	

experience and adaptation. The feedback part of the model shown in Figure 3.3 illustrates this point schematically.

Figure 4.1 provides an extensive check list of the possible elements of basic objectives, guidelines and policies while the column headed 'Function Achieved' in Figure 4.25 illustrates the idea of the functional approach to the question: 'What business are we in?'

In essence the basic objectives are general statements concerning the area of intended business, and the size and profitability to be aimed at. Guidelines and policies are the principles it will follow in observing external affairs, especially its responsibilities, and the way it will conduct its internal affairs from the professional point of view. In other words they may be regarded as the 'rules of the game' which top management lay down for operators to follow.

4.3 INFORMATION BASE

4.3.1. General remarks

A preliminary description of the contents and the purpose of the information base is given in Section 3.1.2. Here it is necessary to repeat its importance not only for the identification of the sort and size of business opportunities which lie before the firm, but also for the purpose of decision making in the phases of the planning process which follow—the setting of objectives, the choice of strategy and the specification of action programmes.

At the outset it must be realized that there are several aspects of an information base. In principle they are shown by the following matrix:

	A Past	B Future
1 External events	Factual	Forecast of events—outside company control
2 Internal events	Factual	Opportunities and objectives arising—inside company control

Of these four elements both the past events named as factual in 1A and 2A are obviously historical in origin. The first should be assembled as fully as data on external matters are available, and the second as far as the information records of the company permit. The events in 1 B are forecasts of the trends of the past external events in 1A. Those in 2B provide the basis of the company's future, that is, they show what business opportunities are to be expected, and what advantages the company will take of them.

The elements are valuable because:

1 They portray the past conditions under which the company operated (1A).
2 The company performance data in 2A may be analysed to identify any important, albeit past, relationships (causes and effects) to the external events in 1A.

3 They comprise the forecasting of the external conditions of the future environment, that is, the trend from 1A to 1B.

4 They indicate opportunities in the planning of the company's future activities (2B).

The crunch of the planning process in this workbook lies in the treatment of items 1B and 2B.

Item 1B calls for the making of assumptions, or actual forecasting, a vital stage since the outcome will demonstrate the time scale and the sort of dimensions of the factors which will influence the firm's opportunities and hence the scale of its objectives.

Proceeding with this approach, 2B indicates the levels of the firm's future activities which would also be in harmony with those forecast in 1B to the extent that a past relationship had been shown to exist between 2A and 1A, and that the same sort of efforts and relationship would continue.

(The identification of a quantitative relationship between the data in 1A and 1B is desirable, its existence being demonstrated by the method of regression (least squares) analysis, described in most textbooks on statistics. In the first instance any relationship may be obtained roughly by plotting the data as coordinates on squared paper, giving a line from which a value for the second item, the first being known, may be obtained by direct reading. More sophisticated methods call for the determination of the equation describing the line, using computer formulae and desk calculators. The usefulness of the method depends upon the availability of adequate starting information. These methods are involved in preparing certain parts of the information base, when data of the time-series nature is to hand. An example will be found in Figure 4.8, which shows the actual changes in the gross domestic product (GDP), the index of industrial production, the output of an industry of significance to the company and its sales thereto. In the example quoted, it is the textile industry. The past relationships are analysed, and on the basis of an assumed increase in the first item, a forecast is developed of the demand from the textile industry for the firm's products).

In other words, this sequence of forecasting becomes a basic indicator of the future operational levels of the firm which are possible. They may merely be a continuation of the past sort of activities, that is, reacting to the foreseen environment in its traditional manner, or, and this is the linch-pin of corporate planning, there may be a fundamental change in attitude. In taking up planning, the firm should elect to improve on its 'trended' future; it may, as originally defined in Section 1.1, but expanded here, 'systematically develop action programmes aimed at reaching agreed business objectives by a process of analysing, evaluating and selecting from among the opportunities which are foreseen', but which are more ambitious and profitable than would arise simply by continuing its past style and degree of effort.

In the meaning of the models of the planning process shown in Figures 3.2 to 3.4 the information base may even be regarded as a precursor to the evolution, not only of specific objectives, but of the basic objectives and policy of a firm. Certainly in subsequent planning cycles, the information bases will have an important feedback to this particular part of Figures 3.2 to 3.4 and should thus have a beneficial influence in updating and reshaping the original goals of the business and the ideas of its founders.

These principles account for the need for a sound information base but this will rarely be achieved during a first cycle of planning. In any case, contributions to a base are a continuing process, systematically and formally acquired, often involving special studies outside the standard phases of the planning cycle.

The following sections in Section 4 of the workbook, especially Sections 4.3.2 to 4.3.9, deal with the elements of information bases which are common to most sorts of concerns. The extent to which they can be determined during a first cycle will be limited. Some are more important that others, but in the absence of forecasts of external events, the first cycle of planning may have to be restricted in practice to planning by extra-polative methods, that is, simply by extensions of the firm's past activities, their kind and degree. This in fact applies in most cases to companies when inaugurating a planning system. A firm will rarely have available all the types of information which are called for and which it ought to have, in order to arrange its business in relation to the background of external affairs.

The scheme for kinds of plans dealt with in Section 3.2 can also be used to indicate the kinds of information bases required. This is elaborated still further in Figure 4.23 which lists the various kinds of information bases and who prepares them, whether alone or in cooperation with others.

It is only after broader and deeper information bases have been established that really good plans and improvements in the direction of the development of the firm can be made. Nevertheless the first cycle of planning, carried out on more limited lines, confers considerable benefits for it has great educational value. It is often surprising to learn what gaps there are in the items of business intelligence which an operating department ought to have. The first cycle also provides the chief executive with experi-ence in the process of planning as a means of management.

(*Practical notes:* In Section 4.3 dealing with the development of the information base, most of the forms carry a heavily lined top left-hand box carrying a form title. These boxes, after adaptation to the special needs of a planning unit when necessary, are to be completed and assembled as the information base of one or other unit, in accordance with the suggestions given in Section 4.3.11. In view of the need in long-range planning to deal with annual and compound growth data, attention is drawn to Appendix III, an easy-to-use chart. It shows the relationship between an annual rate of increase and the cumulative increase over a number of years and is useful in preparing various sections of the information base which involve annual growth calculations.)

4.3.2 General external events—economic, industrial production, fiscal and monetary, sociological and political indicators at international and national levels

Forecasts of the trends in the first two of these elements of the external environment are important both in the short and the long term; political issues are of short-term importance if, at the time of stocktaking, changes of government are probable. Changes in fiscal elements, especially taxation, usually occur annually at the time of national budgets, though monetary changes (availability of credit, interest rates and so on) may occur at any time. Both may be allied to the political element and, in turn, to inter-national influences. Sociological changes are usually of a longer-term nature but may be seen building up gradually.

The recording of the past levels of these events and the making of forecasts as *to how the indices of the quantifiable items are likely to change* is an early part in the assembly of the information base concerning general external events. These considera-tions also form the basis of agreed assumptions on which planning is based. Assumptions are dealt with further in Section 4.3.10.

The phrase a change in index means the percentage change in a given year, in one or other sort of activity, compared to the level of an earlier year. Most national and trade statistics are given in absolute terms, such as monetary units and units of size such as tons, yards or gallons and also as a percentage of the level in an earlier year. Never-theless the use of particular indices which show the relative changes year by year is highly convenient in the early stages of planning. Indices and indicators are words that are used almost interchangeably in the workbook and the language of planning, though the first refers to actual numbers while the second is sometimes used in a more qualitative sense.

As the work in the practical phases of planning proceeds nearer to the stage of budgets, so the indices of change are gradually converted to absolute units. Even so, it is still convenient to include ratios and percentage data to enable quick comparisons to be made not only in the planning process but in the control process as well. The format of budgets and control reports is designed for this purpose.

International indicators

The forecasting or the making of assumptions on these items is important for firms with international operations, but less so for firms concerned only with home markets and events in their own country.

Typical items in this part of the information base, against which attitudes need to be taken, are listed in Figure 4.2. Some are basic to corporate planning in all companies and must not be ignored however distant they may appear. The figure provides a check list, with blank spaces to be completed with opinions and assessments. Such forecasting and the proposal of assumptions on intricate questions such as political issues, is a task for the corporate planner, usually aided by specialist advice from outside the company. Sources of external information and opinions are numerous; economic and related data forecasting trends may be obtained directly from those countries which publish such data, and from reports and publications of such organizations as EEC, UNO, IMF and OECD, as suggested in Figure 4.7.

In any case the more important these are, the more likely will it be that local planners in international organizations will be aware of them. Such people also need to prepare their own local information base on these topics, which in turn will contribute to the total information base of the parent company on indicators of general external events.

In connection with Figure 4.2 it should be stressed that the data should be scrutinized and items of likely impact on the business of a particular firm taken into account in the planning work which follows.

National indicators

The principal national economic indicators and recent changes in them are shown in Figure 4.3, though others, such as those for disposable personal income, bank lendings, imports and exports, should be studied if they are considered relevant to the company's planning interests. They are described as macro-indicators, being indicators of general activity at the national level. Forecasts or assumptions on them should be inserted in the spaces under 'Planning assumptions' in Figure 4.3. They are directly meaningful in corporate planning for they provide the key note for general external events.

Thus a multi-product, multi-market company may be so diverse as to be able to link its overall fortunes directly with those of, say, the national growth or decline, as measured by the change of the Gross Domestic Product, or with the growth in population (or changes in its composition), with the income per head and so on. The difference in forecasts of the GDP between 1 and 3 per cent or an awareness of changes in the purchasing power of people of different age groups, can be extremely significant in pointing out the level of future business opportunities for many firms.

Sources of data on UK national indicators are to be found in the publications of the Central Statistical Office, The Department of Trade and Industry and so on as listed in Figure 4.7. Opinions and forecasts on these items are frequently published by organizations such as The National Institute for Economic and Social Research, The Organization for Economic Cooperation and Development, The Department of Economics of the University of Cambridge, The London Graduate School of Business Studies, various economic consultants and the financial press. A review of such forecasts forms the starting points for making corporate assumptions concerning the national economic indicators.

Cost indicators

Macro-level items which are of the nature of cost indicators, as distinct from the indicators of general levels of productive activity, are treated in Figure 4.4. They comprise factors which have a direct or indirect effect on the expenses of a firm and hence serve as indicators of the build-up of the future costs of a firm's raw materials, its labour and services. To some degree they may indicate the trend in selling prices. The figure also includes an index of the firm's own personnel costs over recent years, based on the average annual salary. It may also include the costs of social services. Forecasts of the trends in personnel costs form the basis of agreed planning assumptions which are used equally by all planning sectors in budget calculations for personnel costs. They are mentioned further in Sections 4.3.10 (assumptions) and 4.8 (planning letters).

Major industries and business indicators

The next logical breakdown of the macro-indicators of the level of general activity shown in Figure 4.3 arises from the breakdown of the GDP, leading to indicators of its components, that is the major industries, businesses and public or national organizations in the economy as a whole.

The principal elements of the GDP are the values added by:

1   agriculture, forestry and fishing
2   mining and quarrying
3   manufacturing
4   construction
5   gas, electricity and water
6   transport and communication
7   distributive trades
8   insurance, banking and finance
9   public administration and defence
10   public health and education
11   ownership of dwellings
12   other services.

The identification of the particular component of the GDP relevant to the interest of a company is important. It is the task of the corporate planner to identify the relationships down the hierarchical scale from the GDP, through its components such as manufacturing, construction, or whatever other line is of interest to the company, to the individual industries or business sectors which ultimately form the company's markets and to make planning assumptions concerning them. Later, by the use of further breakdowns shown later in Figure 4.8, and then in Figures 4.9 and 4.10, the corporate planner deals more specifically with the continuation from the concept of the activity within the GDP, to the question of individual market shares held by the firm and its competitors, and to the question of key customers.

Figure 4.5 suggests how to present data, in this case quoting some of the principal components of the GDP, in the standard format of Figures 4.3 and 4.4. It also includes data on the company's overall activities as measured by its sales income. Again, the blank spaces are for planning assumptions. These relate to its total sales of products or services. Sales are measured not only by price but also by volume since the two help to identify changes in price structure arising as a result of inflation and also resulting from changes in the assortment of products, marketing strategy and so on.

In later cycles of planning, attempts should be made, either manually or with calculators, to determine any numerical relationships which existed between the hierarchical levels mentioned in Figures 4.3 and 4.5 and to see whether factors can be identified to account for them or for any abrupt changes which occurred. Even in the first cycle of planning it would be beneficial to know if any correspondence, however rough, existed between the indices of the company's sales and say the indices of the change in GDP, the total of industrial production or of certain sectors of the industrial markets.

The analysis of identifiable relationships, whether general or precise, is the first stage of the basic approach to opportunities and objectives in that they might be calculated to maintain the corporate activity relative to that of the next higher level sector or industry which it serves. Such a basic approach to the setting of objectives as such is dealt with in Section 4.4.3.

The question of improving on this potential by increasing market shares, by the innovation of new products or services, or the reorganization of product assortment according to profitability and so on, becomes the second means of approaching higher objectives in planning.

Collecting the foregoing sort of data in the fashion outlined may not be necessary in a small firm whose fortunes are linked to events lower down the economic scale of business and working in limited localities. It may also be impracticable during the first cycle of planning though it should be part of the information base for the second and subsequent cycles. On the other hand such analyses are essential in larger organizations as they provide primary indications of the countrywide opportunities and hence for divisional and corporate objectives. Such opportunities arise in the export field as well as in home markets.

Opportunities for manoeuvring and independence of action by a small company are usually greater than in a large firm, whose overall destiny is more closely linked with that of the national economy.

Manoeuvring in such cases will need to take place within its various divisions, even within its product groups. Many businesses, such as motor cars, fertilizers, textiles, radio, consumer durables and hence hire purchase, have a very positive link with certain economic indicators. Nevertheless the enterprising concern must always attempt to seek opportunities within the environment in which it is to operate. This topic is the subject of Section 4.4.2.

Other indicators

Fiscal and monetary considerations involve a highly subjective analysis and a forecast of likely changes as they might affect the company is correspondingly difficult. On this account they call more for the making of assumptions in the same manner as many of the macro-economic indicators already discussed. Assumptions are made concerning the balance of payments position and monetary reserves, in that they may foreshadow other changes such as:

1 rates of exchange against other currencies
2 availability of borrowed money, controls on credit
3 interest rates at home and abroad
4 transferability of currencies
5 changes in nature and rates of taxes
6 changes in nature and rates of exercise and customs duties, purchase tax, etc.

Allied to these factors are controls on trade such as quotas or even embargoes on imports and exports and the special tariffs operating between various trade areas (US, EEC, EFTA etc).

Related items on which assumptions should be made for the purpose of standardizing the approach throughout the concern towards costs and other budgetary items are:

1 Depreciation allowances, investment grants, special cases such as for development areas.
2 Cost of social services, national health and related charges, state pensions, etc.
3 Cost of training levies, and the degree of recovery.

Finally an attempt should be made (again this is a subjective study for the corporate planner using whatever advice he can obtain) to make forecasts of any important changes in the political and social fields, and their likely impact on the planning of affairs. Political changes can have deep effects on many of the topics already dealt with in this section.

Social changes are usually slow to develop but can be influential in the long run. Changes in attitudes to leisure (sports, holidays, hobbies and other personal interests), family life, standards of living and so on, are all capable of affording opportunities and posing problems to a firm. These will depend on its sort of activity and on the nearness of the firm's sales point to private individuals. Companies dealing at the industrial level may be more slowly affected by these changes than those whose operations are nearer to the High Street sales counters.

Summary

It is the task of the corporate planner:

1 To build up the information base on the general external events as factually as possible concerning their past movements and changes.
2 To attempt to define relationships between these and the firm's past general activities as shown by sales and cost indicators.
3 To identify the external trends in all the areas mentioned and when possible to make forecasts concerning them, failing which,
4 To propose assumptions for acceptance at corporate level.
5 To inform all participants in the company's planning work of these basic assumptions and to ensure they are taken into account at an early stage in the preparation of their unit plans.

Basic assumptions on items of direct importance to the company, and which have been agreed upon for general recognition, are notified to all the planning units through the planning letter of the chief executive, as described in Sections 4.3.10 and 4.7.

Figure 4.6 gives an extensive check list of the numerous items which come into account in this part of the information base, some of which have been quoted in the preceding figures as the basis of important indicators. Figure 4.7 refers to the principal public sources of information on general external events, though this is not meant to be exhaustive.

4.3.3 Industry, markets, and own performance of products or services

After the analysis of the various national indicators and the firm's total sales, we now go to similar but lower-level analyses which involve the growth of the company's divisional and product group sales and profitability in relation to specific industries and to specific markets. This is a more precise consideration of each of the divisions of the company, their product groups (even individual products if they are of key importance) or services, in relation to the sub-sectors of industry and to single markets. As in the analysis of the data in Figures 4.3 and 4.5, we need to see how each has changed, what are the trends that are forecast and the sort of characteristics which link the firm's progress with that of its markets.

Again it is useful to use indices for the measurement of changes and trends, doing this for the past five years followed by five year planning projections.

The completion of this part of the information base calls for studies on:

1 Total markets of specific interest to the company, and its sales thereto.
2 The breakdown of the total sales of individual products or product groups (by volume and by value) to the sub-sectors of the markets which are served. Alternatively, in the case of non-manufacturing concerns, analyses of services rendered or operations achieved is similarly carried out.
3 The size and growth of the total market, the sub-sectors served and the market share held by the company.
4 The profitability of each of the products or product groups as sold to the different sectors of the market.

Figures 4.8, 4.9 and 4.10 are used to present data on these items.

The example of Figure 4.8 dealing with item 1 above starts with quotations from Figure 4.3 (GDP and the Index of Industrial Production), followed by actual national data for a typical sub-industry, the textile industry. Assumptions are made in the first instance concerning the growth of the GDP. Then come assumptions on the growth of industrial production and of the textile industry which bear the relationships shown by the past actual performance. The development of the forecast of the company's sales to the textile industry follows similarly and provides the basis for the setting of minimum objectives in the planning process, that is, a volume growth which preserves the past relationships to the market. The volume basis in turn serves for production planning, then in the determination of costs which, with considerations of pricing policy, finally lead to data on the growth in the value of sales and profits.

At the stage of the information base called for by Figure 4.8, several analyses and formats may be needed, depending upon the number of different industries or markets which are served by the company as such, or by its various business divisions.

A small concern may only need to make one or two analyses of this kind, whereas a large company may be involved in five, ten or possibly more. The workload is not in proportion to the number, since the basic assumptions made on the macro-indicators, as in Section 4.3.2, serve equally for all the formats which are called for.

In practice many companies may be unable to identify definite relationships between many of the levels depicted in this series of quests for a good information base. A company working under such conditions is operating in a vacuum and cannot plan; it is obliged to work on a day-to-day basis, reacting only to events as they come to its notice. On the other hand the lack of an apparent relationship may be due to the use of sales values instead of volume data, in making comparisons with industry and business indicators. There is always the need to compare like with like, and then to identify remaining deviations with the effects of inflation, changes in the pricing of the assortment of products, or market shares, or some other factor. Furthermore, the use of volume indices (tons, yards or gallons) is necessary when forecasts of sales levels are used as the basis of production planning as in capacity calculations in the plan for production.

Forms of the type of Figures 4.9 can be used to show the breakdown of sales as required by the studies in 2 and 3 above. Headings are designed to reflect the particular interests of the firm, and in the case of an export oriented company can show exports to various countries or regions.

Taking as an example a firm producing and selling plastic materials, the corresponding version of Figure 4.9 would show the sales of the different types of plastics (polyethylene, polypropylene, polystyrene, PVC) possibly also sub-divided into different qualities. Separate forms would show these product sales to different sectors of the industrial markets (electric cables, floor coverings, artificial leathercloth). The sales would be given in terms of volume (weight in tons) and of value (£'000) for the last five years from which the two growth rates would be adduced. The forecast of future sales by volume would have its origin in the sort of data developed and shown in Figure 4.8, and as a minimum would be in harmony with the projected growth of the market as a whole.

The form of Figure 4.9 specifically includes market shares as an essential part of the information base. Accounting for all the suppliers to a market through the assignment of market shares occurs again in the competitor analysis dealt with in Section 4.3.8.

Several methods are available for the determination of market shares.

The 'top-down' methods arise from the analysis of statistics on industrial outputs. Publicly available reports such as those named in Figure 4.7 are invaluable for this purpose, especially the '101' production reports of the Department of Trade and Industry, sold as *Business Monitors*. These are available either monthly or quarterly and usually give value and volume data for past years in detail. The analysis in some cases may need to be made in the light of the imports and exports of the products under study. Many other sources of indicators of market size are available through membership of trade associations, much of whose findings is published in financial journals.

The UK Government publications listed in Figure 4.7 are necessary reference books to the corporate planner in building up the information base.

When official data is not available on market sizes, the 'bottom upwards' methods of market research are involved, either through the firm's own resources or jointly with others through the service of one or other of the marketing consultants and information-gathering agencies.

Profitability, as called for in item 4 above, is shown by Figure 4.10 which corresponds with Figure 4.9 in that the same products and market sectors are listed. Profitability at this stage is shown as a percentage of the sales income, this being defined as the gross or operating profit, that is, taking into account all the allocatable costs (cost of goods as manufactured, packages, delivery and marketing costs) but excluding corporate charges such as headquarters costs, interest payments, taxes and so on.

ACTION PLANNING TEST LIST 10

QUESTIONS	RESPONSE BY	TIMING OF ACTION ARISING
1 Why is information on (a) the trends of the past activities of the firm (b) trends in the past growth of the environment, and (c) any relationship identified between them important in the planning process?	All management	
2 Which items in the following lists are relevant to the company's business (a) international indicators (Figure 4.2) (b) national (macro-) indicators (Figures 4.3 and 4.5) (c) national cost indicators (Figure 4.4) (d) other indicators (Figure 4.6)? Identify any further indicators of relevance to the firm	Corporate planner	
3 Does the company or its departments, have data on (a) the past size and growth of its markets and sub-markets in terms of value, volume and profitability for each of its products or product groups, and (b) the *forward* trends of these items? (Figures 4.9 and 4.10) If not, what steps will be taken to acquire this information?	Corporate planner and business heads	
4 Has any correlation been found between the past activities of the firm and the various indicators? If not, can reasons be adduced to account for this?	Corporate planner and business heads	
5 Has reference to, and use been made of, the information sources of Figure 4.7 for the purpose of decision taking in the above questions? Record the particular sources which it is proposed to monitor regularly for planning purposes	Corporate planner	

While the guidelines given as points 1 to 5 in the summary at the end of Section 4.3.2 still apply in principle, it is no longer a task for the corporate planner alone to prepare the data charts of Figures 4.8, 4.9 and 4.10. At this stage the responsibility moves to the heads of the divisions of the company who must ensure that their staff, market research and management information personnel acquire this sort of material information on the lines laid down. The data sources quoted in Figures 4.6 and 4.7 should still be of use at this stage. The role of the corporate planner is one of cooperation, system making and, finally, coordination between units of the concern. Naturally the division of work depends on the type and organization of the company, since in smaller concerns the planner may himself still have the responsibility of assembling the data and of making the forecasts called for in Section 4.3.3.

The build-up of information base data of one or other of these kinds, according to particular circumstances, is essential if the firm is to see how and where it stands in relation to its past and projected market environment and for dealing with the further phases of practical planning. The data is always based on past relationships and on the trends which emerge. They form the basis on which the planner superimposes other factors of likely impact so that the best possible picture is built up within which realistic opportunities can be foreseen. It is within these opportunities that further initiative can be applied to ensure that sales and profits trends can be surpassed and that planning can thus be truly growth oriented.

4.3.4 Resources

The cataloguing and analysis of the company's resources both by value and working utility are essential features of the information base phase of the planning process, since they indicate not only the present state and use of the company's assets but the potential ability or otherwise to provide for growth according to the way that the objectives develop in the planning process. Their analysis will show the existence of a reserve in resources or a need for further resources, that is, whether a gap in capacity is identified which requires to be filled if growth objectives are to be achieved.

From the point of view of the corporate planner, the following areas are those in which the scheduling and analysis of resources is necessary, though in practice this work is carried out in conjunction with the appropriate divisional or functional head in whose area of responsibility they fall:

1   Resources in fixed assets—land, buildings of all sorts, plant, equipment, machinery etc.
2   Resources in personnel—management and staff, and other main classes of workers.
3   Resources in finance—actual cash, existing and potential, that is, credit or borrowing ability.
4   Goodwill, patents and special sorts of know-how which are also regarded as valuable resources in certain types of concerns.

More specifically, the resource analysis will show:

1   The key areas in which corporate capital is employed.
2   The percentage of its utilization in the past, and hence
3   The extent of reserves available to support growth without further need for capital.
4   What strengths and weaknesses are evident (Section 4.3.7).

5 Opportunities which exist for more profitable use.

6 The need for new resources according to the evolution of strategies to meet planning objectives.

Again, it will not always be possible in a first cycle of planning to prepare a comprehensive catalogue of all these items and to analyse them, but an attempt needs to be made in the first cycle, if only to identify the major items.

Resources in fixed assets

The production facilities of a company usually represent the larger part of the allocation of its capital, certainly in the case of capital intensive industries such as oil refining, heavy chemicals, plastics and synthetic fibres, highly automated engineering and related industries. It is less so in financial and kindred concerns whose fixed assets mainly comprise office buildings for sales and administrative purposes. Between these extremes, there are many stages involving the use of capital, such as in buildings and equipment for warehouses, laboratories, service centres and transport.

Although this section of the workbook deals primarily with the cataloguing and analysis of the manufacturing resources of a concern, it should also serve to indicate the method of approach to other areas where the yardstick for the measurement of utility is not productive capacity.

An overall schedule for manufacturing resources should be compiled on the lines of Figure 4.11, comprising:

1 Land. The first tabulation of the total land area in acres for each site would also contain comments about its cost, quality and locational advantages, whether it were owned outright or leased, and whether convenient neighbouring land might be available in the event of long range planning calling for completely new space directly linked to an existing site.

2 The second tabulation would show the principal land uses of each site according to the ground area used for:

    manufacture, divided into product or product groups, or functions

    warehouses, for raw materials and for finished products

    offices, for site administration, production or services

    laboratories, for production or raw material control, or perhaps for pilot plants

      or development purposes

    roads and communications, car parks etc

    services: energy, effluents, water cooling etc

    welfare: canteens, first aid, locker rooms etc.

Finally the area of unused land would be given both in acres and as a percentage of the total site area. It would also show the impact of any developments either in hand or already scheduled.

3 Buildings, equipment and machinery. Third tabulations deal with each of the buildings listed in 2 above in respect of each site. The buildings and equipment are described as to original costs and replacement value. Additionally, the rated capacity in specific units per annum is given for the installed machinery or equipment. Again the extent of the unused space within each building would be given together with a statement of the average degree of use of the installed plant in the previous year. This item would indicate the extent of unused plant.

At this stage some guidance may be necessary concerning the measurement of plant capacity and the degree of utilization of a given manufacturing unit.

The first point calls for the annual time use of the plant which should be given in relation to its use on the basis of 24 hours per day for, say, 300 days per annum, or a number of days less than 365 after allowing for maintenance, shift rotation and the incidence of annual closures for holidays. Too often capacities are calculated on the basis of one or two shifts only. Equally often, reserves of capacity for volume growth are available through increased shift-working but are ignored for minor reasons such as lack of supervisory staff or a false appreciation of the economic balance between higher shift rates for working personnel and the profits arising from the greater use of capital resources.

The second point arises when units are capable of making different products and thus have different capacities according to the assortment manufactured. In these cases it is a task of the planner in cooperation with the production management to identify a common denominator. This is needed:

1 To assign a total capacity to the unit in question.
2 Then to describe the degree of usage at various times to enable the amount of spare capacity to be known.
3 To determine if a more attractive assortment may be produced.
4 To determine if completely new capacity needs to be planned in response to higher sales objectives. In this event, a very important point will be the minimum size of the next economic increase in productive capacity.

The aspect of the common denominator for describing capacity can be clarified by the following examples:

1 A packing machine may be able to pack three times as many half-size packs as a larger one. Here give the capacity in terms of either size but state the conversion factor between them in the event of a mixed assortment being processed.
2 A machine tool will handle three times more work done in one metal than in another. Again state the capacity in either one but give the conversion factor.
3 A chemical unit will produce half as much again of product A than of product B on account of a shorter residence time. Give the list of products of the type which can be produced in the unit (A, B, C, etc.) together with their respective conversion factors to product A according to the different residence times.

In the case of the works infrastructure, assessments should be made of the total resources, that is the capacity for steam raising, energy generation, water cooling, storage of raw materials and finished products, welfare facilities and so on. The assessments should be made in well-known or easily recognizable units of measurement. Alongside this data, the degree of usage in recent years must be shown against the level of production in each period in order to indicate any reserve of these resources.

The key factors shown in the three-part schedule of Figure 4.11 are needed in the first cycle of planning. In subsequent cycles the format of Figure 4.12, production capacity analysis, becomes more useful. The hypothetical example in it shows the past and planned production for a given unit and how the reserve or free capacity is taken up and eventually needs to be supplemented by new capacity installed during the five year planning period. Forms of this type may be used not only for each production unit, but also for the total on each site and then for all the manufacturing resources of the firm by the integration of the key resources of land, buildings and machinery and equipment.

Later we shall see in Section 5.3 that the unit plans for the production management will contain forms of this nature of Figure 4.12, extended timewise to show planned changes from the past and present levels through the five year planning period.

It is worthwhile recalling that such forms serve for:

1 The formal listing of the various sorts and capacities of production resources and the infrastructure associated with them.
2 Indicating the amount of capital employed in each one, and hence the key uses of capital.
3 Indicating opportunities for the better use of these resources by both production management and marketing management. Such liaison between departments in a firm is a beneficial feature of corporate planning.
4 Responding in the feedback or looping process during the phases of planning, when higher sales objectives are coordinated with the present total capacity and the need is seen for new investment in additional resources, if the free reserve is low or non-existent.

An important aspect of the listing of the resources of the firm in respect of fixed assets in manufacturing operations is the corporate policy towards the value of the capital element involved. This is important firstly for costing purposes in that the component of depreciation depends upon it, and secondly for the purpose of estimating the financing of extensions—in the light of the inflationary element in costs.

There are numerous methods available to show this, but as well as knowing the original cost of the investment, and any depreciation which has been credited, it is desirable to know its replacement cost. This is not only a conservative basis for the determination of production costs but is also a prudent policy for the firm to follow. A frequently used source of data on up-to-date depreciation rates, and hence for calculating replacement costs, for buildings and plant installations, is the periodic indices published by the Economist Intelligence Unit (London).

This sort of information may be needed when reviewing products whose sales are meeting price competition or which are becoming obsolete. In these cases the plant investment may be treated as a wasting asset and special pricing may be developed.

Other facilities

Although the treatment of this part of the information base has been for the purpose of listing production and related resources by the use of Figure 4.11, a similar approach should be taken to the listing of other facilities such as offices, warehouses, service centres and transport outside production sites in order that a formal stocktaking occurs for all the other centres in which capital is employed.

In such cases, the common denominators of the working utility of the resources will be on the lines of:

1 Area in square feet for offices and the number of workers which can be accommodated.
2 Area of floor space, or volume in cubic feet of warehouses, and gallonage in the case of bulk liquid storage units.
3 Counter and window space in retail selling operations.

4 Computer capacity in electronic data processing equipment, or
5 Numbers of persons catered for in welfare units.

Similar statements of the total resources minus utilization, giving the available free reserves, are prepared on the lines of those described for land, buildings and machinery in the field of manufacturing resources.

Resources in personnel

All categories of corporate personnel are regarded as assets. This applies without exception to management, staff and other levels of workers in all departments. The value of the assets of personnel depends upon the continued availability to the firm of their skills, experience and know-how. This in turn depends upon their loyalty and adherence to the company which is promoted by adequate remuneration and motivation in their work. The rate of turnover of various classes of worker is regarded as an index of the continuance of the asset value of personnel. These more personal elements are dealt with further in Section 5.2.3, when the preparation of the personnel plan is described.

A catalogue of recent and present personnel resources by numbers, classes and costs, together with the turnover percentages, forms the information base for the planning of future personnel matters, which follow on the growth plans for the company as a whole.

Figure 4.13 is a typical schedule for the recording of information (and later for planning in Section 5.2.3) in respect of numbers, classes and costs of personnel in the various units of the company. The form is basic in its layout since it can be used at the lowest organizational levels such as a cost centre, then to show summarized data for departments, divisions and functions, and finally in more general form, for the company as a whole.

The question of categories of personnel used in this form will depend upon the nature of the unit reporting. Some units may need to classify their staff by qualifications, though classification by function is more logical.

Thus:

1 A R & D unit may use the classification of PhD (trained and experienced in research), graduates (trained), and laboratory technicians (assistants only), and others.
2 A marketing department may use more of a functional classification such as administration, sales, promotion and sales service, while
3 A production department may use the classification of works and plant managers, foremen, section leaders and other workers.

One of the problems to be faced is in the integration of personnel data at the level of the corporate plan without involving too many categories. At the corporate level it may be restricted to the two classes shown as items 9 and 10 in Figure 4.4, that is, manual workers and those in administrative, technical and clerical grades. Alternatively, four categories of personnel may be preferred—senior management, general management, supervisory and operatives. At lower levels the categories will follow the classification by function as already suggested in the examples 1 to 3 above.

The task of adapting the form for the information base on personnel is one for both the corporate planner and the head of the department who has to plan. In organizations which have a personnel department the task is clearly one for the head of personnel, the corporate planner and the head of the operating department, all three collaborating to ensure not only that the corporate picture is built up, but also that the data base serves as a practical working document for the head of the department concerned.

An important feature of the personnel planning form of Figure 4.13 is the inclusion of cost information, personnel ratios and trends.

Cost of personnel in most concerns, and especially in labour intensive firms, is a key item of expenditure. This becomes more so if costs *associated* with personnel are included. Items such as social security contributions, pension charges, welfare and canteen costs all serve to augment this item of corporate expense.

The preparation of an information base showing data such as:

1   Average cost per person per annum throughout the firm
2   Average cost per person per annum in various categories
3   The percentage change in these items over recent years
4   Forecasts of the future changes in these items

is needed for the preparation of personnel cost budgets in the planning cycle.

Reference to the economic and other forecasts in Section 4.3.2, especially on cost indicators (inflation and the cost of living) and to the company record of past increases in the indices of personnel costs (some due to annual increments on a well-defined scale, and others due to changes in the assortment of workers) provides a basis for the forecasting of personnel costs which are a feature of the planning documents of all the units of the firm.

It is necessary that the corporate planner should propose an assumption concerning the increase in the company index of personnel costs. This is then used throughout all the departments of the firm in the course of preparing the budgets in the five year plan. Such an assumption, after approval which might be that certain personnel costs will increase at an average rate of 9 per cent per annum for the first two years, thereafter at 7 per cent for the five year plan, would be issued by the chief executive in his planning letters for general acceptance throughout the firm (see Sections 4.3.10 and 4.7).

Personnel data of the sort discussed in this section is the basis also for interfirm comparisons with other industries and especially with competitors, when the appropriate data is available. Key ratios in this connection which can be taken into account, even in the first cycle of planning, are:

1   Average salary per employee per annum
2   Average annual increments in the above for the past five years
3   Total sales per employee
4   Assets used per employee
5   Personnel costs as a percentage of total costs, or of total sales.

In this way personnel data can give rise to opportunities and provide yardsticks for the setting of objectives. It also assists in shaping corporate policy in respect of the remuneration of all classes of workers.

Resources in finance

The original financial resources of a company derive from the starting capital subscribed by the shareholders so that at this stage we shall do well to recall that the basic objectives of a company are to safeguard this interest of the shareholders and to enhance its value.

Safeguarding is achieved by the allocation, from its sales or other income, of an amount for the renewal of that part of the original shareholding which is applied to fixed assets or, according to the policy of the firm, applied to such items as R & D expenditure, purchase of know-how or licences, for initial promotional activities and so on.

As a newly-founded company proceeds, its financial policy, especially in respect of the inclusion of adequate provisions for depreciation in its product costing, will more and more show recoveries of the capital used in these start-up expenses and hence ensure its preservation in the form of reserves as such or in the form of other investments in fixed assets. Further, an allocation of a share of profits will be designed to provide additional investment in resources for the overall growth of its activities.

As the company proceeds, it may need to look to other sources for finance. In the first case these will be simple short-term borrowings from banks, from the economic handling of its credit and debit accounts, and so on. Eventually its growth may call for more funds than these sources permit, when it will look in the direction of longer-term loans, other sorts of shares, debentures or to an increase in its basic share capital.

In practice the responsibility for the proper handling, and hence the planning of these affairs, is that of the head of the finance function. Nevertheless he will only be able to plan these affairs if the basic corporate policy and guidelines in respect of financial and funding matters have been laid down, that is, if the 'rules of the game' have been spelled out by the chief executive.

The corporate planner has a part to play in the setting of basic policy rather than in actual operations, and in ensuring that the planning processes in all areas are conducted in the light of this policy.

It is with this background that a catalogue of the financial resources of the firm should be compiled, usually by the head of finance in all but the smallest concerns when it may be a task for the corporate planner himself.

The origin of the financial resources is listed according to whether it is actual or potential. The use of existing monies, that is of the first named type, calls only for a decision on its allocation in the planning process, while the second calls for a previous corporate decision as a matter of policy, to exploit an opportunity to make money available in order to enable a resource allocation to be made. Both procedures arise during the various phases of planning.

Financial resources from cash flow (profits, depreciation and so on) will be shown as emerging, year by year, in the budget section of plans, usually those at corporate level 1 (see Section 5.2.5).

Nevertheless the checklist in Figure 4.14—which is not necessarily exhaustive—should be used for the preparation of the information base on financial resources, however roughly some may be estimated. Whether any or all of the potential sources are realized depends on the demand and the policy of the firm. The list itself will suggest direct opportunities for the finance department head to contribute to corporate profitability by the better deployment and gearing of the resources foreseen.

The ready availability of the quantified list during the practical phases of planning is important, especially during the feed-back stages when alternative strategies are being evaluated and questions arise for information on financial resources.

Final note on resources

Catalogues of the various types of resources described in this section, provide a basis for the identification of opportunities by the heads of the respective areas of the

ACTION PLANNING TEST LIST 11   **Section 4.3.4**

QUESTIONS	RESPONSE BY	TIMING OF ACTION ARISING
1 Prepare catalogues of the resources of the firm using formats as quoted, or others designed to show specific corporate resource categories (a) fixed assets Figure 4.11 and 4.12 (b) personnel Figure 4.13 (c) finance Figure 4.14 and, (d) others as required	Corporate planner and appropriate units	
2 Agree upon a formula for showing the production capacity analysis and provide this information to the corresponding business head	Corporate planner and head of production	
3 Identify the major items in 1 and 2 above, for use during the first cycle of planning, and take steps for the completion of the catalogue for the second cycle	Corporate planner and appropriate units	
4 Make a decision for organizing the function of management (executive) development (a) within the existing personnel function, or, (b) as an independent function	Chief executive	

business which are analysed. They also serve for a rapid estimation of the costs of new projects, especially involving fixed assets in manufacturing and other facilities, and the personnel to man them, when plans for growth call for new investments.

4.3.5 Technology

A vital part of the information base is the assessment of the trends of technological change (technological forecasting). Few organizations are outside this influence which is considered to be the principal source of changes of all kinds.

Developments in technology have been and will continue to be the mainspring of developments in most areas of life and of business. They are the prime causes of social, environmental and economic change; they can also influence political attitudes, and obviously have a crucial part to play in businesses and industries which are technologically oriented. In the context of this workbook they are regarded as the chief source of progress towards growth, profitability and security in most companies, even in companies whose affairs do not immediately appear to have a high technological content. Accordingly they figure highly in planning.

An assessment of technological trends becomes an important part of the information base in that they are analysed, forecasts need to be made and conclusions drawn. Depending on their nature they can:

1 Present opportunities—or threats—to the company as a whole or to a part or parts of its business.
2 Influence basic corporate objectives and policy.
3 Affect the operating units in that they need to respond to the changes in corporate level objectives.
4 Direcly affect the technology employed in individual operating departments.

Developments can pose threats to a firm through changes in market demand, obsolescence of its products and the processes of manufacture, and of the services it renders. The use of the questionnaire in Figure 4.25, which deals with 'What business are we in' and 'Opportunities for growth', can profitably be used as a basis for assessments of this kind. Developments which are suggested as growth opportunities can, when effected by competitors, be a source of threats.

The responsibility of preparing the information base on technological developments is an obvious one for the technically competent staff in a firm, but not necessarily theirs alone. Many other personnel can bring in new information and ideas, especially the marketing staff, through their contacts with customers and hence with external developments. There is a particular part for market research staff to play in this work. An awareness of developments through the scanning of the lists of patents in the publications of the Patent Office is an obvious one for the R & D staff itself.

Under these conditions the corporate planner has an overall function, best summarized as being responsible for methodology, administration and the motivation of colleagues.

The minimum action required is the systematic evaluation of all the technological changes already perceived or forecast as likely to have an impact on the company's interest. The changes may equally relate to any of the following:

1 Products made and sold.
2 Nature and calibre of services sold.

74

3 Processes used in the manufacture of a company's products.
4 The products and processes employed by the customer.
5 Services and materials bought in by the company (energy, packing, transport and raw materials).
6 The services rendered to the customer as suggested by the examples in the last main column of Figure 4.25.

The key conclusions from these studies should ideally be quantified in a series of technological forecasts on the following four lines:

1 Qualitatively, that is as to their nature, described in narrative form.
2 Quantitatively, which is the level of activity in terms of technical performance, or their economic influence on, for example, market shares. Part two of a technological forecast should be given in numerical values.
3 As to the time scale in years over which the development is expected to materialize.
4 An overall assessment of the probability of the development, as so far described, coming to pass. By this is meant the degree of likelihood of the occurrence. This is expressed on a scale of 0 (no likelihood in say, 25 years) to 1.0 (100 per cent certain in the time span quoted).

While it is not always possible to prepare such an ideal description of technological developments, efforts should be made to describe the last three stages of technological forecasts in numerical terms in order to give the best basis for decision making in the planning process.

The developments may be external to the company, reported in journals or by marketing people, or they may be completely internal in origin in which case successful developments from R & D or production departments afford the company an opportunity to innovate in prices, products or processes, and possibly become market leaders.

The areas in which technological change can be influential are obviously too wide and too numerous to be listed in this workbook but cogent reminders of the past impact of technological changes whose effects are still likely to continue, are:

1 The sequence of radio valves—transistors—integrated circuitry (solid state physics) in the electronic and computer industries.
2 The concept of disposable garments which affect paper, textile, plastics, garment and merchandising businesses.
3 Anti-pollution legislation which is forcing technological changes in such areas as waste disposal, car exhaust emission and conservation of nature reserves.
4 The historic sequence of travel by foot—horse—steam train—motor car—aeroplane and rocket; similarly by sail to powered boats and ships to hovercraft.
5 Developments in food processing and handling—canning, chilled meats, deep freezing, dehydrated foods, precooking, synthetic protein from oil etc. with corresponding influences on packaging, storage and handling. .
6 Telecommunications and information storage on tapes and in cassettes and their influence on education, newspapers, journals, radio etc.
7 Polymer research, as distinct from agricultural research, which has led to synthetic textile fibres and rubbers from non-biological sources.
8 Psychiatry has been greatly assisted by development in pharmaceutical products.
9 Packaging—glass, cans, tin, aluminium foil, plastics.

ACTION PLANNING TEST LIST 12   Section 4.3.5

QUESTIONS	RESPONSE BY	TIMING OF ACTION ARISING
1 Is the company technologically oriented with respect to products, processes used, services and customer interest?	Corporate planner	
2 If not, identify external technological developments, which can have an impact on the firm's interests	All management	
3 Recall the four elements of technological forecasting and state why probabilistic qualifications are needed	Corporate planner and R & D	
4 Prepare a scheme for the introduction of technological forecasting in the firm based on the procedures of Appendix II. When would this be scheduled?	Corporate planner and R & D	

What are now described as signals of technological change must also be noted: whether they are near, that is already taking shape and maturing, or are distant and barely discernible. The following are given as examples, the analogies to which must be sought for the information base on technology, according to the particular interests of a company:

synthetic tobacco	increased human longevity
plastic paper	synthetic lawns
population control in western countries	forging of plastics
lasers	synthetic white pigments
solar heat sources	carbon and other new fibres
fuel cells	biodegradable plastics
minerals from the sea bed	underwater living
weather control	traffic-free cities
non-tarnish metals	frictionless machine parts
powder metallurgy	taped video magazines

It is the joint responsibility of the corporate planner and the R & D staff to make a systematic survey of all the technical interests of the firm and to identify the key developments, both internal and external, and to note any signals of change, however distant. The use of the technique of relevance trees, described in the literature of technological forecasting, is useful in this sort of analysis.

Once the developments are identified, attempts to quantify them are made on the four lines already described, whereupon conclusions have to be drawn and attitudes taken according to whether they represent opportunities or threats to the business of the firm. The time scale and the associated estimates of probability in such technological forecasts determine whether immediate company action is called for, or whether this is deferred to a later cycle of planning, when the subject develops sufficiently to justify action.

The action which follows goes on the formal lines of opportunity, objective and strategy at corporate level, the strategy being to initiate objectives for one or other planning units of the firm. Although in most cases the strategy will lead to objectives for the R & D units, others may arise. Thus the questions of the licensing of new processes from the original inventors or the takeover of the innovating company become of interest and will form objectives for other planning units.

In view of the importance of the input of technological developments to the overall planning process and the need to have a systematic approach to the information base, a listing of the methods of technological forecasting is provided in Appendix II, together with procedures for the introduction of the methods to a firm and their subsequent development as formal planning tools. Technological forecasting not only serves for the information base on technology but in certain cases provides a highly systematic source of new concepts and projects for the R & D departments.

4.3.6 Key factors for success

Growth in profitability is synonymous with success and here we are involved with how it is achieved in practice. The first stage is to identify the key factors which contribute to profits, directly or indirectly. The second stage is to measure them, and to measure how well the performance of the company or its units stands in relation to them, and finally to set them up as opportunities in the planning process.

The following Section 4.3.7, which deals with strengths and weaknesses, should be approached in the light of the key factors for success, since the measurement of strengths and weaknesses is really a measurement of how well the company performs in respect of these critical elements.

Key factors in business have been referred to as strategic factors; they are the critical major elements in business operations which can reveal the opportunities to be taken and the weaknesses which must be overcome. To identify these factors calls for a close study of all the influences on the supply and demand position of a business, and the identification of the major items which are unique to a given set of circumstances. Frequently there is more than one key factor.

Wherever possible key factors and their influence should be identified in measurable terms. The experience of Pareto's Law shows that 80 per cent of effect results from 20 per cent in number of items or effort. The review of the firm's activities in relation to key factors should be carried out in the light of this relationship.

The aim is to identify the factors which, though few in number, have a large effect, and then to exploit them at the appropriate planning stage. The fewer and more important they are, the better; in fact, in dealing with the concepts of opportunities and how they are presented in the actual plans (Section 5 deals with the format and presentation of plans) it is suggested that the number be purposely limited. Four to six opportunities based on key factors are ample, provided they are of the right degree of importance.

Measurable key factors

The general approach to measurable key factors is through the examination of all kinds of business activities which can be quantified and to which important business ratios, and ultimately monetary values, can be applied.

They appear at all levels of a concern, at the corporate level, at divisional or functional levels and at the levels of departments and cost centres. They appear in all the operations of the company, in production, marketing, finance and so on.

At the corporate level, they are usually in wider terms and more broadly based than at lower operating levels. They normally form the basis of opportunities and objectives at level 1 and are then translated to strategies to be passed to one or other division or function for acceptance as their objective level 2.

Key business ratios at the corporate level 1, stem from the basic objective of profitability, that is, profits earned in relation to the resources used. Important secondary ratios which stem from this primary ratio are:

1 sales to capital used
2 profit on sales
3 fixed assets to capital used
4 current assets to capital used
5 stocks to sales
6 sales per employee
7 fixed assets per employee (in manufacturing firms)
8 financial assets per employee (in other businesses)
9 R & D expenditure to sales.

In larger organizations which comprise self-contained business divisions, these ratios may still be applicable at this level, but as more operational levels are studied, other ratios of a more domestic nature will be called for. Thus, depending upon the sort of business involved, any one or more of the following may prove to be key factors:

1   sales per representative and per customer
2   production cost to sales price
3   marketing costs to sales
4   promotional costs to sales
5   service costs to sales
6   transport, packaging etc costs to sales
7   delivery time on orders received.

Manufacturing departments will be involved in ratios of particular revelance to their own activities. The overriding consideration in this case will start with the chief elements which form the cost of production, their relative impact and whether they are inside or outside the control of the works management.
Examples of specific ratios in this case are:

1   raw materials stocks to total output values
2   finished product stocks to total output and to sales
3   raw material usage and wastage
4   conversion efficiencies
5   process labour costs to total costs
6   maintenance costs to total costs
7   minimum economic size of plant for competitive production costs.

The activities of other departments of a functional nature should also be subject to studies of this kind. Further ideas on the levels of business ratios for the corporate planner to adopt, especially at corporate and divisional levels, can be obtained from the publications of the Centre for Interfirm Comparison (London), the Dunn and Bradstreet Reports on Key Business Ratios (New York and at one time in London) or from special studies carried out by stock exchange analysts or trade associations.

Other key factors

In many cases key factors are difficult to measure and indeed are much more difficult to identify in the first instance. They are more abstract than those which arise from well-known and logical business ratios of the type already described. Nevertheless the search for them is important. Like good concepts in innovation, their recognition and success in exploiting them can transform the results of almost any company.
Thus in the field of ethical pharmaceuticals, it is imperative to have products which have been approved and classified by the National Health Service. Once this approval is obtained it is the promotional effort which commands sales, income and profit. An analysis of the various forms of promotion available shows that success depends on the verbal presentation of medical data to a practising doctor by a firm's representative. Promotion by all other means is of secondary value. In view of the limited time that a doctor allows for interviews, the key factor is the amount of time obtained by the representative and the way he uses it to present medical data on his firm's products. Successful promotion under these conditions leads to the subsequent prescription by the doctor and then a sale through the pharmacy. Promotion directed to the pharmacists or patients is valueless.

For 'over-the-counter' pharmaceuticals the key factor is different: it is the amount of counter space allotted to promotional materials provided by the maker, and is more akin to the promotion of High Street retail sales.

In the case of other industries and businesses, quite different key factors may operate, as the following suggest:

1 styling in clothing or motor cars
2 type of packaging, for example aerosols for convenience
3 easy product maintenance (or none at all!)
4 rapid convertibility of deposits to cash in finance businesses
5 attractive credit terms in selling machine tools to small concerns
6 good plant location for heavy materials industries.

Assessments of such factors is a highly subjective process especially in dealing with key factors such as the value of a corporate image, a brand name and so on. For this reason it may be desirable in later stages of planning to use outside resources for their identification and evaluation.

In practice this procedure can conveniently be merged with studies of the type described in Section 4.3.8, when making appraisals of the strengths and weaknesses of one's competitors. Internal managements may not themselves be wholly objective in making any of these assessments and the collection of data by independent interviewers from an outside agency overcomes the problem. Such appraisals, for example, could find that:

1 A key factor is the use of a technical representative as distinct from a sales representative.
2 Product standardization and reliability of quality have more effect on order placement than price cutting.
3 The procedure of following an imitator is welcomed because a buyer has a choice of supplier—if only as a standby, since he values this in his efforts to measure prices and to buy goods more competitively.
4 Product advertising of industrial goods has a low value.
5 Buying decisions are made in a customer firm by someone other than the official buyer, for example, by a shop-floor foreman, the technical manager or even the managing director!

Figures 4.15 to 4.19 deal with strengths and weaknesses of five important areas and each carries a column to enable key factors to be marked as the check lists in it are reviewed. The lists themselves suggest a wide range of business elements (some of which have already been mentioned) which should be studied by the corporate planner in cooperation with his planning colleagues, in order to help identify factors which may be unique to the business areas they control. The lists contain both measurable and non-measurable elements.

A sound analysis of the key factors for success may not be achieved in the first cycle of planning, but a preliminary attempt should certainly be made to determine the obvious and outstanding factors, and to agree upon them. A more detailed study should be made during the preparation of the information base for the second cycle of planning, that is, during the currency of the first five-year plan.

The schedules in Figures 4.15 to 4.19 are not intended to be authoritative or exhaustive, but to act as illustrations of the sort of areas and the topics within them which need to be probed. Many of those listed are measurable and others are less so. Nevertheless suggestions are made in them, by the indication of numbers or value ratios, of what are good or bad levels of performance. The analysis of schedules such as these and *prepared according to the nature of the company's business,* should be made on the lines of:

1 Is this a key factor in our business?
2 How good, or bad, are we in respect of it?
3 Does it offer an opportunity to be followed up in business planning?

In summary, key factors for success are critical elements and the degree of response that a company or one of its units is capable of making towards their exploitation is a measure of its strengths and weaknesses, aspects of the information base which are dealt with further in the following section.

4.3.7 Strengths and weaknesses

It is a tenet of successful management that strengths are to be exploited and weaknesses overcome. Equally, corporate planning requires that critical and unbiased analyses be made of the quality of the company's resources and its behaviour as an entity. In this way strengths and weaknesses in all areas and at all levels are identified and spelled out in measurable terms if possible, as part of the information base. Their recognition in this way is an aid to the identification of opportunities and the setting of objectives in the planning process.

The preceding section which dealt with key factors for success, indicates which activities are important and which are really critical. The aim of the present section is to assess the extent to which the company through its departments and personnel responds to the key factors, and hence how capably it can exploit them. A high capability is one of its strengths; a low capability is a weakness.

In many cases, especially with elements which are difficult to quantify, the assessment is somewhat similar to the psychoanalysis of people, but here applied to the company and its operations. Nevertheless, by introducing scales of numerical values, the problems of subjectivity are lessened, and what amounts in many cases to self criticism becomes more dispassionate.

The schedules in Figures 4.15 to 4.19 on strengths and weaknesses are designed to overcome the problems of assessment through the use of a four point scale of values constituting very good, good, fair and poor performance levels. In planning language, the first would clearly indicate a strength and the last a weakness. In different words, they would indicate 'What are we good at?' and 'What are we bad at?'

As explained in the preceding section on key factors for success, the lists of Figures 4.15 to 4.19 are not intended to be exhaustive. This would be impossible on account of the widely differing activities of the many companies embarking upon assessments for corporate planning purposes. Furthermore, in some cases, the numerical scale of values suggested is almost arbitrary. They are to be taken as average values, drawn sufficiently wide to enable distinctions to be made between good and bad performances.

A preliminary attempt should be made in the first cycle of planning to identify the outstanding strengths and weaknesses of the company. This can be done at the same time as the key factor analysis: indeed the two quests should proceed simultaneously. Although only a preliminary attempt may be feasible in the first cycle of planning, it

ACTION PLANNING TEST LIST 13 — Sections 4.3.6 and 4.3.7

QUESTIONS	RESPONSE BY	TIMING OF ACTION ARISING
1 Distinguish between measurable and non-measurable key factors Organize dialogues with heads of business divisions and functions to identify the latter in their areas of operation	All management led by chief executive	
2 Identify the key factors for success in the firm's sphere of activity, using the questions in Figures 4.15 to 4.19 as starting points	Corporate planner and appropriate management	
3 If the cases named in Figures 4.15 to 4.19 do not cover all your activities, prepare relevant questionnaires eg for such businesses as, banking, insurance, retailing, service activities etc Identify the key factors in any new list	Corporate planner and appropriate management	
4 How does your company and/or its units measure up against the key factors?	All management led by chief executive	
5 Which sources of key business ratios and inter-firm comparisons have been used? What gaps in information are there and what steps will you take to fill them?	Corporate planner	

will have a great educational value and develop an awareness which can be cultivated on later occasions.

It is the responsibility of the corporate planner after the first cycle of planning is over and while the first year's business activity is under way to study these lists and to:

1 decide which topics are relevant to the company, and by selection and additions,
2 prepare appropriate listings for future use, and
3 suggest the scale of values which is realistic and meaningful to the firm and its sort of activities.

In this work he should be supported by the chief executive. The resulting questionnaires, suitably tailored to the company's sort of activities, are studied and completed in cooperation with the heads of each of the planning units in the organization. It is also a responsibility of the chief executive to contribute to the discussions which are involved in order to assist in the objective evaluation of what are the key factors and how well his company and its staff perform against the standards laid down. In the case of larger organizations typified in Figures 3.6 and 3.7, this becomes a task for the head of the business or function with the corporate planner making objective contributions.

It is not unusual in appraisals of this nature—certainly in the early stages of planning —to find that adequate data are not available on which to make assessments, and still less so on which to make decisions. This applies to many parts of the build-up of information bases. Important statistics and working data on the company's past activities are often lacking. However, information bases are rarely complete at any point in time and are ongoing parts of each planning cycle. The omissions and inabilities revealed in early planning cycles point the way to the production of more purposeful management information for the future. Often it is only after such searches and compilations are complete that worthwhile schedules for management information systems are devised and worthwhile information bases for planning purposes are built up.

A good information base, especially in relation to key factors, and to strengths and weaknesses, is a continuing responsibility. It becomes more and more valuable when trends and changes in the firm's behaviour become evident through changes in one or other of the business ratios of the type discussed in Sections 4.3.6 and 4.3.7 of the workbook.

4.3.8 Competitor analysis

The preceding sections of the information base, especially those dealing with resources, key factors for success and strengths and weaknesses, point the way to judge the standing of the company and its operating departments in many business areas. The application of the same yardsticks to a firm's competitors, on the basis of knowing one's enemies, is a further item of importance in the development of the information base.

The analysis of this sort of data, carried out alongside that of one's own position, highlights the comparison between the character profiles of the two or more companies and can become a critical source of opportunities and, needless to say, of problems to be solved. Much can be learned from this kind of exercise but it is not one which is likely to be conducted in depth until the second cycle of planning is started. Once it has been compiled it only remains to be updated as further news appears.

The responsibility of gathering the data on competitors is that of the corporate planner working firstly with the appropriate heads of business divisions, especially those with marketing responsibilities, and then with others who may have access to different information from that which comes from sales and customer contacts. It should be organized on the lines of marketing activities, that is, by competitors in given products or product groups, or by markets, if the products are sold to different users, then followed by more general data on competitors so that a picture of their corporate standing is built up.

Data sheets on the lines of Figures 4.20 and 4.21 should be completed as far as possible for all these sectors of the competitor analysis. A good information base will contain a large number of such forms, covering the major competitors in each marketing or product group sales area.

The collection of information concerning competitor firms is obviously a more difficult task than providing data about one's own affairs. In practice the net needs to be cast very widely. There are many sources to be tapped, and the following should be considered in this search for information:

1   Reports from sales and technical representatives working in the field, and suitably primed as to the sort of information required.
2   Order placement patterns by the customers.
3   Promotional literature and trade samples or illustrations.
4   Credit reports from financial houses.
5   Annual reports and accounts.
6   Newspaper reports, especially from interviews published in financial journals.
7   Local newspapers reporting on the inauguration of new projects, company celebrations etc.
8   Business intelligence reports (Moodies, Extel etc).
9   Publication of papers in trade and other journals by the professional staff of the competitors.
10 The *Office Patents Journal*.
11 Market research agencies.

The procedure of using outside market research agencies on the lines mentioned in Section 4.3.6 dealing with key factors for success and strengths and weaknesses has a unique attraction in the search for competitor data. The anonymity of the sponsoring organization can be preserved while the interviewer puts an agreed series of questions to a chosen list of customers.

The customer is asked to rank his major suppliers (including the sponsoring company) in some sort of arbitrary order (on a point scale say of 5 for excellent down to 0 for bad), against the agreed series of questions. Such anonymity and the fact of consulting a third party, the customer, gives more objectivity to the assessment of the competitive organization, so the outcome is not only an outsider's view of one's own company but of its competitors as well.

The 11 items listed above suggest which other personnel and departments of the firm may be called upon to cooperate with the corporate planner in collecting and assembling the information base on the principal competitors. In important cases the planner would institute a library of files, each one dealing with a given competitor, as distinct from the information base provided by Figure 4.20 which deals with several competitors in a particular market area.

Such a library of files, analysing facts and trends concerning the resources and characteristics of competing firms, becomes doubly useful when the firm begins to contemplate growth by acquisition or merger. When the dichotomy of the planning

ACTION PLANNING TEST LIST 14   **Section 4.3.8**

QUESTIONS	RESPONSE BY	TIMING OF ACTION ARISING
1 Does the format of Figure 4.20 cover your firm's interests? If not, devise one appropriate to the circumstances	Corporate planner	
2 Institute a procedure for collecting information on competitors (Figure 4.20)	Corporate planner	
3 What steps should be taken to obtain an *objective* appraisal of the strengths and weaknesses of your company's activities and those of its competitors? When would you propose to take such steps?	Corporate planner and chief executive	
4 What are the first steps in developing an Information Base on 'other parties', when the strategy of merger or acquisition is contemplated?	Corporate planner	

organization develops to the point of corporate development, this is a task for the head of corporate development within the whole planning department.

The information so built up helps answer the questions, 'What can they do that we cannot?', 'What have they got that we should like to have?', 'Do their activities and resources complement ours?', and so on. Such questions arise in strategic studies on merger and acquisition possibilities.

Like many of the data sheets on the information base, the forms derived from the use of Figure 4.20 should be on the table when discussions take place on opportunities and objectives.

When analysing the strengths and weaknesses of competitors, it is worthwhile to make a similar analysis of a firm's suppliers of raw materials or services. This is a task for the purchasing function of a firm, in the build-up of its own information base. The production of profiles on this type of third party becomes another valuable source of information when the strategy of a merger or acquisition arises and the policy of 'backwards' diversification is being studied.

A further way in which the analysis of the characteristics of third parties can be approached is through the use of a profile questionnaire of the type in Figure 4.21. This summarizes in a practical way the strengths and weaknesses of one's own company and those of a competitor or supplier, or indeed of any other outside party, and provides a starting point for the selection of candidates in the study of merger and acquisition possibilities. The listings of Figure 4.21, which are on the lines of what we have, what they have and what we want, is slanted in terms of a specific sort of business but can easily be adapted by the corporate planner for use in other directions.

4.3.9 Portrait of a business

After the extensive search for information about the company's business, both internal and external, the analysis of how it has behaved in the past in relation to the environment and forecasts of how things are expected to go in the future, it becomes necessary to sift out the salient features and to epitomize them so that management can see their scale and importance. Such tabulations, called portraits of a business, are a useful procedure at this phase of the planning process.

An example of the features of a business is given in Figure 4.22 which portrays, in the form of an executive summary, the key aspects of its affairs and interests in relation to its markets. The particular text used applies to a company which is either wholly concerned with the business of printing inks, or has a business division which is so concerned.

The business portraits discussed here relate to the several businesses of a company or its sub-businesses in the event that divisions have a number of separable commercial activities and interests. The definition given in Section 3.2 is that a business is a corporate or divisional activity which essentially involves marketing. The business portraits are therefore market oriented and should be prepared for each of the major marketing areas of interest to a business.

The term marketing in this section and throughout the book is used in its widest sense and may refer to the marketing of:

1 Products, for example motor cars, chemicals, toiletries.
2 Services, for example postal and other forms of communication, transport, leisure.
3 Facilities, for example banking and credit facilities of all kinds, insurance.

ACTION PLANNING TEST LIST 15

QUESTIONS	RESPONSE BY	TIMING OF ACTION ARISING
1 Issue forms, modelled on Figure 4.22, to each business head for completion in respect of each of their markets and sub-markets by product groups Assist the business head in preparing the summaries as far as possible in the first cycle of planning, and take steps to verify the facts or fill any gaps in preparation for the second cycle	Corporate planner and business heads	
2 In the event of acquisition being a strategy of interest, assemble preliminary information on the lines of: (a) competitor analysis Figure 4.20 (b) 'other party' analysis Figure 4.21, and (c) portrait of a business Figure 4.22	Corporate planner	

Such tabulations as shown in the format and text of Figure 4.22, rendered at company level for a single business company, or for each of its businesses in the case of a multi-divisional concern, should be prepared by the corporate planner himself in the first named case, or in cooperation with the appropriate business head in the second case.

The bringing together of the essential parts of the information base on the lines of Figure 4.22 is the culmination of the work done and gives a final perspective to the whole situation. The summaries show the highlights of the past and present economic aspects, and the forecasts of the development of the key features.

They provide a thumbnail sketch of the overall activity and so indicate to top management the sort and scale of the factors in order that attention in the quest for profit growth can be focused on them.

4.3.10 Assumptions and their levels

General remarks

In Section 5 the formal presentation of plans is standardized on the basis that each plan contains six sections or chapters. One of these is called assumptions. Here we are concerned with how they have arisen during the practical phases of planning and where and how they fit into different sorts of plans.

Various sorts of forecasts which appear as parts of the information base form the basis of assumptions. In many cases the forecasts will have a high degree of probability and subsequent plans will be prepared on the basis that this will be high enough to warrant their acceptance and as justifying action programmes in consequence. In other words, we plan on the basis that the situation forecast is very likely to occur.

In spite of this however there will be certain elements in the information base which are either difficult to forecast or which may be regarded, at least within the competency of the planning staff, as being incapable of being forecast with any degree of reliability. In many instances attitudes may need to be taken on matters wholly outside the control of the firm.

In these cases a communal stance is taken in order that all units adopt the same approach and that all plans can be integrated to form the corporate plan. It is for these difficult elements, for which there is no sound basis in forecasting, that specific assumptions are adopted.

Elements difficult or impossible to forecast are naturally those most distant from the firm's operations—international events and events at a national level. Both are discussed in Section 4.3.2.

In such problem areas, a 'most reasonable or expected' level, or a simple yes or no to the question of any change, is specified and used equally throughout the firm as an agreed assumption. Very often there will be items which can be quantified and which enter directly into the operating statements in the budget chapters of plans. Rates of inflation and cost increases, levels of taxation and duties, charges for social security benefits and foreign exchange rates, are simple examples of items on which assumptions need to be made for these purposes.

Under these conditions, variances from the budgeted levels of profit performance during the period of implementation of the plans are measured against the agreed assumptions. Changes in the assumptions which occur during the currency of the plan and which are, of course, outside the control of the company or its departments are accepted in explaining operating variances during the currency of the plan. Such deviations are not held to the account of the operating head who prepared a plan based on agreed corporate assumptions.

Naturally it is the responsibility of all concerned to make the best possible assumptions and if doubts exist it is prudent to tend to conservatism. Changes which occur in practice are taken strictly into account during the control procedure. Section 6 deals more fully with these stages, but the following hypothetical examples illustrate the way they may occur:

1   An assumption is made that corporation tax will be 40 per cent. In the event it proves to be $42\frac{1}{2}$ per cent, with a corresponding reduction in profits.
2   An assumption that investment grants will be 35 per cent is made but it proves to be only 25 per cent, leading to a reduction in cash flow.
3   Assumptions are made that the rate of tariff reductions between the UK and the EEC during the transition period of entry will be 40, 35 and 30 per cent over the three year period; actual events might prove otherwise.
4   Assumptions are made that there will be no change in the level of selective employment tax: a downwards change actually occurs, giving lower personnel costs and an increase in profits.
5   Assumptions are made that the value of the pound sterling will be $2.30 US but in practice it stays above this level, with beneficial effects on export earnings.

None of the benefits or disadvantages resulting from these changes are held to the account of the chief executive or of the heads of departments, when actual performance against plan is measured during the monitoring and control stages. They are outside their control.

Specific corporate assumptions of this character are key features of planning. Agreement is necessary so that all departmental plans will be based on common and uniform starting points and the process of control during the period of implementation of plans can be effected in a measurable way and directed to the activities over which executives can exercise control in their operational work, and for which they make commitments in their plans.

Assumption levels

A further aspect of assumptions is that they should be identified as originating at the different planning levels of the company described in Section 3.3 and by Figure 3.8.

Assumptions at level 1 affect the company as a whole. They generally arise from the information base, Section 4.3.2 which deals with external events at international and national levels. They are accepted uniformly throughout the firm. Five examples of this kind have been given. They are expressly stated and are notified to the heads of planning units by inclusion in the planning letters of the chief executive as specific corporate assumptions.

Assumptions at level 2 affect a business division or a functional unit. They arise from the information base (Section 4.3.3 which deals with industries and markets) which are linked more closely with the affairs of the department in question. They are more likely to be based on forecasts of outside events, but more reliably prepared. More accountability can therefore be attached to them during the control period. A high sales and profit performance in the light of divisional assumptions concerning a low market growth is not necessarily praiseworthy and will undoubtedly justify the 'downwards' setting of objectives by top management in later cycles of planning, as

ACTION PLANNING TEST LIST 16 Section 4.3.10

QUESTION	RESPONSE BY	TIMING OF ACTION ARISING
1 Distinguish between assumptions and forecasts How is the factor of probability reflected in either of them?	All management	
2 List all the items on which assumptions will be necessary and made, as at corporate level 1	Corporate planner	
3 Who makes, and who acts upon assumptions at various levels?	All management	

described in Section 4.4.3, part 3. In this case it is due to poor forecasting, or an unduly conservative outlook. In either case, it does not constitute good planning.

Assumptions at level 3 affect a department. They are of an even more domestic nature than those at level 2, which affect the middle level of the company's operations. Nevertheless, it behoves the manager of a marketing unit to make realistic assumptions concerning the availability of new specialized staff and the manager of a production unit to face up to trade union demands.

The formal plan of the company includes a list of the assumptions made for the firm as a whole. Those of divisions and functions need only refer to the corporate assumptions but they should itemize those which directly relate to their own operations at level 2, and on which their plans were based. A similar procedure is followed between divisional assumptions and those of any of its departments at level 3.

Under these conditions, assumptions are seen to appear at three levels. Figure 4.23 in Section 4.3.11 includes a duty list of who prepares different parts of the information base as such (which includes forecasts) and it also confirms the principle of the three levels of assumptions. Agreement on assumptions at levels 2 and 3 is made at the point when the preliminary plans are submitted and the corresponding dialogue occurs, whereupon they are approved and used in the preparation of the final versions of plans on the lines of the timetable of planning phases during each annual cycle.

The appropriate assumptions should be familiar to all who contribute to the development of plans, whatever their level.

4.3.11 Who produces which information base, forecasts and assumptions

It will be evident from the extensive treatment given in the workbook to the quest for information that a sound base is a cornerstone in the practical stages of corporate planning as followed in this workbook.

Planning without adequate and reliable information and sound forecasts is a waste of time. To avoid information gathering and sound forecasting is to pay mere lip service to planning as a tool of management.

Furthermore the work involved, apart from being logical and basic to any concern, is salutary in itself, both at company and departmental levels. Firstly, it obliges all the management to face and answer important questions, some of which may be embarrassing, and secondly, it forces them to take an attitude towards the future conditions under which they foresee the company operating. In particular it produces a highly valuable analysis of the company as a living entity and of its personnel and resources.

Although the purpose is naturally to make sound assessments and forecasts, it is probable that in the first cycle of planning the results may not be all that are desired. Nevertheless the very process of attempting these studies has benefits, for it obliges executives to think full-cycle, that is, to consider all the sorts of things which are relevant and likely to have an impact on their affairs. More of the benefits of this sort of mental approach will arise later when dealing with the selection and choice of strategies in Section 4.4 and later.

Overall these procedures, which are intrinsic to corporate planning, are also some of its practical attractions in that a wide range of people are involved from the chief executive down to departmental heads.

Figure 4.23 charts the principal components of the information base as described in Section 4.3 of the workbook and it indicates who is responsible, either singly or severally, for their compilation.

ACTION PLANNING TEST LIST 17

QUESTION	RESPONSE BY	TIMING OF ACTION ARISING
1 After reviewing the elements of the Information Base in Section 4.3, and having devised formats of special importance to the firm's interest, issue a list (on the lines of Figure 4.23) to all participants in planning State the dates by which each should be complete in the case of: (*a*) the first cycle of planning, or, (*b*) other cycles	Corporate planner	
2 What are the formal and the functional responsibilities of the corporate planner in respect of the Information Base?	Corporate planner	

Apart from motivating his colleagues, the corporate planner, in the practical phases of building up the information base, has the following responsibilities:

1 Provide the methodology; the forms, charts and check lists in this section of the workbook are regarded as models from which others oriented to the particular interests of a firm are derived.
2 Conduct the quest for information and make forecasts for all the higher level factors which have an impact on the firm as a whole. These are the macro-indicators of activity at the national level, or at the level of sectors such as industry or agriculture, which go to form the national activity as components of the GDP.
3 Conduct the quest for information and make forecasts for business divisions concerning the individual markets within those mentioned in 2 above, when these departments do not have competent or adequate staff themselves.
4 Produce a summary of the main points of all the information bases and forecasts, as an annual report for use at corporate level 1.
5 Include in the foregoing report all the agreed corporate assumptions of level 1, which apply equally and without exception to all planning units in the firm. This especially applies to the general economic assumptions which form the basis of budget calculations on costs and expenditure, such as wage and material price inflation, levels of taxation, social welfare subscriptions, as suggested in the preceding section in Section 4.3.10.

(The items mentioned in 4 and 5 are part of the packet of planning documents which are issued with the planning letters of the chief executive in order to provide the corporate background and the common basis for planning.)

6 Cooperate with others having a personal responsibility for the production of an information base and for forecasting in their respective areas.
7 Ensure the continuous updating of the corporate information base.
8 Cooperate with others to ensure the continuous updating and amendment of their lower level bases and forecasts.

4.4 OPPORTUNITIES, OBJECTIVES AND STRATEGIES

4.4.1 General remarks

The elements of planning given at the outset in Section 1.1 call for the analysis, evaluation and selection from among the opportunities which are foreseen. The three stages called for in this part aim to do this in practice, the corporate planner providing the lead in the adoption of the three stage approach and encouraging his colleagues to pursue the same sort of thinking in building up their plans, since the actual format of plans, outlined later in Section 5, involves their presentation in exactly the same sequence.

The following are reminders of what is involved:

Opportunities arise from the analysis of the information base, and are identified areas of potential business growth over and above those in which the company or one of its units has already performed. They represent performance levels towards which the unit can direct its efforts. Ordinarily they represent the maximum which can be foreseen.

Objectives are levels of activity which are taken as goals and which preferably lie beyond past performance levels but within the limits prescribed·by the opportunities.

Strategies follow on the chosen level of objectives and broadly are the means which it is proposed to employ in order to reach the level of objectives set within the upper limits of possibilities represented by the opportunities.

In practice the achievement of objective levels depends on the resources, both present and potential, that the company can deploy. Higher level objectives are expected to call for appropriately more resources. The practical process of planning involves calculations to determine the cost of the resources which are required in relation to the gain expected by the achievement of the objective. Obviously the big question is whether a given strategy calling for a certain use of resources will achieve a given objective and whether there is a net gain in profitability. The testing of various strategies for their ability to contribute to the objectives level, as measured by profitability, is a recurring process until the most effective strategy is selected. The objective chosen in the first case may sometimes be unattainable with the existing resources of the firm, in which case the objective level is modified either by a reduction or a postponement.

In broad terms, the iterative process involved at company level in the setting of objectives and in evaluating and selecting strategies, is effected through the stages of preliminary and final plans (Section 3.2). In this process preliminary plans from the various units of the firm are fed back and integrated at corporate level. If they are then found to be in balance and the corporate objectives are met, the preliminary plans are approved and the final plan is prepared in detail and in conformity with the preliminary plan. The further detail which appears only in the final plans, comprises the action programmes (Section 4.5) and the preparation of the corresponding quarterly budgets (Section 4.6).

In a more intimate way as between the various departments of the firm, the timetable network of Figure 4.32 in Section 4.8 shows how the iterative process is organized between different planning units. Here again, strategies are tested for their effectiveness and eventually that which provides the desired result is embodied in the preliminary plan of the unit concerned. Examples of such coordinated efforts are:

1 Between the sales manager and the marketing manager concerning strategies for increasing sales in the division by the employment of more salesmen in new geographical areas or in new markets, and the impact of different sorts of promotional activity.
2 Between the marketing manager and his opposite number in the manufacturing area concerning the best use of any spare production capacity or the need to increase capacity in order to support higher sales. In this case the manager for finance becomes involved in the evaluation of a proposed strategy, for he provides financial data on the investment cost of new plant and the provision of finance for the higher level of business (current assets).
3 Between the head of a business and the head of R & D concerning resource allocation with a view to stepping up effort to produce a marketable product by an earlier date.
4 Between the head of a business and the manager for personnel, to assess the likely availability and the phasing-in of new staff as well as their cost.

The following parts of Section 4.4 deal with the practical approach to each part of the triple sequence of opportunities, objectives and strategies. The underlying note is that they are carried out in view of the basic corporate objectives and policy as outlined in Section 4.2, which are communicated to the heads of planning units by means of the formal planning letter issued by the chief executive. The stage of the issue of planning letters is described in Section 4.7.

4.4.2 Opportunities

Each unit of every company will have certain opportunities facing it at any one time. They will be related in principle to future business levels compared with the present situation.

At the corporate level they concern major issues such as the growth of its activities through the better use of its resources; at the divisional level they concern such things as product group profitability, market shares and promotional efforts in marketing, while at still lower levels they concern more domestic matters such as output per machine, number of daily calls per representative, the efficiency of the product delivery service, and so on.

The future profitability of each unit, and of the whole firm, depends largely on how far such individual opportunities and problems can be identified and on the action which is taken to exploit or solve them. For practical purposes problems are regarded as negative opportunities in the sense that action is called for to meet and overcome them.

Opportunities should always be quantified in order that management can recognize their relative importance and decide the degree of importance. A well prepared information base always includes numerical values and the design of many of the questions in the various forms and check lists in Section 4.3 is intended to lead precisely to this effect.

The principal opportunity which arises in the first cycle of planning is the continuation of the past sorts of activity but amended as to direction, dimensions and nature in the light of whatever forecasts have shown up in the various parts of the information base, although this is not necessarily completed in depth at this time.

Even in the first cycle of planning, the possibilities for opportunities are legion. The search for them is extended in later cycles by enlarging the scope of the information base and in particular the range of topics which are shown as examples in Figures 4.15 to 4.19.

Extensions can arise by:

1   The wider use of inter-firm comparisons.
2   The analysis of input-output matrices of the type available from official sources such as the Central Statistical Office and elsewhere.
3   Inter-divisional, or inter-regional comparisons of performance within the company, especially if it has international operations.
4   Comparing earlier standards of management performance within departments of the company to see if any debasement of performance has occurred.
5   The examination of changes over recent years in the build-up of product costs (materials, labour, conversion factors, use of energy, transport, factory overheads etc).
6   Improving the control of expenditure in areas which are traditionally difficult to monitor, such as in R & D, internal management services and technical services to customers.

Any analysis which shows a business ratio below average or is trending in that direction is recognized as a problem and an objective is proposed at the appropriate level, to overcome and improve the situation.

Figure 4.24 quotes a wide range of illustrations of opportunities which, according to the sort of concern involved, may be regarded as corporate or divisional opportunities.

What business are we in?, and opportunities for growth

Apart from the step-by-step analysis of all the items in the information base, recommended in the preceding paragraphs, systematic methods for the identification of opportunities are available. The questionnaire in Figure 4.25 is the starting point for such procedures.

Simple analyses of a firm's business, prepared on this basis, enable questions to be posed which help to identify the present business, or businesses, of the firm, by functions. The functional type of approach is referred to in Section 4.2 in dealing with basic objectives, but in the present context it is used to suggest new areas as opportunities for growth and to foresee threats to the existing business.

The model is used to raise questions in relation to:

1 The products it makes and whose sales are the means by which the company earns its income.
2 The processes employed in producing the present products.
3 The service finally rendered to the user of the firm's product.

In each case, the subjects of the three headings used in Figure 4.25 are examined for their logical growth possibilities, either within the direct compass of the subject or in a field adjacent to it. At the same time the growth possibilities are analysed to determine if they are beneficial, that is, if they really represent opportunities. It can happen, of course, that growth in alternative services already in the hands of competitors can be detrimental when the threat to the business demands some form of counteraction.

In the case of motor cars quoted in Figure 4.25, the function of the business is basically to provide people with means of road transport. An area for growth may be foreseen by using the technology of the internal combustion engine in other media, such as on water or in air, in other words in boats and aircraft. Likewise, there may be possibilities for growth by developing electrically powered vehicles for road transport. On the contrary, the development of electrically powered vehicles by others may, and almost certainly will, constitute a threat to the existing business. Similar situations can stem from the other examples quoted—coal and other forms of energy, and electric bulbs and other sources of light. These are simplified examples which can be extended on the basis of the interests of a company when identifying what business it is really in and, having done this, determining the growth factors and the potential threats to its existing business.

By the particular sort of questioning used in Figure 4.25, opportunities can be identified which arise from the basic activities of the firm. While the examples given are simple, it behoves the planner (himself, in the case of a small organization, or jointly with the heads of divisions and their staffs in larger companies) to conduct similar analyses, firstly to identify the functional nature of their business and secondly to identify opportunities for growth through new uses for the products or processes or services with which they are concerned.

Strengths in certain areas may be key factors in other sorts of businesses and thus point the way to new opportunities. For example, special expertise in such widely differing departments as the following can indicate growth points for existing parts of the business, or by exploitation through third parties:

1 special aspects of R & D
2 management services of a particular variety

3   packaging systems
4   patents and licensing
5   personnel development and training
6   safety systems
7   engineering design
8   market promotion

The approach used in this section on opportunities also serves as a basis for the planning of *diversification*, a topic not likely to rank highly in initial cycles of planning, but which is an essential feature of later work after the planning system has been established and when the concepts of corporate development start to take effect. The data acquired during the phase of the information base, especially the type of analysis provided by the questionnaire of Figure 4.25, is invaluable when the approach to growth through mergers and diversification takes shape.

How far the firm wishes to go and to participate in exploiting the opportunities which are revealed by the processes of building up of the information base in Section 4.2 leads to the question of objective levels. So far the opportunities have had the appearance of growth—at least in terms of size or volume, but this may not be consistent with growth in profits. More quantification and evaluation are needed before these can be accepted as attractive profit opportunities. The resources of the firm, especially the skills of its personnel and its financial resources, need to be appraised before concrete strategies to support the objectives which initially seem possible can finally be framed.

Other opportunities, derived from the study of business ratios already mentioned in this section and thus already measured in profit terms, will be self-evident. The following Section 4.4.3 deals with the process of setting specific objectives for the company and for its departments.

4.4.3   Objectives

Following the phase of opportunities which are quantified as far as possible, we have now to consider the extent to which the firm may be able to exploit them and to set objectives within the limits which have been identified but at levels which are higher than those of its past performance and which will represent lines to follow in its quest for the growth of profitability.

The information base compiled according to the procedures of Section 4.3, especially by the requirements of Figures 4.3 to 4.22, should provide a background of the performance of the concern in its past environment. It should also provide forecasts on the business conditions under which it will operate in the future. These will help to quantify the limits to which the organization may go, that is the extent of its opportunities.

The business conditions which have been forecast are of external events which in most cases lie outside the control of the firm. There is a notable exception, which should be taken up more fully in later cycles of planning. This is when the firm is capable of innovation which actually influences the development of outside affairs. Such an achievement is one of the important aspects of goal setting and is intrinsic to growth planning as the theme of this workbook. A company that can influence outside events by the introduction of new business concepts and technologies, and hence create new industries and markets, is a pacemaker and has advantages over a firm which merely follows and reacts to the development of others. Already in the earlier part of this workbook (Section 2.1) the keynote was sounded that corporate planning is a means not only of doing things in anticipation of events which are forecast, but of making

97

things happen to its advantage. This applies to external as well as to internal affairs. In the language of the workbook, it corresponds to the creation of its own opportunities—opportunities which may be unique. The R & D functions have special objectives in this respect.

We now consider specific business objectives which lie within the limits mentioned in the first two paragraphs above. The next important question is exactly at which level they shall be aimed.

There are several approaches.

The first deals with that of profitability as such, and what are considered to be minimum, or threshold, and ideal objectives as measured by profitability, that is, the return on the capital used. This is a necessary approach, not only in the first cycle of planning but in every cycle. It applies not only at the corporate level 1 but as business division level 2.

A more basic method involves the setting of future levels of activity using data on the past performance of the firm in relation to its past environment, and, after forecasting the future environmental conditions, calls for the selection of its growth targets. Usually the objectives which arise are in terms of a corporate or divisional activity such as sales, whose acceptance needs to be measured in terms of profits before they can be included in the plan as specific objectives. They need to be tested by comparison with other companies operating in the same fields of business. The basic approach can only be used after experience has been gained in the planning process. It takes time and experience to develop adequate information on which to base objectives but, subject to the tests of profitability, it should become the standard method of operation after the first cycle of planning is over.

The third method to be described is the simplest in practice and is most appropriate in the first cycle of planning, in that it seeks to improve on the firm's past performance, whatever that might have been. Nevertheless, this method should also be subject to the screening test of profitability used in the first method, even in the first cycle of planning.

This approach is based on the corporate objective of improving profitability by an arbitrary amount of say, 10 or 20 per cent per annum. This is coupled with a request to business executives to make contributions through their own proposals of business objectives. The divisional contributions which arise may vary in effect, but when integrated at corporate level 1, the net result may fall in the range of profit levels desired. This is the 'bottom upwards' method of planning, and is realistic practice for the first cycle of planning. It is distinct from the 'top downwards' approach which begins to apply in later cycles when a good information base has been built up and when top management can knowledgeably nominate objectives for the firm's planning units.

Overall corporate profitability and its growth

The first approach to overall corporate objectives is a simple statement of profitability and its growth. It is derived after a study of the following which serve as yardsticks.

The total profitability to be achieved, which, after certain diminutions, enables a satisfactory return to be made to the shareholders for their investment in the equity of the company. The principal diminutions consist of sums allocated for the renewal of existing assets (depreciation), an amount for re-investment in additional assets for the purpose of growth, and an allowance for corporate or other taxes. The following is a simplified illustration of this calculation.

Assume that the sale/capital ratio is 1:1, and the gross profit on sales is 30 per cent. After allowing 10 per cent for renewals, 10 per cent for investment, and 6 per cent for taxes, there is 4 per cent available for dividend payments to the shareholders. In addition, the shareholders can expect a growth of 10 per cent per annum since the value of their equity is being increased by the second diminution mentioned, investment.

The appropriate minimum and ideal ratios in a given case depend upon the risk element and the factor of inflation. A high risk business ('cosmetics in Timbuktu') justifies much higher profit ratios in order to give correspondingly shorter pay-back times on account of the high capital risk involved. Another high risk and high cost business, in this case involving lengthy research and development costs, is that of pharmaceutical chemicals. This also justifies a higher profitability on the sales of its successful products, while a more stable business, dealing with basic commodities in regular demand (food, shelter and clothing) may be content with lower ratios.

The 'flooring' of profitability may be measured by the minimum return of 7 per cent expected by the UK Government of projects in the nationalized industries. In the case of a typical nationalized industry, the profit objective, after allowing 6 per cent for depreciation, is 7 per cent on the net capital assets which permits the payment of interest to the owners of borrowed capital, there being no equity capital in such cases, and leaves a modest surplus of 1 to 2 per cent which is put to reserve.

The third measure is the *level of return* which may be obtained by investing the company's funds elsewhere. At the time of writing, 7 per cent is not at all uncommon for borrowed money at little or no risk. During inflationary times this figure can be exceeded.

The level of profitability to be set may be determined by *comparison with similar businesses,* operating under similar environmental conditions. The starting points for these comparisons are inter-firm comparisons from centres for inter-firm comparisons, and the Key Business Ratios of Dunn and Bradstreet, from the earnings data in *Financial Times* Actuaries Share Index lists for various industries, from the published accounts of individual firms and from *The Times'* and *Fortune's* surveys of industry.

The minimum or threshold objective for corporate profitability to be set should first of all be on the lines of the averages shown by the last-named criteria. According to the exact relationship to them, the basic policies of the firm and the nature of its operations, it may be set higher than the industrial average. Indeed this concept of an ideal objective is fundamental to the purpose of corporate planning. Implicitly, this is not only to grow, but to grow as well as or better than others in the same field.

Later, the basic objective of overall corporate profitability will require to be broken down into the various corporate strategies which will in turn become specific objectives for each of the firm's operating departments. This procedure will again be on the lines of the scheme of opportunity, objective and strategy levels described in Section 3.3 and illustrated by Figure 3.8.

The basic approach

Schemes 1 and 2 of Figure 4.26 depict the situation with reference to the sort of data which are collected in the information base. They are meant to be illustrative and should be used as models for the key activities at any level in the firm.

In the explanations which follow, the word activity is used to describe one or other sort of operation. To make the examples clear, Scheme 1 takes the total value of a market and the actual company sales, and shows them as indices. Thus the level of the activity in the planning year would be quoted as 100, levels in the preceding years would probably be less, while indices forecast for the future years might range to 120 or more, if annual growths were greater than 4 per cent per annum. These are shown on a time scale, say for five or more years prior to the planning year and for five years later.

Scheme 2 is analogous to Scheme 1, but applies when an absolute theoretical or practical economic limit is available as a yardstick. The percentage indices of activities in such cases might be:

1 raw material utilization in manufacturing processes
2 labour turnover
3 patents applied for against patent granted
4 number of customer calls per day
5 orders delivered on day of receipt
6 inverse of the number of rejects in production.

Reverting now to the format of Scheme 1, the points A, B show indices of the past progress of external affairs, in this case the total market value, together with the planner's forecast of this activity in the future period of planning, that is the line from B to C.

The line from point D to E shows indices of the past progress of the firm's sales or profit performance in relation to the indices of the market change. The extension of the line D-E, that is, the line E-F, is in harmony with the forecast of the related external event shown by B-C. It provides the first and obvious basis for the setting of specific objectives in the five year period of the plan. Such objectives would be consistent with no relative change in corporate behaviour and effort. Under these conditions the strategy would be to continue with the past style and level of management activity. It would represent growth of sales or profitability but under these conditions it would only be keeping pace with external events and maintaining a past level of efficiency. In the case of the example shown in Figure 4.26, the market share would be maintained, even though this were as low as 5 per cent. It would not represent growth over and above that which would occur simply be keeping pace with the market. Furthermore, if the factor of inflation, as analysed in lines 1 and 2 of Figure 4.3, were brought into account, it could well be that there would be no growth in profitability.

By many tokens, the setting of objectives to the level of point F is not unrealistic in the first cycle of planning, and subject to the inflationary factor may well be adopted as the minimum or threshold objective.

In the case of a company besought with weaknesses and competion, such an objective level may be as far as it can reach until its weaknesses have been surmounted and further strengths acquired and deployed.

However, the purpose of corporate planning is not only to achieve growth according to the line E-F, but more than this, it is to achieve growth in real terms beyond this point by, say, a rate shown by the level of point G.

An objective of the sort shown by the point G is described as a *normative* or ideal objective, as distinct from one which merely follows a trend line by extrapolation. Normative planning means planning which involves objectives independent of the trend line and commensurately of higher calibre than would simply harmonize with the sort of relationships shown by the line E-F.

The area between the lines E-F and E-G (the normative goal), is usually referred to as the gap. It is an extremely useful concept in planning, especially in the setting of objectives. Where the point G should lie and hence how large the gap should be hinges on the basic corporate objectives which will in most cases call for the objective of performing at least as profitably as its competitors in their common fields of business. To exceed this level is desirable and calls for objectives which are challenging and stretching. In any case the setting of normative goals has the advantage that more intense efforts and ingenuity are demanded than would be the case if lower objectives were set on the trend line (to point F) from the record of past performance.

Similar considerations apply to the other activities already suggested as examples for use in Scheme 2 and which can be shown as percentages of the efficiency with which Activity 'X' is carried out. Other indices than percentages may be used in both schemes: they may be set up using key business ratios or even simple numbers indicating economic or other values.

A final check on the basic method of setting objectives calls for the following:

1   Establish the external growth levels on the lines of A-B in Scheme 1 of Figure 4.26, or the practical limits of the other working ratios symbolized in Scheme 2.
2   Compare the company results D-E, with A-B.
3   Compare the company results with those of its peers and competitors in similar businesses using data from the information base, especially on inter-firm comparisons, in order to determine whether the firm's results are worse, equal or better than average.
4   If the results are worse than average, drastic increases in objective levels must be embodied in the planning effort. If the results are average there may be cause for satisfaction, but there are still opportunities to set objectives in the upper quartile of performance. If the results are higher than average, there is undoubted cause for satisfaction, but still a need to set objectives to maintain this position with special strategies to defend it.

In summary it is the practical responsibility of the corporate planner and the heads of planning units to review all the elements of the information base and to compare the level of performances of the firm and its divisions with the appropriate external indicators, or other independent working standards. The review shows the extent of the opportunities for business growth and for improvements in performance in the areas of operating ratios. The setting of objectives within the top limits thus shown, but aiming at levels beyond those which the company normally achieved, arises after the analysis of the company's performance against its equals in business or against scales of any known efficiencies against ratios for internal operating activities.

The approach to objectives in the first cycle of planning

The foregoing procedures are fundamental but are only likely to be effected in depth after planning has been practised for more than one annual cycle. We need to outline procedures to serve in the case of the first cycle of planning.

Under these conditions, it would be fortunate if the chief executive were able to spell out not only the basic objectives of the company, but also be able to issue specific objectives to each of his departmental heads.

In practice however the company can be expected to have some record of its recent profit performance and can obtain data to enable comparisons to be made with the average profitability of other concerns in the same line of business. Additionally, there is almost certain to be data, however scanty, on the performance of the departments of the firm, their sales and market shares, production records and the profitability of various products or services. This information, together with preliminary ideas on external affairs, such as the way the market is growing, the likelihood of countrywide increases in wage rates and raw material costs, should enable a practical approach to be made in the quest for improvements in profits.

The collection of this starting information is a task of the first priority for a newly appointed corporate planner.

Thus advised, the chief executive can set a preliminary level of corporate objectives, together with similar preliminary objectives for the divisions, both being, say 20 per cent higher than the last annual level. At the same time he can follow the procedure, now well tried, of inviting his managers to review their work on the information base, at least using whatever contribution it can make at this stage, and to identify opportunities. They can then propose a series of objectives which can be integrated, firstly within their divisions, and then at the corporate level, to show the effect on the overall corporate profitability.

Such a procedure will collect many single objectives from various units. Some may contribute more than others to profitability. Some units may need to accept increases in costs, while others, such as R & D, may need more time or further resources, in order to contribute to higher profitability in later years.

The simplified tabulation shown in Figure 4.27 illustrates how such an array of individual contributions can arise and how they integrate to the corporate total. The profit objective of a 20 to 25 per cent increase in the first year of planning, starts with the known figure for a base year. It shows the positive contributions from the selection of objectives on the part of the main operating units of the firm. It also includes negative contributions which largely arise from forecasts of changes in factors which lie outside the control of the firm. All the contributions are classified as to whether they arise from the action of the management or lie outside its control, a principle which features again in Section 6.

The overall integration of the contributions shows that growth of profitability can be planned for the first year and the chief executive is thus enabled to accept the objectives proposed by his departmental heads and to authorize the production of their final plans.

This approach from the lower working levels has already been described as 'bottom upwards' planning as distinct from 'top downwards' planning. It is a more practical approach for the first year's planning and can be extended over the five year period, by the addition of further columns which will show progressive changes in the items listed, and the emergence, later, of benefits such as from R & D investment. In later cycles of planning, after the top management have acquired a fuller appreciation of the information base and of the opportunities, more emphasis will be placed on the setting of objectives from the top downwards. At the same time the basic objectives of the company will be taking shape in a more realistic fashion for the longer term.

Following the setting of objectives, the next phase in the practical work of planning is the choice of strategies, that is, the broad means by which the objectives will be achieved. This is the subject matter of the following part of Section 4 of the workbook.

4.4.4 Strategies

Strategy is a term which has been widely used in connection with planning. Indeed it has often been used in a wider context than planning itself as the familiar expressions of 'strategic planning' and 'corporate strategy' illustrate. This is incorrect, since strategy is a part of the overall planning process. More correctly one might speak of the planning of strategy!

Strategies describe the basic approaches to be adopted to reach given objectives. They answer the question 'How do we meet the objectives which have to be achieved?', and they provide a basis for the framing of the detailed action programmes which follow.

This is the meaning of strategy for use in business practice and as already described in this workbook. In total, the choice of strategy involves the identification of alternative methods of reaching a given objective, their analysis, evaluation and the final selection of one (sometimes more) of them to be put into action.

The framework of planning with the preparatory stages of basic objectives, information base, opportunities and objectives, is designed to make decisions on strategy more effective and in harmony with corporate policy. In this context, strategies should be:

1 based on the best possible information
2 made at the right time
3 made at the correct level in the company
4 followed up to ensure effective implementation
5 made after consideration of their effect on all parts of the firm.

These hinge again on the quality of the information base and since strategy concerns action to be adopted in the future, the soundness of the forecasting becomes critical. The information base as compiled in the workbook also serves to provide check lists and counter references which help answer the question 'What if . . . ?' in the analysis and evaluation of alternative courses of action. In other words, the search for the advantages and disadvantages of a given strategy must be a matter for an all-round scrutiny. At first sight a particular route might appear to be attractive but on closer questioning, pitfalls and problems may be foreseen, as well as reactions from other parts of the firm.

Fundamentally, the choice of a strategy is made on the lines of a decision tree when the various branches are evaluated as to their potential in contributing to the set objectives. Apart from a realist evaluation of the alternatives, the key factor in designing the decision tree, is the identification and inclusion of the maximum number of relevant alternatives.

For the practical purposes of the workbook, the procedure on strategy is exemplified by cases. The first is a general approach which attempts to consider all possibilities, while the others are cases at different levels of planning.

General illustration of a systematic approach to objectives and strategy

A broad illustration of the choice of alternative courses of action is shown in Figure 4.28, which embraces the selection of both objectives and strategy. It refers to a hypothetical business situation assumed to be well-furnished by data in the information base and contains questions as to three salient possibilities, each being considered on the basis of a check list. The possibilities represent simplified approaches from extremely different angles. Thus, the list systematically poses questions on the lines of:

1 quitting the business
2 staying in the business but with no further resource allocation, or
3 developing the business.

Although the questionnaire is treated as a case study (The Battery Chicken Co. Ltd), the basic approach should be applied as a routine procedure in planning, even in the first cycle of planning. The concept can be applied to the operations of the company as a whole, to separate businesses or to major product groups or services. It poses standard questions leading to ideas on strategy, which in turn form the basis of action programmes.

Although the questionnaire is of a qualitative nature, it goes back to fundamentals, and is a particularly useful formality to adopt during the introductory cycle of planning in any sort of concern.

Case study in strategy

The following outline of a specific planning situation illustrates the concept of strategy at various levels, firstly at the corporate level and then at those of a business division and a central function. It also illustrates the need to follow the working points in the list given above, especially the questions of timing and coordination.

The case is that of an enginering company, whose basic profitability is below the average level of companies working in similar fields. Its information base shows that it has opportunities for its power transmission division, which has only a 10 per cent share of a market growth at 15 per cent per annum. The division has undoubted strength in marketing. The corporate objective calls for an increase in profitability of 50 per cent in a relatively short time (two years), and then sustaining an annual growth of at least 15 per cent thereafter.

The company identifies a wide range of strategies, of which the following appear to justify evolution:

1 To give to its power transmission division the objective of increasing its profit contribution towards the corporate goal within the first two years of the plan.
2 To give to the central research and development department the objective of accelerating its development and design work on some research products based on hydraulic systems, whose marketing by the power transmission division could contribute to the profitability required by the company in years two onwards.
3 To negotiate licences to parties in other countries for the sale, or the manufacture and sale, of products from the existing range of the transmission division.
4 To acquire licences from parties in other countries for complementary products either for sale, or preferably for manufacture and sale, through the transmission division.
5 To acquire by purchase a second line power transmission company whose products would be complementary to the present range of the transmission division and to which their marketing skills could profitably be deployed.

Any one or more of these strategies—the list is not exhaustive—could be selected and issued to the heads of one or other units of the firm, for evaluation as branches of a decision tree, especially the time scale on which the various contributions to profits would arise. The results of the evaluations would determine the decision to be taken and the approval of the particular strategy or strategies to be built into final plans as action programmes and budgets.

Continuing the practical procedure of objectives and strategies, each of the units in receipt of an objective from the corporate level 1 would proceed at its level to a more detailed analysis of the opportunity in order to develop its own specific objectives, to evaluate the possible alternative strategies and, when approved, to embody the selected ones in action programmes.

Thus the head of the power transmission divisions (level 2) would examine his information base, identify the opportunities and develop objectives, the strategies for which might be on the folowing lines:

1 The manager of the marketing depaartment (level 3) to increase sales by 25 per cent per annum, suggesting the exploitation of new sales regions, engagement of trained staff, the extension of promotional activities, etc. A variation of this might be to develop a marketing strategy to improve the long term profitability of the product mix on the lines of the optimization of the procedure outlined in Section 4.3.
2 The manager of the production department (level 3) to effect cost reductions of at least 7 per cent per annum, suggesting the adoption of group technology in the principal machine shops and increase of shift working.

The head of the R & D department (level 2) would review his situation and develop objectives and strategies for his particular section leaders, for example:

1 The manager, research section (level 3), to speed up the outstanding research and evaluation work on hydraulic products, select the most effective one from amongst those under study and issue design details and specifications.
2 The manager, development section (level 3), to prepare full drawings and specifications for production purposes, make cost estimates, prepare prototypes and organize field testing.

Finally, strategies 3, 4 and 5 would be given as objectives to appropriate units in the firm who would make studies for the licensing possibilities mentioned. In some organizations these would be issued to the actual business division concerned if it had the resources for such tasks, while in other cases the strategies might be taken for action by top management itself.

Throughout this process each key operator at his level needs to identify the possible alternatives and to assess their value in contributing to the specified objectives. The evaluation of the upwards flow of information shows how far the corporate objective at level 1 will be met.

In the practical phases of planning the upwards flow will be shown in the preliminary plans which emerge during the intermediate stages of the annual planning schedule or network (Section 4.8). If the proposals are acceptable to the top management and conform to the policies of the firm, being within its resources, approval is indicated in the planning letter no. 2 whereupon the items are incorporated in the final plans of the units concerned. At this time action programmes will also be prepared for inclusion in the final plan, while the budgets will be more detailed than those in the preliminary plan in order to take full account of these intentions.

Marketing strategy for profit growth

The third illustration of procedures for the elaboration of strategy is in respect of marketing and would be appropriate for the head of the business division described in the preceding case study, to suggest to his marketing manager as at level 3 in the

ACTION PLANNING TEST LIST 18 Sections 4.4.1–4.4.4

QUESTIONS	RESPONSE BY	TIMING OF ACTION ARISING
1 Recapitulate Questions 1–3 in Action Planning Test List 9	Corporate planner	
2 Has the concept of 'opportunities-objectives-strategy' been appreciated by all who have to produce plans? If not, what steps will be taken to clarify this approach?	Corporate planner	
3 Has agreement been reached as to 'what business are we in?' (functional objectives) and 'opportunities for growth', using the analysis of Figure 4.25, in respect of: (a) the company, (b) business divisions and sub-businesses, (c) products, processes and services?	Chief executive and all management	
4 In the procedure of item 3, have threats been identified? If so, list them for counter action in the appropriate plan	Corporate planner	
5 What external opportunities have been identified for exploitation of the strengths of any *functional* unit of the firm?	Corporate planner	
6 What are the principal approaches to the setting of objectives? Which features are common to all, and which are suitable for use in the first or other cycles of planning?	Chief executive and corporate planner	
7 Assess the various components of the firm's business as high, medium and low risk activities How will this information affect the setting of financial objectives?	Corporate planner	
8 In reviewing the past performance of the company, or its units, against the external environment: (a) have sales kept pace with changes in the market and the economy in general, or (b) have sales grown at a different rate, and if so what are the reasons?	All management	
9 Have *all* the firm's executives reviewed the key business ratios in respect of their spheres of responsibility? Have they identified any areas of low performance and accounted for them?	All management	
10 Into which quartile of performance, measured against its peers, or against absolute levels in the case of functional units, does the company, or each of its business divisions fall?	All management	

ACTION PLANNING TEST LIST 18 continued

QUESTIONS	RESPONSE BY	TIMING OF ACTION ARISING
10 (a) If in the upper quartile, what special strategies will be needed, if any, to maintain its position? (b) If in a lower quartile, which of its strengths, in order of priority, will be deployed to fill the gap?	All management	
11 On what factors does the success of strategy as a decision-making process in planning, depend?	All management	
12 What are the three basic questions to be posed in the systematic choice of alternative courses of action in the procedure of objectives and strategies?	Corporate planner	
13 Recall the elements needed to develop a long range sales/profit strategy. In your case, can the data be handled manually, or will you need to write a program for handling by computer?	Corporate planner and business heads	

organization. It would be particularly apt when a range of products is sold to several markets each with different characteristics.

The objective given would be to improve the sales assortment in respect of present and future profitability having regard to a number of items in the information base. The strategy would be to develop a detailed sales programme based on an analysis of the following elements:

1 The profitability of each product (or product groups), as sold to the different markets.
2 The present market shares of each product in the various markets.
3 The forecast of the annual growth, or otherwise, of each market served.
4 The production capacity for each product and the extent of reserve capacity in the planning year.
5 The minimum economic unit of production, in the event that the sales programme outran the capacity of the installed manufacturing resources within the planning period and further investment in fixed assets was called for on the lines of Figure 4.12.

The calculations involved are those of optimization, while the outcome would be a strategy which would improve market shares wherever these were below the objective level in mind, and to do this in markets showing the greatest growth and in terms of products which yielded higher profits than others. The use of spare capacity would be in the same terms, and a picture should emerge which would be decisive in the planning of further manufacturing resources or in the selection of products from third parties under one or other of the licensing or acquisition strategies mentioned in the case study.

In simple cases, the identification of the optimum sales strategy and the consequent action programmes might be done manually, but in more complex cases the precise determination of the optimum selling mix, the markets to be aimed at and investments to be made in further production would call for the use of a computer.

The stage of decision making on strategy is one of the most important in management and planning. It no doubt serves to account for the importance given to it in the literature of management, and the fact that at first sight it almost appears to dominate the whole subject of planning. Certainly the setting of objectives, though a responsible actiivty, appears to be less onerous than that of identifying the right strategy and following it up with action programmes. In other words it is sometimes simpler to say what we wish to achieve than to prescribe exactly how it will be achieved.

The success of strategies as decision-making processes, depends on:

1 The degree of ingenuity which is brought to bear on the identification of alternatives.
2 The amount and quality of data which is available to evaluate each alternative.
3 The extent to which action programmes are framed in support of the chosen strategy.

At this stage in the practical phases of planning, we need to recall that top management approval of the strategies which have been developed takes place after the preliminary plans from all the planning units of the firm have been integrated and have been found, in total, to meet the corporate objectives of level 1. Approval of the preliminary plans calls for the preparation of the final edition of plans which include, for the first time, the corresponding action programmes. The framing of action programmes is the subject of the next section.

4.5 ACTION PROGRAMMES

Action programmes have already been stated in Section 3.1.4. to be among the most important working documents of the formal planning process. They specify the actual tasks which various people are to perform (who, when, where, how and, of course, why) in order to give effect to the chosen strategy which in turn goes to achieve the specific objectives. They form the final link in the chain of management starting with the chief executive, going through his divisional and functional managers, to those in the departments of the latter who actually accomplish the tasks at the working level 3. It is the step of action programmes which distinguishes the corporate plan from mere forecasts of possibilities and probabilities. Their compiling is a part of the way of making things happen instead of reacting to events as they occur. They form the basis of agreed instructions and for the measuring of the performance of the staff concerned, that is, for control purposes during the currency of the plan as described in Section 6.1 of the workbook.

Although they are a formal part of the system of planning, the programmes are working documents and they must contain the following key elements:

1 A reference to the objective they are intended to achieve and the strategy chosen.
2 A list of the specific action steps to be followed.
3 Statements of which person is responsible for each particular step.
4 A timetable, which also shows the time demand, for example in man-days.
5 Who is responsible for the immediate overseeing of the activities.
6 A statement of the financial impact, that is, profit contribution.

There are many ways in which action programmes may be laid out. Treatises on management by objectives frequently show examples. The format given in Figure 4.29 should serve as a basis for the corporate planner at least in the first cycle of planning, after which it may be extended or modified to suit the particular organization in which he is working.

The following are guidelines to the setting up of action programmes in the practical phases of planning and for the use of the format of Figure 4.29.

1 A given objective may involve more than one strategy, and hence more than one action programme will be called for. In the case study on strategy described in Section 4.4.4, action programmes would eventually be set up to give effect to whatever strategies were adopted. In the first case there would be two involving the head of the business division (power transmission), one each for the marketing and production strategies. In the second case there would again be two involving the head of R & D, one each for the separate research and development strategies. In the case of the strategies involving licensing and acquisition, action programmes would be set up for the person to whom the responsibility was allocated. In some firms this might be the chief executive himself, while in others the business head might be given the responsibility. In either case they would be aided by the corporate planner and his assistant on corporate development, and the head of corporate finance.
2 The format of Figure 4.29 will be seen to:
    call for reference to the originating objective and the strategy chosen to achieve it
    list the various steps to be taken in order of time, by whom and when
    indicate whether supporting parties (SP) from other units of the firm are involved

ACTION PLANNING TEST LIST 19   **Section 4.5**

QUESTIONS	RESPONSE BY	TIMING OF ACTION ARISING
1 What are the basic features of an action programme?	All management	
2 How many are desirable in the plan of each unit?	All management	
3 What purpose do they serve?	All management	

who has supervisory responsibility for the overall action programme and will
report upon it during the monitoring and control procedures, and

contain a statement on the financial benefit of the programme in terms of the
increase in profitability and the costs of the work to be done.

3 Only the most important programmes need to be included in the final plans of a
unit; in practice, up to four and not more than six should cover the key opportunities.
Further, these should be those in which the head of the unit is involved as the
responsible supervisor.

4 Action programmes of lower rank than those mentioned in 3 above need only to
be listed in the final plan. These are usually programmes for sub-units at level 3
in the firm.

5 Action programmes are only prepared for the first year of a five year plan.
Subsequent annual plans will call for action programmes for the second or further
years.

6 Action programmes do not need to be prepared until the strategies in the preliminary
plans have been approved, but they are an essential part of final plans.

7 Before an action programme can be approved for inclusion in a final plan, the
head of the unit who supervises it must ensure that the manpower and other
resources called for are available, or will be allocated when necessary from supporting departments, also that the timetable is consistent and practicable with the
objective in view.

4.6 BUDGETS

Budgets are not plans; they are numerical statements, usually, though not exclusively, in
financial terms, which describe planned activities and goals. These may relate to a variety
of topics—sales, production, personnel, R & D, finance and so on. They have an
economic basis and are prepared by all the key operating units of the firm, the
progressive totalling of which leads firstly to the budgets of divisions and functions,
and finally to the overall company budget. Corporate budgets thus represent a synthesis,
though highly summarized, from all the individual cost and income centres of the firm.
Their value depends upon, and is a reflection of, the soundness of the documentation
of planned activities at all levels.

An important feature of corporate planning is the provision of a framework for
management purposes, not for accounting purposes. Accordingly, the budget sections of
plans are not necessarily prepared by accountants, though they have an important
part to play in the methodology involved in order to ensure they harmonize with company accounts required for other purposes. The head of finance is responsible for the
most beneficial handling of the company funds as befits his functional responsibility
and which is the subject of his own departmental plan.

Budgets as planning documents are not necessarily in the form that is required for
legal, tax and other purposes. In the first cycle of planning they may well be kept
separate from the already established accounting system of the firm, but in progressive
cycles of planning it will be found that the budgets derived from the planning system will
go far to supplant the older accounting methods. They will be much more oriented to
the objectives of the company. Eventually there will only be a limited need for the
preparation of separate accounts for other purposes.

Apart from serving to project the planned performance of the company and its sub-
units in terms of its goals, budgets provide a basis for management control during

the currency of a plan. Thus they provide for the monitoring of progress by the comparison of actual performance with the budget levels of the plan (Section 6).

In designing the particular budget forms for his company the corporate planner should endeavour to include space to show indices or ratios against financial or other data. These should relate to the sort of working business ratios discused in Section 4.3. For example, the inclusions of percentages of various costs against sales, the return on investment, and numbers of weeks of stocks or debtors, all help to give a better and quicker appreciation of the growth in the plan than do absolute figures. They also serve in this way when control reports are prepared for comparison against planned results.

Since every plan will contain a final section concerning budgets, (Section 5.2 deals with this in more detail), every person who has the responsibility to produce a plan must produce the corresponding budget. Cost centres forming part of a planning unit will each prepare budgets which will be consolidated to show the budget of the planning unit as a whole.

In the first case, budgets will appear in the plans of the:

1   Company p.p. the chief executive, as at level 1.
2   Divisions p.p. the heads of businesses, as at level 2.
3   Functions p.p. the heads of functions, as at level 2.

Thereafter, and depending upon the sort and complexity of the corporate organization, plans and their budgets will also be prepared from sub-units of the level 2 stages shown above. Thus the budget of a business division which has its own departments for R & D, as well as marketing sub-businesses, will contain summaries of these departmental budgets at their level 3.

The format of the financial budgets will depend on the policy of the firm with respect to the particular accounting procedures used, and also on the organizational structure. In the simplest and ideal cases, the parts of the budget section of each planning unit dealing with income and expenditure as an operating statement should be designed to show profitability as a ratio, not only of the sales activity, but also in relation to the capital employed in the operation. Such an operating statement can also be designed to include further ratios such as sales to capital employed.

In some organizations there may be the alternative of the use, as a matter of policy, of the principle of 'contributions'. This is especially useful when a corporate unit only incurs costs, that is, makes a negative contribution, or shows a gain or a profit, that is, makes a positive contribution. Either may be under conditions when little or no capital is involved. The R & D department is an example of the former case, a marketing unit of the second.

Wherever possible the corporate planner should link the outcome of planned activities in terms of profits, with the resources that are used but unless the correct basis is involved, the figures may be meaningless. Thus, a simple marketing division may show an inordinate return on investment when the profit is attributed to the assets used in the unit itself and excludes those used in its associated manufacturing division. On the other hand, the analogous data for the manufacturing division will be non-existent when its products are simply transferred to the marketing unit at an ex-works cost level.

It is therefore a matter of corporate policy as to how these affairs are arranged. In most cases the principle of using contributions helps to provide a good basis for the control procedures if it is applied at the budget stage of planning. Furthermore, it avoids the arguable task of adding the profit element to each stage of the corporate organization according to the assets used in each of these stages; it also overcomes the problem of setting special transfer prices within the organization.

Nevertheless it should always be the endeavour of the corporate planner, if necessary in cooperation with the head of finance, to prepare divisional budgets on the basis of profitability, that is, in relation to the assets and resources used. A business division of the type defined in the workbook in Section 3.2, having marketing and probably other departments such as manufacture and R & D, is the next lower level than the corporate level at which this becomes feasible and logical.

At this stage we need to distinguish between the evaluation of a business division as a sub-business of the company as a whole and the principle of integrated management planning. For the former we need to take into account both its own activities and the resources it can directly control itself, and the associated corporate services which it enjoys and over which it may or may not have any control. Integrated management planning only stresses the items which come under the direct control of the head of the planning unit and for which he makes commitments in his plan. This basic principle is elaborated further in Section 6 which deals with the control and reporting procedures during the currency of the planning period.

If there are corporate or associated expenses which can logically be calculated and charged to a planning unit on the basis that they are an agreed purchase, then these are included as a controllable item. If this is not possible, they should not be allocated. An arbitrary or flat rate is meaningless for the purpose of management planning and the costs of such services should be restricted to the unit for whom some other planning head is responsible.

As operating units of the firm are progressively linked together to form the divisional budgets, and ultimately the corporate budget, the growing picture of the net sum of the negative and positive contributions given as ROI, or as earnings per share of the equity capital, becomes clearer and more meaningful.

In practice budgets are prepared in at least two ways:

1   As annual budgets for each of the five years of the planning period. (These show the overall progress towards the growth of profitability in the long run.)
2   As quarterly budgets derived from the budget of the first planning year.

If the policy of the firm in exercising its control procedures, as discussed in Section 6, calls for other reporting times, then the first annual budget is broken down appropriately. However, quarterly reporting is most common in the practice of integrated management planning.

The budget which is included in preliminary plans is not prepared in detail. Sufficient of the key features is given in order to show if the planned activities go to meet the objectives given in the planning letters of the chief executive and which indicate the required effort of the unit towards the corporate objectives.

After the approval of the preliminary plan, the budget can be refined and the quarterly breakdown can be prepared as a basis for the control system which will operate during the currency of the plan.

In addition to this preliminary description of the place of budgets in the planning process, more detailed guidance on the formulation of budgets, and the control system which corresponds to them, is given in the appropriate sections of the workbook:

1   Section 5.1 on the use of standardized forms for various aspects of planning.

ACTION PLANNING TEST LIST 20

Section 4.6

QUESTIONS	RESPONSE BY	TIMING OF ACTION ARISING
1 Explain why budgets are *not* plans	All management	
2 Why do their formats contain: (*a*) key ratios (*b*) percentage analyses?	All management	
3 What budgets other than financial budgets, are required?	All management	
4 What do all budgets have in common?	All management	

2   Section 5.2.6 which deals with the treatment accorded to budgets in part 6 of each plan.

3   Section 6.2 which describes the format of control reports used during the currency of the first planning year.

4   Appendix 1 which provides illustrations of the format of all planning and control forms and a table which indicates their use by particular planning units. They are on the lines of:

'P' forms   — used to summarize plans.

'B' forms   — standard budget forms for five year plans.

'B-Q' forms— standard quarterly budge forms for the first planning year of each plan, derived from the foregoing 'B' forms.

'C' forms   — the quarterly control forms corresponding to the preceding 'B-Q' forms.

In Appendix 1 six key planning summaries have been completed, as at corporate level, with illustrative numerical data designed to show growth in profit through objectives for increasing the rate of growth of sales, better use of earlier investments in production capacity and improvements in performance revealed by working business ratios.

4.7 PLANNING LETTERS

Planning letters, already described in Section 2.3 and elsewhere as a personal responsibility of the chief executive, are issued by him to each executive in the organization responsible for the preparation of a management plan for his particular area of operations. They are one of the first overt acts of management and provide a formal start to each annual planning cycle. Each one serves as an official vehicle for communicating to executives the basic objectives and policies of the firm, and the objectives that are proposed for each unit, together with the agreed assumptions at the corporate level. Also included are the particular timetable and other administrative details for the planning work which is called for.

During the annual cycle of planning, the schedules for which are shown in Figures 4.32 and 4.33 of the following Section 4.8, the issue of planning letters occurs twice.

The first planning letters are on the lines shown in the first paragraph, whereas the second letters are issued after the preliminary plans have been submitted and the preliminary plan of the company has been drafted.

Provided that the contribution of a unit, as shown in its preliminary plan, is in compliance with the objectives given to it in the first letter, the second is merely one of formal approval, instructing the recipient to proceed with the preparation of the final version of his plan on the lines already submitted and to do this in accordance with the timetable already published.

Whenever the contribution of a planning unit does not meet with the objectives given, or calls for criticism, planning letter no. 2 deals with these matters on a formal basis. It is possible that in view of dialogues which may have taken place, that the chief executive may accept the preliminary plan with certain reservations, asking the head of the unit to embody revisions or to consider still other strategies in a better attempt to reach the objectives first given. Any changes in corporate objectives, with corresponding revisions in its strategies which may become necessary following the integration of all the unit plans, are notified in second planning letters, with requests for appropriate modifications.

ACTION PLANNING TEST LIST 21

QUESTIONS	RESPONSE BY	TIMING OF ACTION ARISING
1 What are the purposes of Planning Letters No. 1 and No. 2, respectively?	Chief executive and all management	
2 What are their essential contents?	Chief executive	
3 Who: (a) drafts planning letters (b) finalizes and signs them (c) receives them – for action?	Corporate planner and chief executive	

The essential contents of a planning letter are listed in Figure 4.30. In practice, most of them appear better as appendices or enclosures with the letter which then forms a cover note to the whole packet of items, and which gives the more personal comments of the chief executive.

Naturally there is much in common between the various planning letters that are issued to different divisional and functional heads in a firm; for example, items 1 (in part), 2, 3 and 6 of Figure 4.30 would be included in all cases.

Otherwise the letters are oriented to their particular recipients and their fields of responsibility, that is, they are confined to the items of corporate strategy which are passed on as objectives at level 2. In this way, items 1, 5 and 7 of Figure 4.30 would be specific to the planning unit in question.

In larger multi-divisional or multi-functional organizations, the principle of the use of an official planning letter between the chief executive and the heads of units at level 2 may be extended. Thus the head of a large business division which contained its own manufacturing and R & D departments might choose the medium of a planning letter to convey analogous items to the heads of his manufacturing and R & D units. This procedure is certainly called for if the organization consists of a group of companies, perhaps separated nationally, when the chief executive of the group issues planning letters to the chief executive of each subsidiary company. They in turn issue the appropriate planning letters to the heads of the individual units in the subsidiary concerned.

An example of a planning letter to the head of a business division of a firm is given in Figure 4.31. In this case it would be typical of the situation when planning had already been introduced. In practice such a letter would be supported by annexures corresponding to the seven essential items of a planning letter according to Figure 4.30 and which would tabulate the particular details in the case of a given company.

In the case of a planning letter issued in a first cycle of planning, the general comments in the first item of Figure 4.30 would still refer to the recent progress and standing of the firm, and of the unit to which the letter was addressed. As a matter of policy it would recall the decision of the top management to introduce corporate planning as a way of management throughout the firm and the various meetings which had already taken place in order to familiarize the executives with the procedures which would be involved. These would be of the sort suggested earlier in the work-book—Section 2.5—'How to introduce corporate planning to a company'. In this event, item 5 in the contents of a planning letter of Figure 4.30 would be re-slanted on the lines of the 'bottom-upwards' method of determining objectives described in Section 4.4.3, page 102 (The approach to objectives in the first cycle of planning). The other parts of the planning letter would follow the remaining items listed in Figure 4.30.

In view of the earlier explanations concerning second planning letters, no example is quoted or deemed necessary, since each would be designed according to individual circumstances.

The staff work in connection with planning letters is performed by the corporate planner. He prepares drafts for the chief executive whose final version is issued over his own signature, according to the list of responsibilities of a chief executive shown in Figure 2.1.

4.8 SCHEDULES IN THE ANNUAL PLANNING CYCLE

For the timetable of events in each annual cycle of planning, at least two sorts of schedules are available, between which, there are many practical variations:

1   A simple timetable as shown by the bar chart of Figure 4.32, which gives the calendar of events with the time in weeks allowed for each phase of planning.
2   A network scheme, based on the principle of a critical path network, showing the overall calendar of events as in Figure 4.32, but giving more detail on the individual phases and on the interactions between the various planning units in the organization.

Figure 4.33 shows a simplified network scheme. An organization with more than one division would call for a planning network with an appropriate number of cells, showing also any interlinking if they had interests in common. The network scheme shown illustrates the first recycling point (numbered 14/15) when product profitabilities are established. Once these are in acceptable order the planning units can proceed in the preparation of their preliminary plans.

The first sort of schedule may be appropriate for the first cycle of planning in the introductory year, while a network scheme may be developed later when the participants had acquired some sophistication and more was known of the requirements of a particular organization.

The basic features of any scheme are the stages of:

1   The work leading up to the preparation and issue of the first planning letters.
2   The preparation of the preliminary plans of the units in the company.
3   The integration of the unit plans to the corporate plan, and the issue of the second planning letters.
4   The preparation of the final five year unit plans with the first year in detail.
5   The integration of the final unit plans to the corporate plan and the issue of formal approvals.

Once the first cycle of planning is over, the build-up of the information base continues as a standard procedure, but it is 'frozen' at certain points in the calendar of events. Attitudes and decisions have to be taken at these points in time regarding critical factors on which planning depends, for example, the assumptions at various levels and the adoption of forecasts at the start of the sequence of opportunities, objectives and strategies.

Likewise, when the organization of corporate development as a part of the whole planning system has been established, this too becomes a continuing process but based more on *ad hoc* studies. These are aimed to harmonize with the overall calendar in which decision points occur, although in practice this is not always feasible. Under such conditions, the state of the know-how in any corporate development study is frozen and assumptions are made, feeding into the annual cycle of integrated management planning in a way similar to items from the more routine parts of the information base.

These models of the calendar of events contain the fundamental phases of annual planning but their timing during the year is a matter for discretion. Smaller and less complex organizations can operate on shorter time schedules. The interactions between units is more personal and is faster. In the case of the larger organization of the type shown in Figures 3.5, 3.6 and 3.7, the calendar of events, due to physical constraints (communications, the need for travel for the purpose of dialogue and so on) may occupy a full year's working in total. Under such conditions planning work does not necessarily engage all the participants for all of the time, since the location of various phases of activity change and there are obvious waiting periods. The smaller organization has important advantages in this respect but on the other hand, the overall management of a large organization can be greatly simplified by following such network procedures as are proposed.

In the case of the smaller organization, the events in the annual cycle of events may not need to occupy more than six months from start to finish. In this case the count-down time may start on 1 July with the issue of the first planning letters. In the case of the larger organization, planning letters will need to be issued during the first quarter and the schedule devised so that the second letter is issued in July or August.

Such schedules enable the head of a planning unit to have the benefit of the first half year's trading results to hand. Furthermore, since he will then be 'closer' to the coming events of the first year of the five year plan, the reliability of the detail called for in the final plan, especially the action programmes and the quarterly form of the budgets, will be that much better.

Between the two sorts of schedules described, there will be many degrees of difference in the phasing of events and in the length of the timetable involved. In addition, as experience is gained through several cycles of planning, the actual workload is reduced. Compliance with planning procedures becomes more acceptable as a way of life, and those who plan even begin to wonder how they managed before!

ACTION PLANNING TEST LIST 22

QUESTIONS	RESPONSE BY	TIMING OF ACTION ARISING
1 After reviewing the organization and the location of the units of the concern, what time-table of annual planning events will you propose?	Corporate planner	
2 How will this be communicated to those who have planning responsibilities?	Corporate planner	
3 When will the formal 'countdown' time commence?	Corporate planner	
4 With reference to the network scheme of Figure 4.33 (a) how many decisions points are there in the production of preliminary plans (b) how many opportunities for recycling and integrating preliminary and final plans?	Corporate planner	

BASIC OBJECTIVES, GUIDELINES AND POLICIES	
Basic objectives and obligations to be recognized and defined:	Decisions are desirable on guidelines and policies towards:
Shareholders	
1 Security of the business 2 Growth in terms of ROI and EPS 3 Growth in terms of assets 4 Rewards 5 Functional objectives	1 Self-financing and independence 2 Retentions and reinvestments 3 Capital gearing 4 Information and communication 5 Employee profit participation etc
Employees	
1 Job satisfaction 2 Motivation and rewards 3 Welfare 4 Pensions 5 Safety and hygiene in works and offices 6 Race relations 7 Relations with organized labour	1 Training schemes 2 After-service welfare 3 Job security 4 Health services 5 Holidays with pay 6 Job rotation 7 Encouragement to participate in community affairs 8 Information and communications 9 House journal etc
Customers and/or suppliers	
1 Fair dealing 2 Give and expect service 3 Give and expect product reliability	1 Pace setting on prices 2 Aim to be brand leaders 3 Aggressive/soft marketing 4 Innovativeness 5 Never compete with customer or supplier 6 Problem solving either way 7 Prompt settlements of accounts 8 Early settlements with discounts etc

Figure 4.1 Basic objectives, guidelines and policies.
Check list of basic corporate objectives (and obligations) and items on which decisions are desirable concerning guidelines and policy with respect to shareholders, employees, customers and suppliers, the general public and internal operations

BASIC OBJECTIVES, GUIDELINES AND POLICIES	
Basic objectives and obligations to be recognized and defined:	Decisions are desirable on guidelines and policy towards:
General and public	
1 Good image and public relations 2 Environmental problems 3 Law abiding 4 Support of trade organizations	1 Support of charities 2 Support of political parties 3 Prestige advertising 4 Support of local community affairs 5 Support of local religious organizations 6 Support of education by scholarships, university research etc etc
Internal operations	
1 Promotion from within 2 Delegation and giving of authority in defined terms 3 Corporate organization	1 Mass production, low cost — high productivity — low margins 2 Speciality, high cost — low production — high margins 3 Accounting methods — depreciation — costing methods 4 Basic research 5 Innovation from own R & D 6 Licensing in and out 7 Imitative development 8 Support of trade research associations 9 Patents 10 Corporate planning, integrated management planning and corporate development 11 Management succession programmes etc

Fig. 4.1 cont.

INFORMATION BASE INTERNATIONAL INDICATORS – CHECK LIST FOR ASSUMPTIONS	RELEVANCE	
	?	ASSUMPTIONS
1 Political Major military conflicts Regional conflicts and effects East-West relations – Warsaw Pact countries, China etc East and West Germany Nationalization of industry, sequestration of assets, etc		

2 World economy
 	
General economic trend, recession or growth
Cycle of world trade
Pace and centres of inflation
Expected growth in GNP (real and current) in:
    UK
    EEC
    Other European countries
    USA
    Canada
    South American countries
    Africa and Asia
    Japan
    Australia and New Zealand
    'Eastern Bloc'
    China
    Any specific country of importance		

3 Trade policies Impending trade agreements Tariff and quota proposals GATT and Kennedy round Tariff reduction schedules on EEC entries US anti-trust legislation US average selling price basis for tariffs		
4 New groupings Extensions to EEC Position with old EFTA members Integration possibilities in other areas: South America, Middle East, Africa, S E Asia, Japan and Australia		
5 Monetary trends Relationship of gold and US dollar values Rates of exchange of currencies Controls on convertibility of currencies: movements of capital, payments of dividents, etc		

Figure 4.2   Information base: international indicators check list for assumptions

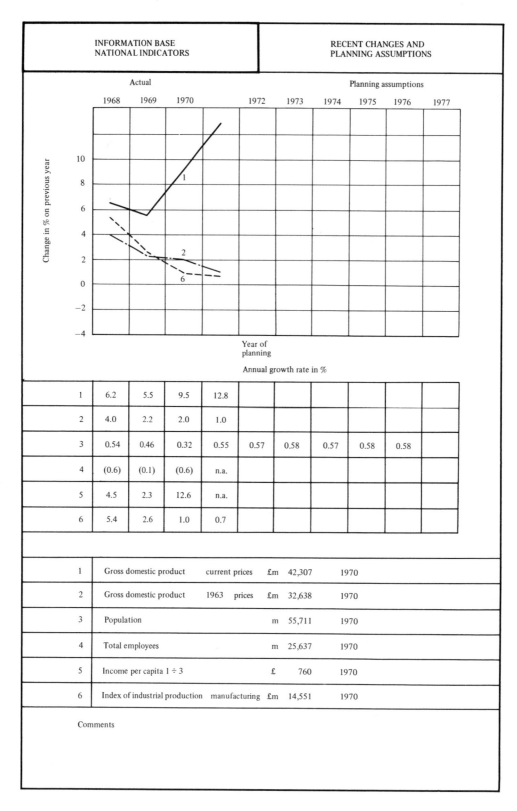

Figure 4.3 Information base: actual changes in the principal national indicators as a basis for planning assumptions

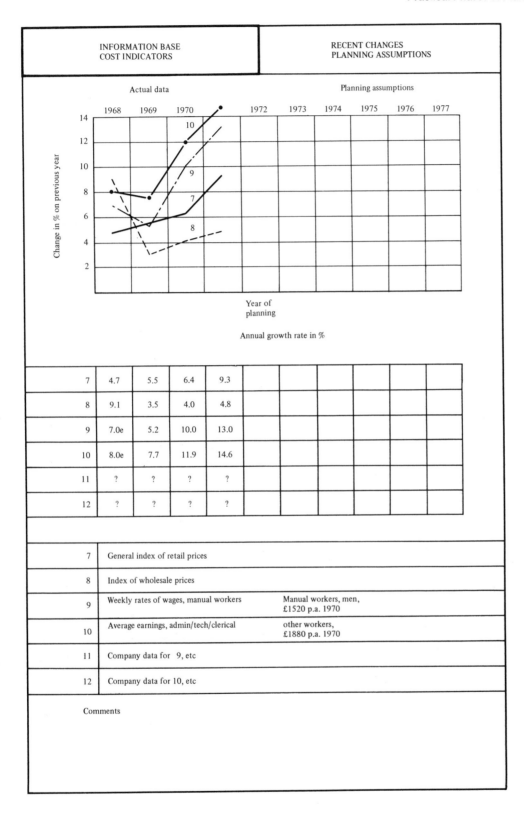

	INFORMATION BASE COST INDICATORS				RECENT CHANGES PLANNING ASSUMPTIONS				

Actual data

Planning assumptions

	1968	1969	1970	1972	1973	1974	1975	1976	1977
7	4.7	5.5	6.4	9.3					
8	9.1	3.5	4.0	4.8					
9	7.0e	5.2	10.0	13.0					
10	8.0e	7.7	11.9	14.6					
11	?	?	?	?					
12	?	?	?	?					

7	General index of retail prices	
8	Index of wholesale prices	
9	Weekly rates of wages, manual workers	Manual workers, men, £1520 p.a. 1970
10	Average earnings, admin/tech/clerical	other workers, £1880 p.a. 1970
11	Company data for 9, etc	
12	Company data for 10, etc	

Comments

Figure 4.4 Information base: actual changes in cost indicators as a basis for planning assumptions

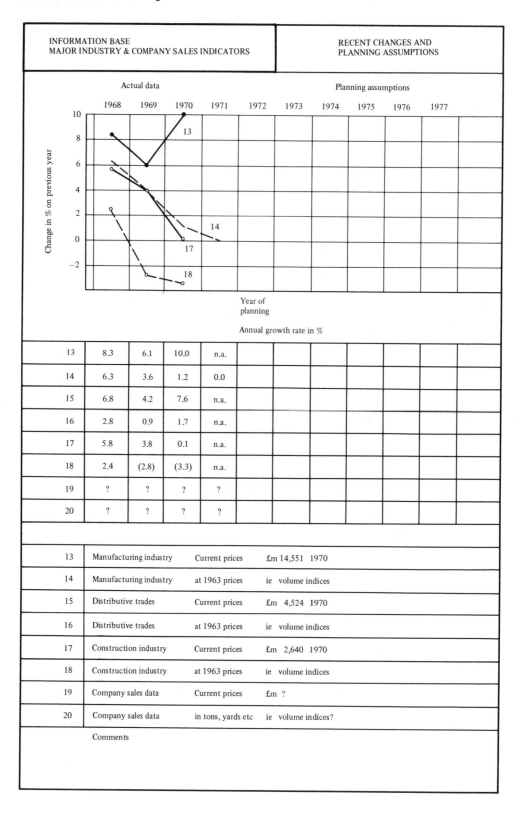

INFORMATION BASE MAJOR INDUSTRY & COMPANY SALES INDICATORS				RECENT CHANGES AND PLANNING ASSUMPTIONS					

Actual data   Planning assumptions

	1968	1969	1970	1971	1972	1973	1974	1975	1976	1977
13	8.3	6.1	10.0	n.a.						
14	6.3	3.6	1.2	0.0						
15	6.8	4.2	7.6	n.a.						
16	2.8	0.9	1.7	n.a.						
17	5.8	3.8	0.1	n.a.						
18	2.4	(2.8)	(3.3)	n.a.						
19	?	?	?	?						
20	?	?	?	?						

Annual growth rate in %

13	Manufacturing industry	Current prices	£m 14,551 1970
14	Manufacturing industry	at 1963 prices	ie volume indices
15	Distributive trades	Current prices	£m 4,524 1970
16	Distributive trades	at 1963 prices	ie volume indices
17	Construction industry	Current prices	£m 2,640 1970
18	Construction industry	at 1963 prices	ie volume indices
19	Company sales data	Current prices	£m ?
20	Company sales data	in tons, yards etc	ie volume indices?

Comments

Figure 4.5   Information base: actual changes in some major industry output indicators as a basis for planning assumptions

INFORMATION BASE GENERAL EXTERNAL INDICATORS – CHECK LIST FOR ASSUMPTIONS	RELEVANCE	
	?	ASSUMPTIONS
1 International indicators see Figure 4.2 for check list		
2 National indicators 2.1 Gross National Product 2.2 Gross Domestic Product 　　　　current prices 　　　　fixed prices 2.3 Industrial production 　　　　all industries 　　　　manufacturing industry 2.4 Population 　　　　age groups, sexes, etc. 2.6 Employed labour force 2.7 Per capita income 2.8 Personal disposable income 2.9 Volume of retail trade 2.10 New car registrations 2.11 Investment in various sectors 　　　　private, public, manufacturing, 　　　　buildings, etc		
3 Cost indicators 3.1 Indices of inflation 3.2 Basic hourly wage rates 3.3 Average earnings of all employees 3.4 General index of retail sales 3.5 Wholesale price indices 　　　　basic materials, output of manufacturing 　　　　industry, etc 3.6 Interest rates 　　　　short-term and long-term		
4 Industry indicators 4.1 Trade cycles 4.2 Mining and quarrying 4.3 Construction 4.4 Gas, electricity and water 4.5 Manufacturing industries 　　　　food, drink and tobacco 　　　　coal and petroleum products, chemicals, etc 　　　　engineering sectors 　　　　metals 　　　　textiles, leather and clothing 　　　　bricks, pottery and glass 　　　　timber, furniture, etc 　　　　paper, printing and publishing		

Figure 4.6   Information base: check list of general external indicators

INFORMATION BASE GENERAL EXTERNAL INDICATORS – CHECK LIST FOR ASSUMPTIONS	RELEVANCE	
	?	ASSUMPTIONS
5 *Fiscal and monetary indicators* 5.1 Effects from balance of payments position, monetary reserves, and devaluation possibilities 5.2 Rates of exchange of currencies 5.3 Availability of capital borrowings, controls on credit, etc 5.4 Interest rates at home and abroad 5.5 Transferability of currencies, foreign payments, capital transfer, exchange controls, etc 5.6 Nature and rates of taxes – corporate, personal, purchase, SET, VAT, etc 5.7 Nature and rate of customs and excise duties 5.8 Depreciation allowances, investment grants, development areas, etc 5.9 Social service costs – national health, state and private pensions, etc 5.10 Cost of training levies and their recovery 5.11 Special bank deposits with Bank of England		

6   *Political indicators*
 	
6.1   Nationalization policies
6.2   Regional policies
         subsidies, depreciation and
         investment allowances etc
6.3   Industrial relations
6.4   Taxation policy
6.5   National Planning
6.6   Government controls
6.7   Ecology – pollution etc
6.8   Import-export controls and incentives
6.9   Monopolies policy
6.10 National undertakings use of markets for finance
6.11 EEC and other regional developments in trade, etc		

7 *Social and other indicators* 7.1 Sports 7.2 Leisure activities in general 7.3 Holiday developments 7.4 Family life 7.5 Standard of living, food, clothing, etc 7.6 Religion 7.7 Community living, houses, flats, etc 7.8 Developments in education, health, etc 7.9 Books, papers, radio and TV 7.10 Social welfare policy 7.11 Hours of working		

Fig. 4.6 cont.

1   United Kingdom

   1.1 *Annual Abstract of Statistics,* Central Statistical Office,
   1.2 *National Income and Expenditure,* Central Statistical Office (annual)
   1.3 *Monthly Digest of Statistics,* Central Statistical Office
   1.4 *Economic Trends,* Central Statistical Office (monthly)
   1.5 Business Monitors
          Production, Civil Aviation,
          Miscellaneous and Service
          and Distribution, Department of Trade and Industry (HMSO)
   1.6 Trade and business associations, financial journals, etc, various
   1.7 *Social Trends,* Central Statistical Office (annual)

2   EEC

   2.1 *Graphs and Notes on the Economic Situation on the Community,* Directorate General for Economic
          and Financial Affairs (Monthly)
   2.2 *Economic Situation in the Community,* Directorate General for Economic and Financial Affairs (quarterly)
   2.3 *General Statistical Bulletin,* Statistical office of the European Communities (11 times a year)
   2.4 *Foreign Trade Monthly Statistics,* Statistical office of the European Communities
   2.5 *Social Statistics,* Statistical Office of the European Communities (bi-monthly)

3   International Monetary Fund (IMF)

   3.1 *Direction of Trade (11 issues a year and annual summary)*
   3.2 *International Financial Statistics* (monthly)

4   Organization for Economic Cooperation and Development (OECD)

   4.1 *Main Economic Indicators* (monthly)
   4.2 *Economic Survey of Member Countries (19 to 21 issues a year)*
   4.3 *Foreign Trade Statistical Bulletins* (in 3 series)

5   United Nations Organization (UNO)

   5.1 *Commodity Trade Statistics* (fortnightly)
   5.2 *Monthly Bulletin of Statistics*
   5.3 *Population and Vital Statistics Report* (quarterly)

6   United Nations Educational, Scientific and Cultural Organization (UNESCO)

   6.1 Review of Information, and others

7   World Health Organization (WHO)

   7.1 *Bulletin* (monthly)
   7.2 *Chronicle* (monthly)
   7.3 *International Digest of Health Legislation* (quarterly)

Figure 4.7   Public sources of information on general external indicators.
All publications (except those for trade and business associations)
are available from Her Majesty's Stationery Office

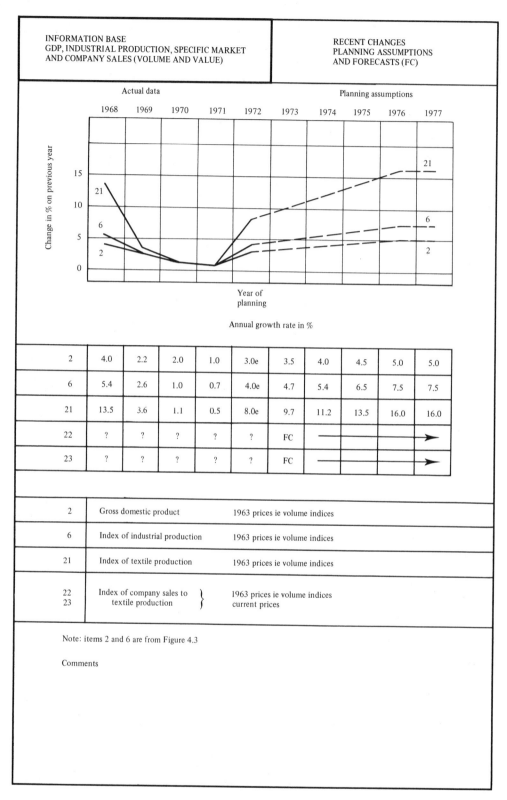

INFORMATION BASE GDP, INDUSTRIAL PRODUCTION, SPECIFIC MARKET AND COMPANY SALES (VOLUME AND VALUE)	RECENT CHANGES PLANNING ASSUMPTIONS AND FORECASTS (FC)

Actual data Planning assumptions

Change in % on previous year

Year of planning

Annual growth rate in %

	1968	1969	1970	1971	1972	1973	1974	1975	1976	1977
2	4.0	2.2	2.0	1.0	3.0e	3.5	4.0	4.5	5.0	5.0
6	5.4	2.6	1.0	0.7	4.0e	4.7	5.4	6.5	7.5	7.5
21	13.5	3.6	1.1	0.5	8.0e	9.7	11.2	13.5	16.0	16.0
22	?	?	?	?	?	FC				⟶
23	?	?	?	?	?	FC				⟶

2	Gross domestic product	1963 prices ie volume indices
6	Index of industrial production	1963 prices ie volume indices
21	Index of textile production	1963 prices ie volume indices
22 23	Index of company sales to textile production }	1963 prices ie volume indices current prices

Note: items 2 and 6 are from Figure 4.3

Comments

Figure 4.8 **Information base: recent changes, planning assumptions and forecasts.** Actual changes in the GDP, the index of industrial production, the textile output, and the company sales to the textile industry, followed by assumptions on the growth of the GDP, and related indicators, and forecasts of company sales

INFORMATION BASE MARKETING INFORMATION

COMPANY: ABC Co. Ltd
PRODUCT/S GROUP/S: Plastics Materials
SALES TO SUB-MARKET: Electric Cable Industry

BUSINESS DIVISION: Plastics Division

COMMENTS:

NOTES: M S is market share in %
1968–72 is *actual data*
1973–77 is *projected data*

Year	1968		1969		1970		1971		1972		% Growth 68–72	1973		1974		1975		1976		1977		% Growth 73–77
	T	M/S	T	M/S	T	M/S	T	M/S	T	M/S	M/S	T	M/S	T	M/S	T	M/S	T	M/S	T	M/S	
Sales by volume (tons)																						
1 Polyethylene A																						
2 Polyethylene B																						
3 Polypropylene A																						
4 Polypropylene B																						
5 Poly 'X' A																						
6 Poly 'X' B																						
Total																						
Sales by value £'000																						
1 Polyethylene A																						
2 Polyethylene B																						
3 Polypropylene A																						
4 Polypropylene B																						
5 Poly 'X' A																						
6 Poly 'X' B																						
Total																						

Figure 4.9 Information base: sales of product groups to a sub-market (plastic materials to electric cable industry)

INFORMATION BASE MARKETING INFORMATION	COMPANY: ABC Co. Ltd													BUSINESS DIVISION: Plastics Divisions	COMMENTS:															
	PRODUCT/S GROUP/S: Plastics Materials														NOTES: P is total profit in £'000 % is percentage profit on sales 1968–72 is *actual* data 1973–77 is *projected* data															
	SALES TO SUB-MARKET: Electric Cable Industry																												
Year	1968		1969		1970		1971		1972		% Growth 68–72		1973		1974		1975		1976		1977		% Growth 73–77		
Profit on sales	P	%	P	%	P	%	P	%	P	%			P	%	P	%	P	%	P	%	P	%			
1 Polyethylene A																									
2 Polyethylene B																									
3 Polypropylene A																									
4 Polypropylene B																									
5 Poly 'X' A																									
6 Poly 'X' B																									
Total																									

Figure 4.10   Information base: profitability of sales of product groups to a sub-market

INFORMATION BASE LAND RESOURCES	LOCATION IN COUNTRY	GENERAL PURPOSE	COST/ VALUE (£'000)	TOTAL AREA (ACRES)	AREA USED (ACRES)	AREA FREE (%)	AREA FREE (ACRES)	COMMENTS
Site A								
Site B								
etc								
All sites total								

INFORMATION BASE LAND USES SITE	LOCATION ON SITE PLAN	SPECIFIC PURPOSE	COST VALUE (£'000)	AREA USED (ACRES)	% OF SITE AREA	AREA FREE (%)	AREA FREE (ACRES)	COMMENTS
1 Manufacture A								
B etc								
2 Warehouse RM								
Prod's								
3 Offices A								
B etc								
4 Labs. etc								
5 Roads and communications								
6 Services								
7 Welfare								
8 Others								
Land uses total								
Site total				100				
Site free land								

Figure 4.11 Information base on: (1) land resources; (2) land uses; (3) buildings and capacity resources in production

INFORMATION BASE BUILDING AND CAPACITY RESOURCES SITE	BUILDING COST/ VALUE (£'000)	FLOOR AREA SQ. FT			EQUIPMENT COST/ VALUE (£'000)	CAPACITY			COMMENTS
		TOTAL	USED	FREE		TOTAL	USED	FREE	
1 Manufacture A									
B etc									
2 Warehouse RM									
Prod's									
3 Offices A									
B etc									
4 Labs.									
5 Roads and communications									
6 Services									
7 Welfare									
8 Others									

Notes:

1 All data should refer to a specific year eg the last full year before the planning year (except cost).

2 Cost is original cost; value is replacement or market price.

3 A separate form for land uses is produced for each site.

4 A separate form for building and capacity resources is produced for each site.

5 Capacity is the rated output per annum, in specified units of products, or services such as steam, electrical energy, etc., or in other units such as the number of persons accommodated in offices or laboratories. It refers to *installed* capacity only.

6 Comments in the bottom schedule might include a statement of the maximum capacity of buildings if any free area were fully deployed on existing lines.

Fig. 4.11 cont.

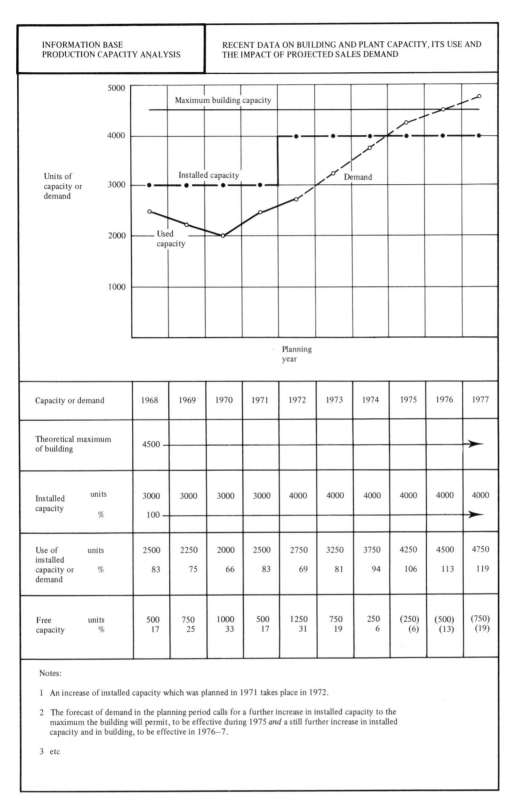

INFORMATION BASE PRODUCTION CAPACITY ANALYSIS	RECENT DATA ON BUILDING AND PLANT CAPACITY, ITS USE AND THE IMPACT OF PROJECTED SALES DEMAND

Capacity or demand		1968	1969	1970	1971	1972	1973	1974	1975	1976	1977
Theoretical maximum of building		4500									→
Installed capacity	units	3000	3000	3000	3000	4000	4000	4000	4000	4000	4000
	%	100									→
Use of installed capacity or demand	units	2500	2250	2000	2500	2750	3250	3750	4250	4500	4750
	%	83	75	66	83	69	81	94	106	113	119
Free capacity	units	500	750	1000	500	1250	750	250	(250)	(500)	(750)
	%	17	25	33	17	31	19	6	(6)	(13)	(19)

Notes:

1 An increase of installed capacity which was planned in 1971 takes place in 1972.

2 The forecast of demand in the planning period calls for a further increase in installed capacity to the maximum the building will permit, to be effective during 1975 *and* a still further increase in installed capacity and in building, to be effective in 1976–7.

3 etc

Figure 4.12 **Information base on production capacity analysis (using illustrative data)**

INFORMATION BASE PERSONNEL NUMBERS, COSTS AND RATIOS	COMPANY BUSINESSES FUNCTIONS								Actual								Projected					BY BUSINESS DIVISIONS AND FUNCTIONS, or BY SUB-BUSINESSES AND FUNCTIONS, or etc	NOTES: Total costs, sales and assets are in £'000. Average costs per person per annum are in £
	1968	1969	1970	1971	1972	% Change 68–72	1973	1974	1975	1976	1977	% Change 73–77	Comments
Divisions and functions: 1 Business division A 2 Business division B etc 3 Function A 4 Function B etc													
Categories: 1 Senior management 2 General management 3 Supervisory 4 Operatives													
Total number of personnel													
Total cost of personnel													
Average cost per person per annum													
% change in average cost on year before													
Sales per employee													
Assets per employee													

Figure 4.13   Information base on personnel prepared for use at corporate level

INFORMATION BASE FINANCIAL RESOURCES	COMPANY YEAR	NOTES: All sums in £'000 A is actually P is potentially available	
Resource		Actually available	Potentially available
1 Unissued ordinary share capital	P		
2 Partially paid up but issued shares	P		
3 New share issues	P		
4 Depreciation account (if the assets represented by it are separately identifiable)	A		
5 Cash	A		
6 Marketable securities	A		
7 Extension of credit from suppliers	P		
8 Reduction of credit to customers (early settlement discounts etc.)	P		
9 Current and planned profits	P		
10 Investments grants	P		
11 Surplus stocks	A		
12 Surplus fixed assets	P		
13 Sale and lease back projects for offices, transport, equipment etc	P		
14 Sale of know-how	P		
Borrowing potential — the appropriate ratio based on the current value of the company's assets in land, buildings etc, stocks and other current assets			
15 Bank overdrafts	P		
16 Long-term loans, debentures, etc	P		
17 Discounting of bills	P		
18 Mortgages	P		
Comments			

Figure 4.14   Information base: check list on financial resources

INFORMATION BASE STRENGTHS AND WEAKNESSES AND KEY FACTORS FOR SUCCESS 4-point scale of 'what we are good/bad at'	COMPANY UNIT NOTE: All figures are %'s unless stated otherwise				IS THIS A KEY FACTOR ?
Financial ratios	Strengths		Weaknesses		Comments
	++	+	–	– –	
1 Return on investment	>20	20/10	10/5	<5	
2 Gross profit on sales	>50	50/20	20/10	<10	
3 Sales on capital used	>200	200/100	100/75	<75	
4 Stocks on sales	<10	10/20	20/50	>50	
5 Debtors on sales	<4	4/6	6/8	>8	
6 Total marketing costs on sales	<5	5/10	10/20	>20	
7 Promotion costs on sales	<2	2/5	5/10	>10	
8 Distribution costs on sales	<1	1/2	2/5	>5	
9 Allocation of sales to R & D	>15	15/5	5/2	<2	
10 Interest rates on borrowed money	<6	6/8	8/10	>10	
11 Sales per employee (£)	10,000	10,000/7,500	7,500/5,000	5,000	
12 Assets per employee (£)	10,000	10,000/7,500	7,500/5,000	5,000	
13 Annual change in ROI over last 5 years (average)	>5	5/0	0/(5)	<(5)	
14 Annual change in gross profit on sales over last 5 years (average)	>10	10/0	0/(10)	<(10)	
15 Financial resources	Maximum	Reasonable	Limited	Tight	

Figure 4.15 Information base: strengths and weaknesses shown by financial ratios

INFORMATION BASE STRENGTHS AND WEAKNESSES AND KEY FACTORS FOR SUCCESS 4-point scale of 'what we are good/bad at'	COMPANY UNIT NOTE: All figures are %'s unless stated otherwise				IS THIS A KEY FACTOR?	
Research & development	Strengths		Weaknesses		Comments	
	+ +	+	–	– –		
1	Sales arising from R & D products introduced in the last 10 years	> 25	25/10	10/0	0	
2	Time for development stages after research is complete	< 6 months	6 months/ 1 year	1/2 years	> 2 years	
3	New products which are completely innovative (ie not imitative)	100	100/50	50/5	5	
4	Number of patents filed per annum per R & D 'unit'	> 3	3/1	1	< 1	
5	Patents granted/patents applied for	100	100/50	50/10	10	
6	R & D contribution to corporate objectives	Strong	Occasional	Rare	Never	
7	Value of R & D in sub-licencing products or processes special skills or expertise	Large	Partial	Limited	None	
8	Is there basic research including liaison with university research	High	Partial	Limited	None	
9	Is R & D a source of personnel for other functions eg marketing, production etc	Often	Occasional	Rare	Never	
10	Are the evaluation resources commensurate with research output	In balance	Partial	Limited	Rare	
11	Coordination of R & D with marketing	Strong	Fair	Poor	Absent	
12	Is R & D planned on risk basis with full financial appraisal of costs and rewards	Fully	Partially	Limited	Never	
13	Deployment of technological forecasting as an input to R & D	Fully	Partially	Limited	Never	
14	Percentage time granted to senior R & D staff for free research	20/10	10/5	5/0	0	

Figure 4.16 Information base: strengths and weaknesses in research and development activities

139

INFORMATION BASE
STRENGTHS AND WEAKNESSES AND KEY FACTORS FOR SUCCESS
4-point scale of 'what we are good/bad at'

COMPANY UNIT

NOTE: All figures are %'s unless stated otherwise

	Production	Strengths ++	Strengths +	Weaknesses −	Weaknesses − −	IS THIS A KEY FACTOR? / Comments
1	Efficiency — Yields or conversions (obverse of wastage)	>95	95/85	85/70	<70	
2	Capital intensive – £ capital investment per worker	>5,000	5,000/2,500	2,500/1,000	<1000	
3	Labour intensive – labour cost on works cost	<5	5/10	10/30	>30	
4	Communications and transport – for products and personnel	Very good	Good	Fair	Poor	
5	Are raw materials vulnerable	None	Minority	Majority	All	
6	Are raw materials 'tied' or basic to the company	All	Majority	Minority	None	
7	Are manufacturing processes derived from own R & D / licensed	All / None	Majority / Minority	Minority / Majority	None / All	
8	Organization of training programmes	Proven	Partial	Starting	None	
9	Average age of plant facilities (years)	<5	5–10	10–20	>20	
10	Time to install new facilities (months)	<12	12–18	18–24	>24	
11	Labour – trade union relationships	Very good	Good	Fair	Poor	
12	Labour turnover per annum	<5	5/10	10/20	>20	
13	Reserve capacity — Plant and machinery / Buildings / Land	5/10 / 5/15 / 5/25	10/20 / 15/25 / 25/50	20/50 / 25/50 / 50/100	50 / 50 / 100	
14						

Figure 4.17 Information base: strengths and weaknesses in production activities

140

Product line	Strengths ++	Strengths +	Weaknesses −	Weaknesses − −	IS THIS A KEY FACTOR? Comments
1 How much could profitably be eliminated	0/10	10/20	20/50	50	
2 How much product 'gap' in the range	0/10	10/20	20/50	50	
3 Have R & D objectives been set for the opportunities in 2	All	Part	Few	None	
4 How many products are / Commodities / Specialities	0/10 / 100	10/20 / 100/50	20/50 / 50/25	50 / 25	
5 How many are patented or have trade names	100	100/50	50/25	25	
6 How many have export potential	100	100/25	25/5	5	
7 Amount having expected life use over 10 years	100	100/25	25/5	< 5	
8 Amount introduced in last 2 years	> 20	20/10	10/5	< 5	
9 How many have outlets in more than 1 market (number of markets)	> 5	5/2	2/1	only 1	
10 Are they synergistic (help sales of other products of the company)	Yes	↑		No	
11 Are the products unique and vital to users	> 50	50/5	5/0	None	
12 How many are brand leaders	50	50/10	10/0	None	
13 Are the following data known / Product profitability / Product market share / Product market growth	Fully	Partially	Limited	No	
14					

INFORMATION BASE
STRENGTH AND WEAKNESSES AND
KEY FACTORS FOR SUCCESS
4-point scale of 'what we are good/bad at'

COMPANY UNIT

NOTE: All figures are %'s unless stated otherwise

Figure 4.18 Information base: strengths and weaknesses of product line

INFORMATION BASE STRENGTHS AND WEAKNESSES AND KEY FACTORS FOR SUCCESS 4-point scale of 'what we are good/bad at'	COMPANY UNIT NOTE: All figures are %'s unless stated otherwise				IS THIS A KEY FACTOR ?	
		Strengths		Weaknesses		Comments
Marketing		++	+	−	− −	
1	Are there 'tied' markets or customers	Many	Several	Few	None	
2	How many potential customers (numbers)	100	100/20	20/5	5	
3	How many accounts taking more than 20% of sales	None	1	2	4	
4	Market research status	Proven	Moderate	Limited	Low	
5	Market growth per annum	>15	15/5	5/0	<0	
6	Share of market	40/20	20/10	10/5	5/0	
7	Competition	Weak	Slight	Moderate	Strong	
8	Reputation for Product leadership Innovation Service Promotion Distribution Packaging, etc	High	Moderate	Poor	Adverse	
9	Have we high level sales contacts	Yes ———→			No	
10	Pricing problems	No ———→			Yes	
11	Are markets seasonal/cyclical	No ———→			Yes	
12	Delivery time v orders	Same day	1/3 days	3/10 days	>10 days	

Figure 4.19 Information base: strengths and weaknesses in marketing activities

142

INFORMATION BASE COMPETITOR ANALYSIS Own company first, major competitors follow	Research and development	Production	Product range	Marketing	M%	Finance, etc
COMPANY: ABC Co. Ltd			**BUSINESS DIVISION: 'M'**			**NOTE:** M% is market share by value
PRODUCT GROUP: 'X'			**MARKET: 'Y'**			
MARKET VALUE: £			**MARKET VOLUME: UNITS**			
1 ABC Co Ltd business division 'M'	Product research is too widely spread; use research is good. Reputation for developing new uses. Little basic research.	Has 5 plants: 2 over 10 years old. Total capacity 10,000 units. Are 50% basic in raw materials. 100 acre site reserve.	Wide range which could profitably be reduced. Have other product ranges which are synergistic in sales. Quality good and reliable.	Good market image. Price followers. Good product use service. Have a share of most accounts. Export 10% of production.	25	Part of a group with £50m capital. Profits growing steadily from 10 to 25% ROI in last three years. Very modern management.
2 DEF Co Ltd	Development is speedy and adaptive. Poor research; no patents or innovations. Imitative.	15,000 unit capacity: 2 plants over 10 years old. Very flexible. No raw materials position. Site fully used.	Mainly commodities of average quality. No leaders in the range.	Price leaders. No technical use service. Delivery is good. Large exports. Aggressive sales personnel.	33	Single business firm: growth hinges on GDP and trade cycles. Recently became public on good record. High sales to capital ratio.
3 GHI Co Ltd business division 'N'	Extensive research with basic support. Strong patent position. Has policy of sub-licensing.	4/5,000 unit capacity. 100% basic in raw materials. Large site reserves.	Limited range: chiefly special-ities of high price and per-formance. Market leaders in product quality and performance.	Soft sellers. Concentrate on home market. No exports in view of sub-licensing policy.	10	Part of international group with extensive resources but poor profit record. High research and corporate costs.
4 KLM Co Ltd	No research; rely on sub-licensing from a US Company. Good and speedy in development.	Capacity about 2,000 units. No raw material pos-ition. Plant is 5 years old. Site is fully used and in built-up area.	Limited to sub-licensed products for a sub-market 'Z'. Quality is very good.	Concentrate on sub-market by inter-company contracting. Low cost marketing operations. No exports of note.	5	Small firm with limited capital but US licensors have 30% shares. Low corporate costs. ROI record over 20%. Well managed.
5 etc Others						

Figure 4.20   Information base: competitor analysis—prepared for hypothetical firm in manufacturing industry

INFORMATION BASE SUMMARY PROFILE OF OWN AND OTHER PARTY BUSINESSES	STRENGTHS AND 'HAVES'		S	W		WEAKNESSES AND 'WANTS'	
	'P' – PRIORITY IN MERGER AND ACQUISITION STUDIES						

Subject area		Own company			Other party		'P'
		Remarks	S/W	S/W	Remarks		
Technical	1 R & D	Excellent resources: also in basic research	▨		None		
Technical	2 Patents	Potentially good: applications pending	▨		None		
Manufacture	3 Raw materials	Yes – from industrial side	▨		None		
Manufacture	4 Finished products	None	▨		Limited range based on 2 key products		
Manufacture	5 Capacity	None but could instal quickly	▨		Limited and out of date		
Manufacture	6 Warehousing	Extensive for general purposes	▨		Use distributors		
Marketing	7 Goodwill/image	Good in industrial markets		▨	Long established: nationally known	P
Marketing	8 Promotion	Have large experience in related fields	▨		Little or no effort today		
Marketing	9 Sales	None in field of interest		▨	Have 20% of market	P
Marketing	10 Distribution	Have good network for related products	▨		Use distributors & agencies		
Products	11 Brand names	None in field of interest		▨	2–3 well known brand names	P
Products	12 Market leaders	None		▨	Losing earlier position	P
Products	13 Range	Potential for comprehensive range	▨		Limited to variations on 2 key products		
Personnel	14 R & D	Excellent	▨		None		
Personnel	15 Manufacture	Potentially good	▨		Outdated: foremen only		
Personnel	16 Marketing	Good experience in related fields	▨		Old directors still in charge		
Personnel	17 Administration etc	Ample modern types	▨		Old directors still in charge		
Financial	18 Sales	None in field of interest		▨	£½m in each of two main ranges		
Financial	19 Profits	None in field of interest		▨	Past record of 25% ROI is decreasing		
Financial	20 Cash position	Excellent	▨		Poor		
Financial	21 Fixed assets	None in field of interest		▨	Outdated plants: but site has good value		
Financial	22 Total assets	Extensive in total: £50m	▨		About £¼m at book value		
Etc	23 Location etc	Has several sites with ample space and buildings	▨		5 acres in East End: no growth possible		

Figure 4.21 **Information base: summary profile of own and other party businesses: semi-quantitative comparison for acquisition study: illustrated for a market oriented activity**

INFORMATION BASE PORTRAIT OF A BUSINESS	COMPANY: BUSINESS DIVISION: PRODUCT GROUP: YEAR:	ABC Co Ltd Paint & Printing Inks Printing Inks 1972	NOTES
Sub-markets / Information	1 Newspapers, magazines etc	2 Packaging	3 Commercial printing and publishing
Size of sub-markets £'000s Tons	£6m 28,000 (17,000 black) (11,000 coloured)	£7m 11,000 (all colours)	£17m 21,000 (all colours)
Growth of sub-markets	Volume not increasing Value increasing on account of increasing use of colour (3%) p.a.	9% per annum in vol. at least twice the growth of the GNP Value growths are 1–2% higher	3.5% per annum in vol. closely linked to growth of the GNP
Own % share of sub-markets Value Volume	40% 20%	11% 10%	16% 15%
Own capacity tons	3500	2500	4000
Technology	Changing more to colour and web offset New plate and printing technology will call for new types of inks Great interest in synthetic paper as a substrate	Printing speeds rising Use of plastic packaging & flexographic inks increasing	New types of plates and printing technology Long range development of electro-static systems in multi-colour. UV curing methods to aid ecology
Marketing	Bulk contracting and delivery Increasing 'in-house' manufacture Black inks are low cost products	In few hands High discount and credit terms prevail High technical service demanded	Many small customers highly fragmented UK is a large exporter of commercial printing Credit terms etc are similar to those in 2
Economics	Printed matter is generally related to gross income per capita		
Economics	Inks for newspapers reached a peak around 1960 but use of colour is growing They are high volume, low cost and low margin products	Gross profits on sales average 25% but marketing and service costs are high	
General	The opportunities for a maker of inks lie in:		
General	Coloured inks to newspapers etc	Increasing shares of growing market	New reproductive processes leading to 'tied-markets' Increasing share of market

Figure 4.22 Information base: portrait of a business (text is approximate and for illustration only)

145

INFORMATION BASE		CORPORATE 1	BUSINESSES AND FUNCTIONS 2	DEPARTMENTS 3	FIGURE TO BE USED
Section	Responsibility / Topic	Corporate planner (CP) indicates cooperative task	Head of business or function	Head of department, staff for market research, controllers etc	
4.3.2	*General external events*				
	International indicators	Corporate planner			4.2
	National indicators	Corporate planner			4.3
	Cost indicators	(CP)	Personnel, purchasing and finance		4.4
	Major industry and business indicators	Corporate planner			4.5
	Other indicators	(CP)	Finance etc		4.6 and 4.7
4.3.3	*Industry, markets and own performance*				
	Industry, market and company sales	Corporate planner			4.8
	Product group sales to markets	(CP)	Business	Marketing	4.9
	Profitability of product group sales to markets	(CP)	Business Finance	Marketing Controller	4.10
4.3.4	*Resources*				
	Land and uses, buildings and capacity	(CP)	Appropriate business or function		4.11, items 1, 2 and 3
	Production capacity analyses	(CP)	Production	Engineering etc	4.12
	Other capacity analysis	(CP)	Appropriate business or function	Appropriate departments	4.12
	Personnel	(CP)	Personnel and appropriate business or function		4.13
	Finance	(CP)	Finance	Controllers	4.14

Figure 4.23 Who prepares which information base (including forecasts) and makes specific assumptions

PLANNING LEVEL / INFORMATION BASE		CORPORATE 1	BUSINESSES AND FUNCTIONS 2	DEPARTMENTS 3	FIGURE TO BE USED
Section	Responsibility / Topic	Corporate planner (CP) indicates cooperative task	Head of business or function	Head of department, staff for market research, controllers etc	
4.3.5	*Technology* Products, processes, services etc Technological forecasts	(CP)	Research and development	Marketing, Process engineers, R & D managers etc	as appropriate
4.3.6 and 4.3.7	*Key factors for success, and strengths and weaknesses* Finance	(CP)	Finance	Controllers	4.15
	Research and development	(CP)	Research and development	R & D managers	4.16
	Production	(CP)	Production etc	Process engineers	4.17
	Product line	(CP)	Business	Marketing	4.18
	Marketing	(CP)	Business	Marketing	4.19
4.3.8	Competitor analysis	(CP)	Business	Marketing, market research, etc	4.20
4.3.9	Portrait of a business	(CP)	Business		4.22
4.3.10	Specific assumptions	Corporate planner	Business or function	Department	as appropriate

Fig. 4.23 cont.

1   A company with a static business in the growing field of household products (10–15% per annum), finds that it lacks an up-to-date corporate image, nor does it offer its products in the form of aerosols as do all its competitors.

2   A high profit product group (50% on sales) for which the firm has a 30% reserve in manufacturing capacity, fills only 5% of its market, which is growing at 20% per annum.

3   The growth in the personal disposable income of persons in the age group 20–25 years is growing faster than any other. The firm produces record players but only high cost commercial models.

4   The firm has undoubted technical strengths in the field of miniature electronic equipment and foresees a growing demand (over 25% market growth per annum) for miniature calculators which would sell at similar prices to the radios which at present form its major outlet.

5   A dyestuffs manufacturer with modern range of products finds that the key factor in selling is the provision of technical service; at present it has less than 7% of the market, most of which is sold through agents.

6   A retail branch company in the grocery trade having over 100 shop sites, most of which are freehold, has a poor capital gearing using large amounts of borrowed money.

7   A firm with a high research and development expenditure (15% of sales income), and an indifferent record of innovation, has strengths in its small but adaptive development department which has successfully imitated 2 out of 5 competition products in the last year.

8   A company has a good market image in the field of pre-cooked foods, a market which is increasing at 20% per annum, but its present assortment is limited to three products which are sold widely but only through small traders.

9   Stocks of finished goods have doubled in the last three years, resulting in a 15% increase in the total capital employed. A reduction to 10 weeks of stocks would increase the firm's ROI by 17%.

10   A company in the field of industrial water treatment sees the growth which is occurring in the use of household water softeners.

11   A firm with long experience and high expertise in handling its own waste disposal problems recognizes the growing interest and the increasing legislation in environmental pollution.

12   A colour pigment maker notes the trend towards the greater use of brilliant colours on motor cars and in other products such as plastic garments and shoes, in promotional displays, etc.

13   During the last five years the number of a firm's customers has decreased by 50% on account of mergers. The output of the user industry is still increasing (7% per annum) but its own sales have dropped by more than this. It has no policy for dealing with the centralized purchasing now practised by the new groups.

14   A pharmaceutical company sells both its range of ethical and non-ethical pharmaceutical products through the same marketing organization.

Figure 4.24   Illustrations of business opportunities derived from the analysis of information bases

15 A floor-covering manufacturer whose product is based on linseed oil notes from national statistics that plastic materials are rapidly replacing the older product. They have no experience in handling plastics but understand that much of the machinery involved is of the same nature.

16 From the national statistics, a firm notes that a market is growing faster in value (15% per annum), even after correcting for inflation, than in volume (5% per annum). Its own data show that its average price per product has only kept place with inflation.

17 A concern with its own building and engineering department finds that new projects take over two years to come into effect and are always more than 20% higher in cost than originally estimated. The department, however, is strong in new design ideas.

18 A firm producing heavyweight commodity materials has its own road delivery service, but fails to increase its sales in areas over 100 miles distant.

19 A concern having a chain of restaurants finds that the 'kitchen cost' of materials is over 50% of the corresponding menu prices.

20 A life insurance company finds that its representatives use 70% of their time in servicing existing policies and only 30% for getting new business.

Fig. 4.24 cont.

	COMPANY BUSINESS DIVISION					
WHAT BUSINESS ARE WE IN? OPPORTUNITIES FOR GROWTH		**PROCESSES**		**WHAT BUSINESS ARE WE IN? FUNCTION ACHIEVED**		or,
PRODUCT						
Present	Growth opportunities	Present	Growth opportunities	Present	Growth opportunities	
Motor cars	Increase sales by volume, increase range of products eg sports cars, taxis, lorries, etc	Engineering and assembly	Other engineering products, refrigerators, office furniture, hydraulic machines, engines for other uses, fibre glass structures, etc	Road transportation	Other forms of transportation, air, sea, canal, etc, electric vehicles, etc	
Coal	Increase sales by volume, smokeless fuel, building materials, etc	Mining	Mining for other minerals, underground civil engineering – tunnels etc, drilling, conveyor belt transport, ventilation, dust prevention, etc	Energy and minerals	Other forms of energy, chemicals from coal, heating appliances, etc	
Electric bulbs	Increase sales by volume, cathode ray tubes, sodium, mercury, etc vapour lamps, etc	Various technologies	Glass shaping, vacuum systems, rare metal and wire technology, adhesive systems based on glass/metal, etc	Illumination	Other forms of illumination, cold light, phosphors, signalling, road, sea, etc	

Figure 4.25 'What business are we in' and 'Opportunities for growth' (using illustrations for three cases)

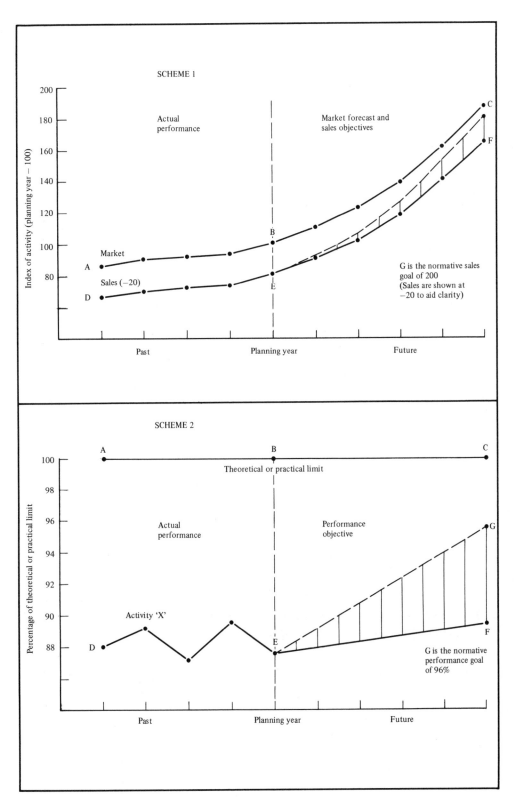

Figure 4.26 Basic approaches to objectives.
Scheme 1 based on indices of market and sales activities
Scheme 2 based on percentages of theoretical or practical limits
of an activity 'X'

151

			£'000
1	Estimated profit for last year		1.000
2	Profits arising from *outside* the control of the company:		
	Increase of size of market by 4%	40	
	Higher volume use of production resources	4	
	Increase in basic wage rate	(25)	
	Increase on raw material costs	(80)	
	Increase in cost of social services	(10)	
	Increase in interest on extra loans	(20)	
		(91)	909
3	Profits arising from items *inside* the control of the company:		
	Increase of market share, 20 to 25%	260	
	Higher volume use of production resources	26	
	Higher manufacturing yields	35	
	Reduction in use of labour	35	
	Increase in costs of management services and training	(20)	
	Increase in costs of R & D	(45)	
		291	
4	Net effective profit for the first planning year		1.200

Simplified assumptions:

Profit on sales in the last year was 20%
Capital used was £5m, made up to £4m in shares and £1m in loans
There is an increase in loans of £0.2m at 10% interest

Outcome:

Earnings per share increase from 25p to 30p whilst,
Return on total investment increases from 20% to 23%

**Figure 4.27   Scheme of profit objectives for the first cycle of planning
(contributions from different units)**

STRATEGY OUTLINE ALTERNATIVE COURSES OF ACTION			COMPANY: The Battery Chicken Co. Ltd BUSINESS/PRODUCT GROUP: Battery reared chickens
	Answer		
Alternatives	Yes	No	Reasons
1 Do we wish to get out of the business? 1.1 Totally 1.2 Partially		 No No	There is substantial capital still invested in this business. Management expertise in production is good. There is a trend to higher incomes and increased living standards in the UK. It is forecast that poultry will increase as part of family budgets. The cost of other protein foods is increasing rapidly. The latter items represent opportunities.
2 Do we wish to maintain the present business (without making capital additions)?	Yes		There is excess battery chicken production facilities in the UK at the present, and pressure on margins. For the short-range future (not less than 3 years) it is felt that no new investment is called for and our objective to maintain the present chicken business, growing with the market but also to diversify by extending the product range to include higher class, higher profit products.
3 Do we wish the business to grow? 3.1 Equal to market growth 3.2 More than market 3.3 By diversification (New uses/new products)	Yes		With no early investment on the chicken side, current growth should be to the point where existing capacity is fully used, whilst the strategy should be towards diversification. A move into day-old chick production (for resale) is being studied as well as the rearing and sale of game produce eg pheasant. This is a logical move in view of our expertise in these areas and would require only a moderate investment. This would also contribute to a smoothing in our seasonal selling cycle. Our existing farm land reserves are still extensive.

Figure 4.28 Strategy—outline alternative courses of action (Illustrative text for The Battery Chicken Co. Ltd.)

153

ACTION PROGRAMME	COMPANY BUSINESS DIVISION/FUNCTION DEPARTMENT	or, or,	ACTION PROGRAMME NUMBER

Objective

Strategy

Overall responsibility
Reporting to

Supporting parties (SP)
1
2
3

By	Start date	Finish date	Number man-weeks

Action steps to be taken

1

2

3

4

5

6

7

Financial benefit

Profit

Costs

Figure 4.29 Standard format for action programmes

CONTENTS OF PLANNING LETTER

1   General comments and key data on recent progress against plans:
    (*a*)   as at corporate level 1
    (*b*)   as at the level of the addressee.
2   Basic corporate objectives, guidelines and policy:
    reiterations and/or emphasis on changes due to new elements appearing in information
    bases.
3   Corporate assumptions at international and national levels.
4   Invitations to propose assumptions:
    specific to the field of the recipient, that is, applying domestically to the business or
    function at level 2.
5   The particular corporate objectives and strategies which apply to the recipient:
    these strategies become in turn the objectives at level 2, the author exercising his right, if
    so desired, to suggest certain strategies for the recipient to follow.
6   Administrative instructions:
    (*a*)   timetables
    (*b*)   format and presentation of plans.
    The latter may be unchanged from the standard procedure laid down in the corporate
    planning manual, or if sections are amended, attention is drawn to tne changes.
7   Coordination:
    Stress on special cases where coordination is needed, for example as between various
    divisions having elements of common interests, or with specific functional executives.

Figure 4.30   Essential contents of a planning letter

ABC Company Limited

D.E.F. Esq.,
Director in Charge,
G Division

1st July 197—

CONFIDENTIAL

Dear Mr F.,

Planning Letter Number 1 for G Division: 1974—8

This letter and the enclosed packet of items is for your guidance in the 1973 cycle of corporate planning embracing the period 1974—8. The items are laid out in detail but I would like to give you my personal comments on some of them.

Although our end of the year estimates of the total corporate income and profitability show increases of 10 and 5% respectively, over the previous year's performance, they both fall below the continuing objectives of increases of 15 and 10%. However, I accept that in the passing year, the limited growth of the economy as a whole, plus the greater degree of inflation than we assumed, are largely responsible for below average increases.

Nevertheless, there were significant differences between the results of our four business divisions, as you will see from the tabulation which is enclosed. From these results, it will be clear that, apart from linking the growth of the firm's businesses with the general progress of the country's economy, the highest profit growths have undoubtedly been in the businesses with the highest innovations, not only of products, but also in respect of markets. Concentration on this policy will be evident to you in the key objectives put to you in this letter.

As you will see from item 2 which is enclosed, a change in the basic policy of the firm has been adopted in that we believe that our financial record and prospects will enable us to raise long term capital, probably up to £2m, on acceptable terms. Our director in charge of finance and I, now have an action programme to conclude the negotiations by the end of the first quarter of 1974 and funds should be available for allocation during the coming cycle of planning. This will ease the past burden of self-financing and enable us to consider a higher rate of investment in production facilities and for a foothold in Europe. This should give you a wider choice of strategies to consider in your business.

Concerning the corporate assumptions set out in enclosure 3, you will see that we anticipate a growth in the real GDP of 4% per annum until 1975 when this rate is assumed to decrease to an average of 3% for the rest of the planning period. At the same time, we have to assume, unfortunately, that the inflationary element of the GDP will be almost 10% for the next two years, at least. I hope the budgets in your plans will overcome this dual problem by showing increases in the real productivity in the various departments of your business. You will also notice that you are requested to take into account changes in the nature of levies and taxation (SET and VAT). There are no changes in the other items on the list of assumptions of enclosure 3.

I have no special comment regarding your own assumptions which are called for by item 4.

The table of financial details enclosed under the heading of item 5, lists the corporate objectives which call for a much greater growth rate in sales income and profitability in view of our assumptions on the growth of the GDP in the UK during the period for which we are now to plan. I hope you will be able to devise strategies and action programmes to meet the objectives given in the lists which are assigned to your division. Increases of 25% in sales and profits are stretching goals but under the conditions of business which are assumed, they are not, I believe, unreasonable.

Figure 4.31   Planning letter no. 1.

Illustrative planning letter no 1 from a chief executive to the head of a business division—in practice supported by annexures corresponding to the seven essential items of a planning letter according to Figure 4.30

Now that the entry of the UK into the EEC, has become a fact, it is a corporate objective to develope our business in Europe more intensively. You will see that our strategy involves an objective for you in this respect. Apart from increasing direct exports, I wish you to pay special attention to the strategy of an acquisition or some other form of local operation on the continent which would include manufacture within the planning period ahead.

A further objective for your division arising from the corporate objective of intensifying our R & D facilities, is an R & D unit within your own division. Later in this letter I mention the coordination which will be called for in this respect. From the enclosure number 5, you will see that we propose to allocate 10% of your sales income to R & D, three quarters of which will be to the new unit, the balance being directed to the Central R & D unit for longer range research. Your plans in respect of this development will be awaited with much interest.

I have no comments to make on the timetables and administrative details in item 6, these being in principle unchanged from the scheme of last year.

Referring now to the question of coordination, this is specially called for in two cases:

1   Although the new R & D unit will be under your control, Mr H.I.J., as head of R & D will have a functional part to play, not only in its establishment, but in the future activities of the unit. Will you please take the responsibility for the action programmes which arise in this area? I shall include these points in my planning letter to him.

2   Likewise, since an analogous objective to your intensification of activity in the EEC, has been given to Mr K.L.M. on behalf of his business division, I would like you to cooperate with him in the groundwork involved. I have in mind the sharing of the quest for acquisitions in that there will be many features in common between the two divisions (infrastructures, administrative facilities etc.). I would, however, like you to take the responsibility for the action programmes which you will set up in this connection, a request I shall make clear to Mr K.L.M. in my planning letter to him.

I look forward to receiving your preliminary plan by Sept. 30, 197— and particularly the choice of strategies you propose to employ for the objectives regarding EEC and R & D developments.

Finally, I would like to repeat that I am always available for discussion on these matters — likewise Mr N.O.P., as head of our corporate planning department, whose services I know you have very fully used in past planning work.

Yours sincerely,

Q.R.S.
Managing Director

Enclosures: Items 1—7

Fig. 4.31 cont.

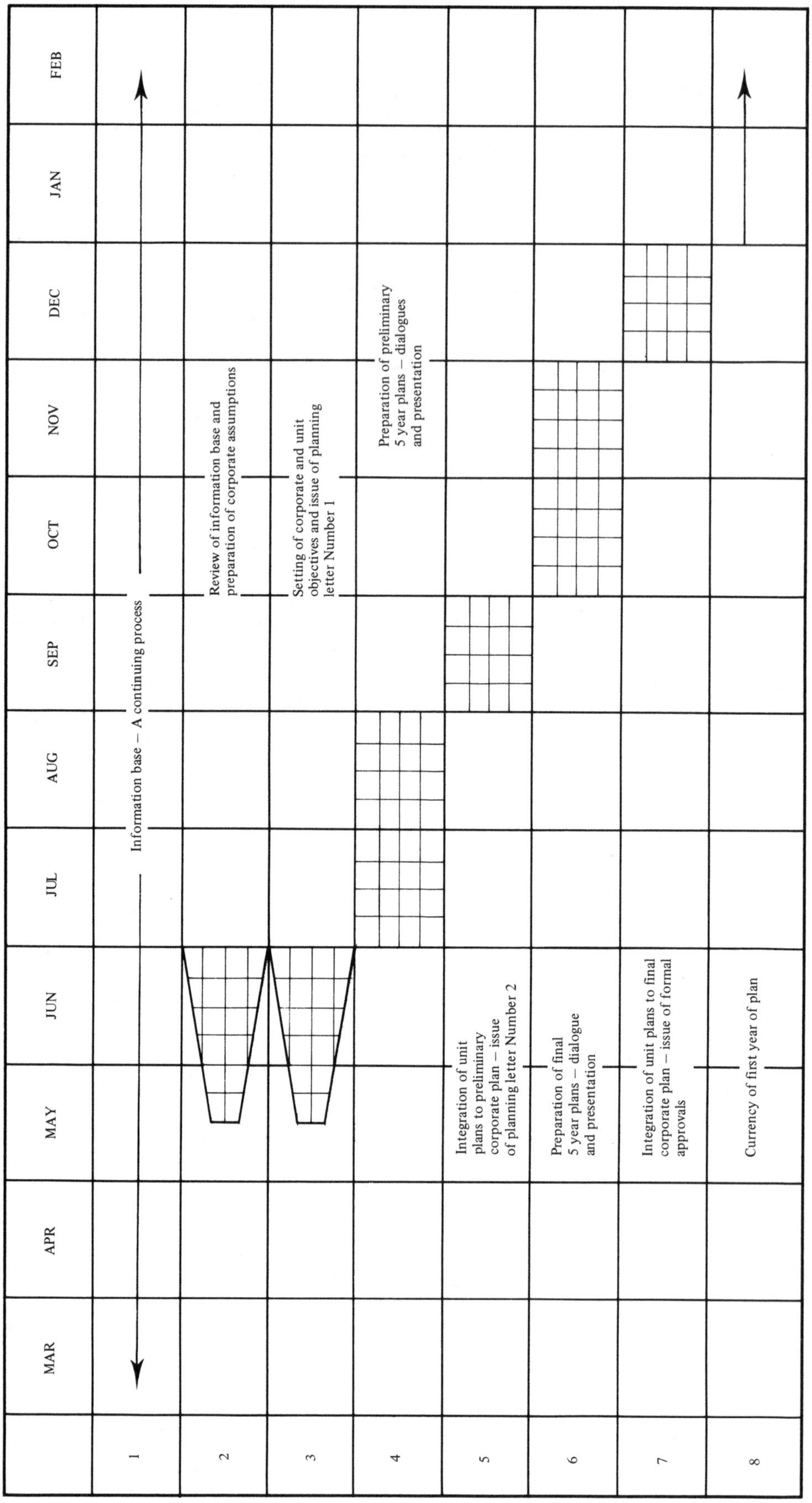

Figure 4.32 Schedule of events in the annual planning cycle

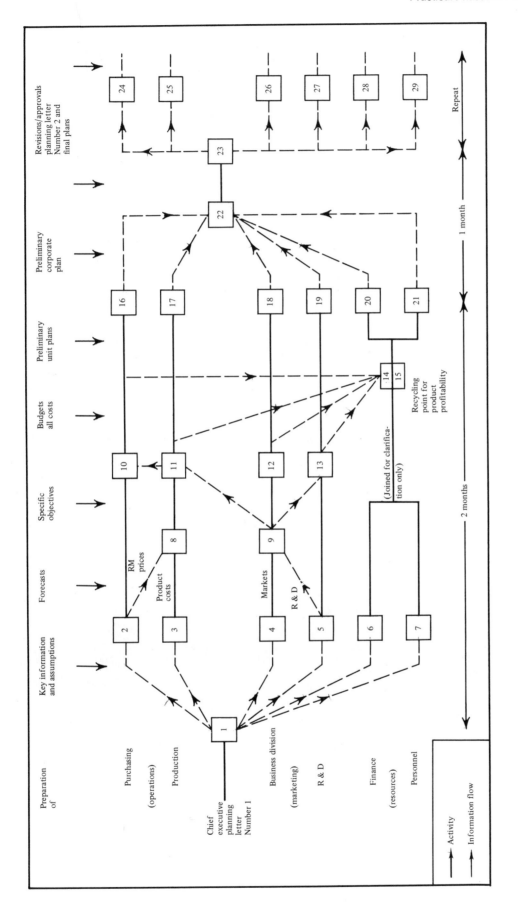

Figure 4.33 Network scheme of events in the annual planning cycle (showing one business division only)

SECTION 5

Format and
Presentation of Plans

5.1	General remarks		163
5.2	Parts of a plan		167
	5.2.1	Summary	168
	5.2.2	Key information and assumptions	168
	5.2.3	Opportunities, objectives and strategies	169
	5.2.4	Action programmes	170
	5.2.5	Resource requirements	170
	5.2.6	Budgets	172
5.3	Unit plans		175
	5.3.1	Corporate plans	175
	5.3.2	Business division plans	179
	5.3.3	Function plans	184
5.4	Coordination of unit plans and approvals		201
	5.4.1	Coordination	201
	5.4.2	Approvals	203

SECTION 5

Format and
Presentation of Plans

5.1 GENERAL REMARKS

According to the opening paragraph of Section 1.1, corporate planning is 'the systematic development of action programmes aimed at reaching agreed business objectives by a process of analysing, evaluating and selecting from among the opportunities which are foreseen'.

The practical phases of planning dealt with in Section 4 of the workbook systematically cover each of these stages. Thus:

1 *The opportunities which have been foreseen* arise from one or other parts of the scrutiny described in the second part of Section 4.4 (which deals with the identification of opportunities in the future environment in which the company intends to operate).

2 *Agreed business objectives* come from within the limits of the quantified opportunities which have been foreseen. The determination of the levels of the objectives is described in the third part of Section 4.4. Agreement on the precise levels of the objectives formally occurs when the preliminary plans are approved and are then refined into final plans, according to the annual schedules given in Section 4.8.

3 *Strategies* arise from the evaluation and selection of the various alternatives which aim at the agreed business objectives, on the lines of the fourth part of Section 4.4.

4 *Action programmes* are scheduled following the selection of the particular strategies, according to the methods in Section 4.5.

5 The strategies and action programmes both take into account the present and potential resources of the firm while all the stages are viewed in the light of the basic corporate objectives, guidelines and policy.

6 Finally, the intended activities are quantified and reflected in the budgets, (Section 4.6) which show the forward trend in profits.

From this recapitulation it will be evident that planning is the summation of all the foregoing stages, each of which is essential and each of which goes to form part of the 'plan' as a whole. In principle, this applies to all kinds of plans whether they be at the corporate level 1 or others at level 2 (business and functions in the company) or at level 3 (departments, or sub-units of level 2 units).

The next stage of the workbook, which describes the format and presentation of plans, recognizes the essential stages of the overall process. It outlines how the chief features have arisen and then how they should be summarized and assembled to give the format of a plan which can serve as a practical document.

At the same time it is necessary to recall that planning is a tool of management, so that the plans themselves should also demonstrate the activities of management: leadership, organization and the delegation of responsibility and authority (and their acceptance as a commitment) should be evident. The other functions of management are effected by the monitoring and control procedures, described in Section 6, when actual results are compared with planned results.

In principle, plans of every kind should be produced with a common structure. That is, they should have the same basic form and layout in order that the sequence of planning levels originating at the corporate level 1 is seen to be taken up and continued through the lower levels which follow. They should use the same sort of forms for the presentation of basic data in order that the integration of sub-unit plans into those of the next higher level can be effected by simple addition. The standard formats for planning data form the basis of the control reports in order to facilitate comparisons between actual and planned results (Section 6).

Ideas and models for the format and presentation of plans vary widely, but general experience and logic show that there should at least be a recital of the particular elements of the information base which yielded the business opportunities, and of the objectives and strategies which have been selected. Action programmes and budgets should be included in sufficient detail to allow measurements of progress during the control period while a résumé of the additional resources needed is part of the story.

Finally, if the author of each plan is permitted to give special views or comments on the basic contents, the structure of a formal plan emerges as having the following six parts:

1 Author's summary and personal remarks
2 Key items from the information base and assumptions
3 Principal opportunities, objectives and strategies
4 Action programmes
5 Resources needed
6 Budgets

Section 5.2 of the workbook deals, in turn, with these six parts of a plan; the common approach and the principles which are followed with respect to each part are outlined as standard features.

Section 5.3 deals with different kinds of unit plans—that is, plans of different levels and of different areas of responsibility.

The characteristics and formats of the six parts of unit plans conform to those outlined in Section 5.3 but are in terms of their particular level and of the particular corporate interests with which they are concerned. In these respects they naturally vary. For example, opportunities in the third part of a business plan are market oriented while those in a personnel plan deal more with people; the budget forms in part 6 of a business plan show details of its sales income and its own divisional expenditure while a function such as R & D has costs and no income to show in the budget in its plan, and so on.

Preliminary and final plans

The distinction between preliminary and final plans, described in Section 3.2.3, hinges on the feedback stage at which the proposals in preliminary plans from units of the firm are reviewed and integrated. Integration ensures that the plans satisfy the requirements of the company as a whole and that they are in line with one another, having been coordinated with the asistance of the corporate planner.

Approvals of preliminary plans, which are contained in planning letter 2, authorize the preparation of final plans on the basis proposed, or with agreed amendments.

Accordingly, a preliminary plan is an outline of an expected final plan. It follows the same format but does not need to contain the part on action programmes, nor the amount of detail that appears in part 6 (budget) of a final plan. For example, quarterly statements, which are the basis of reporting and control procedures, are not needed; these are prepared only after planning letter 2 has been issued indicating approval of the preliminary plan or calling for modifications. Procedures for the approval of plans are clarified further in Section 5.4.

Use of standardized forms

Since planning of any kind calls for a logical and systematic approach to the development of affairs, it is necessary to record key factors and data in a reasoned and organized manner. This helps to avoid the misunderstanding and ambiguity of the spoken word; indeed it ensures clarification. At the same time there is every need for the record to be kept as brief as possible and to see that no more is called for than is absolutely essential. This applies with equal force whether the planning work is carried out manually on paper or, in a highly sophisticated organization, by the use of a computer.

The use of standardized forms, not only in the format and presentation of plans and in the control phase of planning, goes far to ensure that the problem is kept within bounds and that there is a minimum of paperwork.

The principle of the workbook, which runs through the presentation of planning data of all kinds, is the maximum use of standardized forms, adaptable in a simple way for use by all units at all levels of the concern and for all planning years. Such formats facilitate the addition of budget data from the lowest levels, either manually or by data processing methods, to give the total for the next higher level and, ultimately, for the company as a whole. The principle also facilitates direct comparisons between different businesses, or between different years in a given planning unit. It also enables data in control reports to be compared quickly and unambiguously with the corresponding data in the budgets of other plans.

Finally, the use of standard forms helps to condense ideas and data and ensures that key factors emerge. It directs effort along the hierarchical tree, the apex of which is profitability.

Appendix I contains specimens of most of the key planning forms. They are also listed in a table showing which planning units use them and exactly where they can be found in formal plans. Reference should be made to them at this stage, since they are mentioned at appropriate stages during the explanations on the format and presentation of plans which follow.

ACTION PLANNING TEST LIST 23

QUESTIONS	RESPONSE BY	TIMING OF ACTION ARISING
1 What are the essential chapters of preliminary and final plans?	All management	
2 What are the advantages, and objects, of the use of standardized forms throughout the organization for: (*a*) information bases (*b*) planning summaries (*c*) budgets (*d*) quarterly budgets, and (*e*) control procedures?	All management	
3 Prepare a list of executives who should cooperate with the corporate planner in agreeing the format of standard forms for the purposes in item 2, above (see Appendix I).	Corporate planner	

The tabulation in Appendix I shows four basic types of forms:

P forms for data used in parts 1 to 5 of the body of a plan, most of which is presented in graphical summaries for quick appreciation of the salient features of the plan.

B forms used to present the budget data in part 6 of a plan giving details of each of the five years of the planning period.

B-Q forms which show the quarterly breakdown of the budget data for the first of the five planning years shown on the previous B forms. The quarterly forms are prepared only after the preliminary plan is approved, and appear only in final plans.

C forms are used to present data on the actual performance, each quarter, during the first year of action of the plan. They show comparisons of actual results with planned results, and form the basis for any revision to the year-end results when a variance is seen to be developing. They are referred to as 'control forms'.

Further aspects of this type of data presentation are dealt with in Section 6 of the workbook, which is concerned with the procedures of monitoring and control, and in Appendix I where guidance is given about the preparation and use of the various forms.

From a preliminary examination of the examples of B forms, it will be seen that many of them include a form of a key business ratio, either as such, or through the use of extra columns, which show the percentage analysis of key totals. This is to assist in making rapid comparisons with the kind of ratios or percentage analyses used during the practical phases of planning when objectives are established.

A small number in each of the top left-hand boxes of the forms illustrated in Appendix I is the suggested means of coding each basic type of planning form. If a form is used at different levels of a firm, or for different years, the appropriate heading is inserted to show the exact purpose and use of the form in question. In practice, once a scheme of forms has been developed for regular use, it is worthwhile to have such forms duplicated on paper of different colours to enable the forms for different planning units to be identified quickly.

Length of plans

Plans do not need to be lengthy documents if they rely for their presentation on the use of standard forms and treatment. On average, 25 pages of typing, including the use of standard charts or forms, plus an extra five in special cases, should suffice. More precise suggestions concerning the length of individual parts of a plan are given in Sections 5.2.1 to 5.2.6.

5.2 PARTS OF A PLAN

Following on the introduction to the structure of a formal plan, guidelines are now given, to be followed by all planning units in their approach to each of the six parts of their plan:

1 Summary
2 Key information and assumptions

3 Opportunities, objectives and strategies
4 Action programmes
5 Resource requirements
6 Budgets

5.2.1 Summary

The summary is a brief personal commentary by the person taking responsibility for the plan, that is, the executive head (a director or a manager) of the sphere of activity involved. It is written after the other parts of the plan are complete and affords an opportunity for the author to stress important points, to make comparisons with previous plans in cases other than the first cycle of planning, to comment on the various assumptions, and so on.

The summary also includes a résumé of the chief features of the plans of the particular planning unit. Simple tables or graphs are used to provide a succinct picture of the general progress towards profitability, over and above that given in the detail of the budgets. Suggestions and guidance for items of this sort (P forms) appear in the corresponding parts of Section 5.3 which deals with plans of different units.

The summary is always written with the next higher authority in the hierarchy of planning in mind and provides that person with a concise appreciation of the plans of the unit as supported by the other parts of the plan. Apart from the P forms mentioned, the summary of any plan need occupy no more than one or two pages.

The summary of a plan is signed by the author to show his commitment to the achievement of the objectives by the means described in his plan.

5.2.2 Key information and assumptions

This part of a plan starts by highlighting the key items from the information base (the salient facts and forecasts) which have been found to bear on the activities of the particular planning unit, taking into account its level and sphere of responsibility. The nature of these items will naturally vary from unit to unit so that more specific suggestions for each case are put forward in Section 5.3 dealing with individual plans.

The object of setting out the key items of information at this stage of writing a plan is to show the origin of the business opportunity, to show how it has been interpreted and to demonstrate the forecasts which lie at the basis of the subsequent planning activity. At the corporate level they will be more closely connected to the macro-level indicators discussed in Section 4.3 (external events at international and national levels) while in businesses and functions they will originate at the lower (industrial and market) levels of the environment. Those in functional units will be slanted more in their interpretation and meaning towards the professional or technical aspects with which they are concerned, for example, finance, personnel or R & D.

Efforts should be made to record the highlights of information in as concise a manner as possible. Those who need to examine the origins in detail may always look back to the documentation in the information base itself. Only key items are included in part 2 of a plan. According to the unit making the plan, one or two pages, excluding any tables or graphs, are sufficient.

Part 2 of a plan then lists the assumptions which have been made on the lines described in Sections 4.3.10 and 4.3.11.

Three levels of assumptions are dealt with here:

Level 1. The international and national assumptions at the company level, which are provided in the planning letter of the chief executive, are quoted in full in the company plan. Only a reference to them needs to be made in plans at level 2. Nevertheless, such references must specifically acknowledge receipt of the chief executive's assumptions and must state that they have been taken into account in the plans which have evolved.

Level 2. Assumptions at this level are of a more domestic nature than the foregoing. They deal more directly with the affairs of a business or function and are formulated by them at their level. They are approved at the stage of preliminary plans and are quoted in full in the plans of level 2. Specific reference to one or other should be made later in the plans when a particular action arises in consequence.

Level 3. Plans made at level 3 units of the company, for example, by departments of business divisions, depend upon assumptions which closely affect their affairs and are probably unique to them. Part 2 of a level 3 plan refers in the first case to the assumptions of the next higher level unit to which the unit belongs but quotes in full any specific departmental assumptions.

5.2.3 Opportunities, objectives and strategies

This part of a plan embodies the actual creative work of planning in each area and is the key decision stage.

It states the opportunities which have been identified in the key items of the information base, and the corresponding objectives and strategies which have been evolved.

Practical experience and the reasoning given in Section 4.3.6 dealing with key factors for success demand that a plan should concentrate on essentials. Depending on the planning level concerned, the number of opportunities dealt with in this part of a plan will range from four to six, rarely more. They will clearly be related to the accomplishment of the objectives set in the corresponding planning letter and relate to all five planning years. Not more than four pages (excluding any graphs or charts) should suffice for this part of a plan.

The detailed work on the opportunities, objectives and strategies takes place during the practical stages of planning, which are outlined in Sections 4.3 and 4.4. They take into account the corporate assumptions which have been provided and any raised at the level of the author of the plan.

The sequence of work, culminating in the third stage of strategy, forms the basis of the action programmes in part 4 of the plan and is the justification for the statement of resources needed in part 5. Without these the preparation of the budgets of part 6 is pointless.

The sequence of opportunity, objective and strategy is presented in this part of a plan as a unified concept, following the lines of the planning levels described in Section 3.3 and shown in Figure 3.8. This part of a plan generally consists of four to six unified concepts, each containing one short paragraph for each of the three stages. Concepts are numbered—opportunity 1, 2, 3 and so on. The planning unit concerned makes a reference in them to the key item of the information base or the objective it has received from its next higher level through the planning letter, whichever is the starting point of the objective in question.

5.2.4 Action programmes

Action programmes represent the outcome of the strategies emerging from the previous part of a plan and in this sense are the fourth stage of the sequence of opportunities, objectives and strategies. Together with the budgets of part 6 of a plan, they provide the basis for management control during the first year of the planned period. Accordingly, they figure highly at the stage of monitoring and control as described in Section 6.2.

Action programmes are described in full in Section 4.5. Each is presented in part 4 of a plan on a form P-9 in the style of Figure 4.29.

Action programmes are set up only when a strategy is operative at the level of the plan of which it is part.

They are set up at corporate level 1 when the action called for involves the chief executive or his immediate staff. They are then part of part 4 of the corporate plan.

When a strategy at corporate level 1 is given as an objective to the next lower level (for example, to a business division) no action programme is called for until the strategy at level 2 has been evolved. In these circumstances it then is set up and involves the head of the unit or his immediate staff. Such action programmes are included in part 4 of the business division plan.

When planning is organized down to a level 3, as will be the case in larger concerns, a similar procedure is followed.

More than one action programme may need to be set up in response to a given strategy, but only the most important are included in the plan itself.

Accordingly, part 4 of a unit plan simply contains up to six forms covering the major action programmes together with a list of any which are set up in its sub-units Five to seven pages should suffice for this part of a plan, comprising four to six forms for action programmes and one page of lists of others on behalf of sub-units.

5.2.5 Resource requirements

The information base contains a catalogue of the four main classes of existing corporate resources (see Section 4.3.4).

1 Land, buildings, equipment etc as the fixed assets of the firm
2 Personnel
3 Finance
4 Other less tangible items.

Part 5 of a plan is used to present the resources which are required to achieve the objectives of the plan but highlighting the additional requirements. They are quantified during the practical phases of planning when the growth of activities is found to justify increases in the facilities of one or other of the four classes mentioned.

Requirements in fixed assets

In this section of part 5 of a plan the major projects for capital investment are listed, each with a brief note giving its purpose, estimated cost and the time when it is planned to become effective. A reference is also given to the corresponding objective and strategy. The expenditure and timing are summarized on a form P-4 for capital expenditure projects. According to the policy governing investment procedure in the firm, which will usually classify projects as major or minor on some arbitrary scale or other, minor projects are grouped together in this list.

The budget section of the plan (part 6) contains a detailed financial account of major projects, which may still be subject to a strict technical and economic assessment as to why they should be accepted or rejected. Section 5.4 deals with the question of the approval of projects as between preliminary and final plans, and the overriding corporate policy on investment procedures generally. One or two pages are allowed for this section.

Requirements in personnel

Two aspects of personnel planning are shown in this section of part 5 of a plan. The first deals with the quantitative requirements for personnel and the second concerns their location in the organization of the planning unit.

Quantitative. The five-year extensions on the form in Figure 4.13 in the information base on personnel resources in Section 4.3.4 are used on an appropriate planning form P-8, to present the requirements of personnel by numbers, categories and costs, and to show relevant personnel ratios such as sales and assets used per employee. Remarks may be made at this stage, concerning requirements of a special nature, the filling of key positions and so on.

Organization. In addition to showing the foregoing data, two charts are included in this section of part 5 of a plan which show the organization chart of the planning unit, on a hierarchical basis, for the first year of the plan, and the organization chart for the fifth year of the plan. The purpose of the second chart is not only to show the development of the unit concerned, but to highlight key appointments for which plans are made in terms of succession and executive training, or as new appointments.

The charts should show the main sub-units of the particular organization, using boxes in which appear the names of the heads of each sub-unit and the number of persons employed in it. The data should reconcile with the data in the personnel form mentioned above.

Suitable notes are made on the second chart giving the year when any intermediate appointments or echelons of the unit are planned to take effect.

Questions relating to the actual engagement and training of personnel appear in appropriate action programmes, in which cooperation with the head of the personnel department of the firm as a supporting party is specified. Two to three pages suffice for this section of part 5—one personnel form, two charts of organization on one page and appropriate comments.

Requirements in finance

The growth objectives set out in the previous parts of the plan will normally call for increases in financial resources, not only to provide funds for investment in new capital assets (fixed assets), but also to provide working capital for the everyday purposes of business (current assets).

Together the two classes of requirements form the starting point for the planning of the total requirements in finance. The available resources, together with the annual cash flows generated in each of the five planning years, indicate whether and when there is any overall requirement, or if there is an excess of funds. Whether this is determined before or after dividends are paid is a matter of basic corporate policy. An overall need for funds after dividends are paid will need to be treated by one or other of the methods listed in Figure 4.14 in Section 4.3.4. Again, the strategy chosen will depend on corporate policy, the outcome being an action programme at level 1 for the chief executive or for the head of the finance function, for raising further funds.

The overall income and outgoings of a firm are assembled in part 5 of a plan under the heading 'sources and uses of funds' and are presented on form P-5. Normally this form, recording the cash flow and allocation of funds, either for further corporate use or as dividends to the shareholders, is included only in the corporate plan, but according to the nature of the organization, one may be called for in the plans of larger business divisions, regions or companies within groups, whenever these are sufficiently independent and self-accounting.

The requirements for capital investment are dealt with in the first section of this part of a plan while the requirements for working capital emerge after the budget (part 6) is complete and when the level of everyday business transactions is known.

Hence a further topic to be handled in part 5 of all plans is the extent of the total assets, shown as financial resources, required by the particular planning unit for the duration of the plan.

The two elements of assets are shown in a further form, P-3, which is included in this part and which shows the overall use of funds for the company as a whole and, when suitably titled, for each of the working units of the firm. The particular form 'P' is used to summarize requirements in finance, both for the purpose described earlier (capital projects) and for use as working capital in the financing of current assets (receivables, stocks of raw materials and finished products, and so on).

Brief comments are given in this section of part 5 of a plan on special aspects of the need for funds for everyday working purposes.

One page should suffice for this section of part 5 of a plan, in addition to form P-5 for sources and use of funds (corporate plans only) and form P-3 dealing with the total use of financial assets both for fixed investments and for use as current assets (all planning units).

Other resource requirements

Requirements in other spheres, such as for the purchase of know-how or patent rights, are briefly listed together with a note on the justification. Any financial impact will be dealt with in the preceding sections.

5.2.6 Budgets

The sort of budget data which are needed to reflect the five-year objectives of a company and to give a basis for control purposes depend upon the nature and level of the unit concerned. Nevertheless, all units of a company have certain budget features in common. Appendix I contains illustrations of the actual budget forms (types B and B-Q) which are needed, while the table in the appendix indicates which are to be used by particular planning units. In general these are on the following lines:

B-1	Operating statements	by company and business divisions
B-2	Sales planning	by company, business divisions and sub-businesses or marketing units

B-3	Assets (fixed and current)	by company, business divisions and functions
B-4	Capital expenditure	by all units which have planned expenditure projects
B-5	Sources and use of funds	by company only
B-6	Financial statement	by company only
B-7	Use of production capacity	by all manufacturing units
P-8	Personnel	by all units
P-9	Action programmes	by all units

At this stage some explanation is called for concerning the use of the forms showing operating statements. Normally such forms are used by planning units which have both expenditure and income and hence show profits. They are used at corporate and business levels 1 and 2, respectively. The corresponding summary and budget forms P-1 and B-1, shown in Appendix I, provide the standard form for operating statements and are used at either level.

However, each unit needs to prepare a budget section for its plan which shows the planned expenditure in more detail than in an operating statement. To this end, attention is drawn to the standard form of operating statement shown in Appendix I (form B-1) which will be seen to carry a horizontal numbering code, 1 to 20. This relates to the detailed statements of expenditure and so on of the components of a company or the particular business division which is responsible for them.

Accordingly, expenditure forms for each of these units should be prepared as supporting data to be shown only as a total in the operating statement, B-1, of the next higher unit to which they are attached.

Most budgets need to be prepared in two forms. The first, covered in Appendix I by B forms, refers to the data for each of the five planning years; the second, covered by B-Q forms, shows a quarterly breakdown of the data of the first year of the planning period and is used as the basis of the corresponding quarterly control form, C.

The compilation of the budgets in part 6 of a plan is effected in stages.

First, all the forms of class B, dealing with the five-year planning period (which exclude the quarterly budgets for the first year), are produced in a rough form for use at the stage of preliminary plans. At this stage they also form the basis of the summaries of class P forms.

Following approval of preliminary plans, with or without agreed amendments, class B budget data are refined and then serve not only for the preparation of up-to-date versions of class P, but also for the quarterly forms of class B-Q. Forms showing budget data of classes B and B-Q are included in part 6 of each final corporate, business division and functional plan.

The financial policies of the firm and its established accounting procedures are taken into account in preparing the financial data in the budget chapters of various plans. This is ensured in practice, since the task of compiling the preliminary and final versions of budgets falls more to the financial specialist of the planning unit concerned (accountant, controller, or works cost accountant) than to the corporate or divisional planner. Much detailed work is called for before the budgets in a final plan can be completed, but after the first cycle of planning it is usually found that the budgets and the corresponding control reports replace much of the earlier accounting procedures of the firm. It is at the budget stage that such features as the cost of planned variances appear and show the extent of unused resources, such as in production. The exact costing procedures used to determine this item, and indeed whether it is featured or not,

ACTION PLANNING TEST LIST 24

QUESTIONS	RESPONSE BY	TIMING OF ACTION ARISING
1 For what special reasons is the summary of part 1 of a plan prepared and why is it signed?	All management	
2 Recall the two sections in part 2 of each plan; how do they accord with the level of the author?	All management	
3 How many opportunities should be included in part 3, and through which stages are they linked to action programmes?	All management	
4 How many action programmes should appear in a plan — the same number as opportunities? If not, explain why	All management	
5 List the essential resources, and the method of describing each additional requirement in them for the five-year planning period	All management	
6 Apart from notional budget approvals, are there any special procedures in your firm for the approval of items of capital expenditure? Have these been formally communicated to the executive? If not, when will this be done?	All management Corporate planner and chief executive	
7 Why are two versions of the organization chart required in each plan?	All management	
8 Which unit plans contain statements on cash flow?	Corporate planner	
9 If quarterly budgets are not to be called for, what period of reporting will be adopted? State which items call for a different period outside the planning system, and why	Corporate planner and chief executive	
10 What method of costing does your firm employ, and how will you reflect this in the design of your budget forms?	Corporate planner and head of finance	

depend on the established accounting policies and methods of the company in question.

Whether the illustrations shown in Appendix I in the workbook are suitable or whether adaptations are needed to meet the activities of a particular firm, is a matter for the corporate planner to decide, usually in cooperation with the heads of planning units (the head of the finance function regarding financial data, the head of marketing for sales data and the head of manufacture for production budget forms).

Budget forms relating to manufacture are obviously to be replaced by others more appropriate to businesses engaged in, for example, banking, insurance or retailing. The same applies to sales budgets, which are inappropriate to some sorts of concerns, though there will be analogous budget forms which indicate, in some meaningful way, the transactions with the outside world which form the starting point of their income and earnings.

Because personnel budgets and action programmes, on appropriate forms, are already included in parts 4 and 5 respectively, four pages in part 6 of a plan will be the minimum for most planning units. Others, such as businesses, which have sub-businesses for marketing, and manufacturing functions will have more, possibly two to four further forms summarizing sales or production budgets. The precise number will depend upon the way they are organized for operation purposes and the complexity of their market and product range.

5.3 UNIT PLANS

5.3.1 Corporate plans

The corporate plan is the plan of the highest level in the organization, that is, the plan at company level 1 but in the case of larger companies, such as those whose structure is shown in Figure 3.7, it will include special cases such as:

1 A holding company whose overall structure includes several separately constituted companies. In such cases, there will be several corporate plans and one of the holding company.
2 A region, which consists of several companies, all lying in a given country, a group of countries or a continent. This case is analogous to that given in case 1.
3 The headquarters company of an international organization, the management of which is conducted first through its regional structure and then through the constituent companies in a given region. In this case there will be corporate, regional and headquarters corporate plans.

The corporate plan discussed here is taken to be the plan of the highest level of any one of these cases and it stands in relation to others, according to the nature of a particular organization, along the hierarchical lines put forward in Sections 3.2 and 3.3 which deal with kinds of plans and planning levels. The practical examples quoted in the present section on unit plans refer to the simple case of a corporate plan which is the integration of unit plans from business divisions and functions.

The author of the corporate plan is the chief executive, whether he is described as manager, managing director, executive chairman, executive president or executive vice-president. It is the person who takes, at his level 1, the responsibility for the plan and, by implication, the supporting plans of the firm's units. It is his signature which shows to his board of directors his commitment to the corporate plan. The summary in this plan may be regarded as a succinct presentation to the board of the company of the plan of the concern as a whole.

Although the chief executive is the official author of the plan, he relies for its assembly and drafting on the corporate planner as his staff assistant who ensures that it presents a correct and balanced integration of the unit plans of the company and that they reflect the corporate objectives at their level. In this work he is also assisted by other corporate specialists, mainly the head of finance. This especially applies in the compilation of the corporate budget, since it not only reflects the budgets of the component planning units, but also incorporates financial items at corporate level, that is, items which affect the company as a whole (sources and application of funds, dividends, use of liquid funds and so on).

Naturally, the chief executive reserves to himself the choice of key items, his personal comments and the final editing of his plan.

The corporate plan, as indeed is the case with all other plans of the firm, is a valuable document and must be regarded as confidential. It is addressed to the next higher authority, which in this case is the board of the company. Only in special cases is it available to lower levels of management. Such a special case occurs when the chief executive has an executive committee as part of the working of the top management. It is a working document for the chief executive for use in his relations with the board, and by his immediate staff and the members of any executive committee he employs. Such an executive committee often comprises the heads of the main operating units in a small concern, or the headquarters functional heads when the firm is so organized.

The following paragraphs deal more specifically with the standard contents of a corporate plan.

Summary

Here the chief executive has the opportunity to comment briefly on the national and international opportunities which lie before his firm and which have been identified during the phase of forming an information base, to indicate the broad objectives which have been proposed and the strategies he has selected to attain them. Events which prove to have a bearing on the basic objectives, guidelines and policy of the firm are noted, their impact is assessed and any changes are defined.

This is not a simple aggregation of unit plans, but rather an overall view given through the personal comments of the head of the firm's operations. It deals with the elements which affect the concern as a whole, the principal changes in the source of profits and the prospects for their growth.

The forward view of the trends in profitability, and of the financial affairs of the concern in general, is shown in detail by the budgets in part 6 of the corporate plan. However, in the summary, forms carrying simple charts or diagrams, based on the data of part 6, are included to show the following key features:

P-1 Summary of operating statement
P-2 Summary of sales (by business divisions etc.)
P-6 Summary of balance sheet
P-7 Summary of use of production capacity

Key information and assumptions

The outstanding items from the work on the information base and which form the source of its opportunities are briefly listed as portraying the environment in which the company will work and the resources it proposes to employ. Only items of higher level impact are given. They would be drawn from the following:

4.3.2 Forecasts of general external events
4.3.3 Forecasts of industrial and market trends
4.3.4 Corporate resources
4.3.5 Forecasts of technological trends
4.3.6 Key factors for success
4.3.7 Strengths and weaknesses
4.3.8 Analyses of competitor activity.

Apart from the foregoing listings, the specific level 1 assumptions, national and international, which were contained in the planning letters, are quoted, or supplied as an appendix to the plan. Examples of topics which call for assumptions are given in Sections 4.3.2 and 4.3.10, and in Figure 4.6.

Opportunities, objectives and strategies

The most important opportunities which lie before the firm as a whole are stated, together with the objectives which have been set and the strategies chosen. The concepts are classified by numbers, so that the plans of lower level units can in turn refer to one or other of them as the starting points for their own divisional objectives. Their treatment in this part of the corporate plan follows the lines laid down in Section 3.3 dealing with planning levels.

If important opportunities have arisen at the next lower level, notes are included to show the level 2 objectives and strategies which have been proposed and finally approved by the chief executive, in order to complete the overall view of opportunities.

In addition to the broad examples of opportunities at corporate or divisional level, as the case may be, which are provided by Figure 4.24 in Section 4.4.1, the following simplified cases illustrate still further the procedure of opportunities, objectives and strategies which is followed in part 3 of a corporate plan.

After reviewing its general business position, especially the information base on its key competitors and their earnings records, a firm's specific corporate objective is to increase profitability from the past levels of between 8 and 12 per cent to 15 per cent as measured by the return on investment (ROI), and to do this within two years; thereafter, the objective is to increase the ROI by 10 per cent per annum so that by the end of the five-year planning period a level of 20 per cent ROI is reached. The company has three divisions of about equal size as measured by the capital used and past performance in respect of ROI.

Opportunity 1 is similar to that mentioned in Section 3.3 and is the case of a chemical company having a business division A in pharmaceutical chemicals. An opportunity is foreseen to engage in the veterinary chemicals industry which is a logical outcome of the application of the procedures of Figure 4.25 in Section 4.4.2 dealing with opportunities for growth and 'What business are we in?'

Objective 1 is growth by gaining a 20 per cent share of the market in veterinary chemicals with a similar profit return as measured by the ROI on the capital used.

Strategy 1.1 is to achieve a given part of this through its existing pharmaceutical business division A, in view of the undoubted strength of the division in the marketing of biological products. Strategy 1.2 is to provide for the second phase of the growth in objectives to the higher level of ROI, through the R & D department which is asked to develop projects for new veterinary products to be made and marketed by the pharmaceutical division A.

Opportunity 2 relates to division B of the company, whose sales and profitability have been relatively static (8 to 10 per cent ROI) although the index of activity of the principal industry served by it has increased by 5 per cent per annum (100 to 128 units by volume over the last five years) and is forecast to increase by 7 per cent per annum through the five-year planning period (128 to 180 units).

Objective 2 is to increase the company profit by a given amount, through strategy 2 which calls for a contribution from division B at a level of 25 per cent ROI by the fifth year, in view of the fact that it has a large reserve of unused manufacturing capacity (30 to 40 per cent) and a low market share (10 per cent) in the industry it serves.

Other opportunities (3, 4 etc) would be identified involving objectives and strategies for transmission to division C, possibly also to divisions A and B.

The practical effect of these concepts is shown in total in the budget part of the plan, but the commentary in the summary mentions them individually in respect of their profit contributions.

Action programmes

Action programmes which involve the chief executive or members of his staff are included in this part of a corporate plan. They are made on the standard form P-9.

Resource requirements

Fixed assets. The major projects for capital expenditure throughout the organization are summarized according to their nature (land, buildings for production, offices, or other facilities, equipment and so on) and the sector of the firm involved (headquarters, business division or function).

Their justification is quoted briefly, if possible making reference to the particular objective to which they are related. Form B-4, from the budget is the basis of this presentation, summarized here on form P-4.

Personnel—quantitative. Form P-8 showing the total personnel of the company by numbers, categories, and annual costs per person per annum is included here. Any personal comments of the chief executive concerning personnel policy are given at this point.

Personnel—organization. The two charts of organization described in Section 5.2.5 are included here.

Finance. A summary of the disposition of the total financial assets of the firm is shown on form P-3 and the overall picture of the sources and use of funds is shown on form P-5.

Form P-5 shows the cash flow and its use in capital investment projects, in providing working capital, the payment of dividends and for the reduction of borrowed money. The data are shown for the past and for the future five years. According to the balance shown and the basic policy of the firm concerning dividends, short statements are made regarding the application of excess funds (dividends or investments), or concerning the source of further funds if the cash flow is inadequate for the planned growth. Proposals for the acquisition of extra funds (Figure 4.14 deals with possible resources) may justify the setting up of an action programme on behalf of the chief executive or the head of the finance function.

Budgets

In a corporate plan, budgets are presented for a firm as a whole. They will include the following, according to the listing given in Appendix I:

B-1 Operating statement (profit and loss)
B-2 Sales planning, by divisions
B-3 Fixed and current assets shown separately as B-3-FA and B-3-CA
B-4 Planned capital expenditure
B-5 Sources and use of funds
B-6 Financial statement (balance sheet)
B-7 Use of production capacity.

The budgets for personnel and action programmes do not need to be included in part 6 of a corporate plan since they have already been presented on appropriate P-8 and P-9 forms, respectively, in personnel and action programmes.

More budget information is provided in plans of subsidiary units than is given in that of a chief executive which is intended only to provide an overview of his company as a whole. Particular reference in this respect is made to the plans of the finance function, which is the custodian of all financial budgets of a company, that is for all units and at all levels (see the fourth part of Section 5.3.3).

Each five-year budget form is accompanied in a final plan by a breakdown into quarterly budgets. These are shown on form B-Q, which serves as a basis for the quarterly control forms C, used during the first planning year.

5.3.2 Business division plans

In Section 3.2 dealing with kinds of plans, a business unit is defined as a divisional activity which essentially comprises marketing. Larger business divisions, which are themselves organized vertically, may contain more than one marketing unit, which may be recognized as 'sub-businesses', as well as such functions as their own production and R & D activities, in which case they are regarded as departments at level 3 in the corporate organization.

Accordingly, the plans of a business division vary in that:

1 They may contain only marketing plans. This situation occurs in the case of a simple organization of the type shown in Figure 3.5 when it is regarded purely as a marketing unit and when the contents of its plan reflect this single interest.

2 They may encompass marketing and other functional activities of the division. In this case the plans would be analogous to those of a company, with an executive leader who was responsible for several units.

The presentation of the unit plans of a business division therefore varies according to the sort of organization.

The principle of including functional units other than marketing in a business division, so that it is as complete an organization as possible, depends on basic corporate policy. It also depends on the size of the organization, since the size of a functional unit must be a certain viable minimum before even a favourable corporate policy would permit such a unit to fall within the responsibility of the divisional head. The advantage of having self-contained business organizations within a company is that it enables complete responsibility to be given to a single person, in this case a business head, thus avoiding the parochialism and isolation which occur only too often when each functional unit goes its own separate way.

These remarks apply with equal force in the case of a business division having more than one well-defined marketing unit each of which can be regarded as a 'sub-business' if specific production and other resources can be directly associated with it in its operations. Here there is the additional advantage that more precise planning and accountability for profits in relation to resources used can be rendered.

Accordingly this part of Section 5.3 is treated on the lines that a business division is a complete business organization in miniature—that is, complete as far as practical accountability and basic corporate policy permit. Under these circumstances, the essential sub-units comprising a business division would be those of marketing or sub-businesses, production and R & D. The head of the division would have a small staff, including the divisional planner and a controller responsible for the divisional financial budgets and accounts.

As in the case of the corporate plan, the plan of the division in total forms a working document for the head of the unit, his staff and the heads of the subunits in his area of responsibility. Such a group often forms a divisional management committee which assists the head of the division not only in the preparation of plans but in their monitoring and control.

Summary

Here the head of a business division summarizes the plan of his unit in the same manner as the chief executive summarizes that of his company in part 1 of a corporate plan.

In the case of the smaller organization shown in Figure 3.5, the area of responsibility would be confined to marketing.

In the case of the larger organizations, a summary would deal not only with marketing but with the functional and other units which are part of the division.

The summary of a business division plan deals with matters at the level of the author and is addressed to the next higher authority, the chief executive.

By analogy with a corporate plan, the commentary is supported by tables and diagrams which show:

P-1 Summary of operating statement
P-2 Summary of sales (by sub-businesses or marketing units)
P-7 Summary of use of production capacity (when a manufacturing function is included in the divisional organization).

These summary data are drawn from corresponding budget data in part 6 of a divisional plan.

Key information and assumptions

Continuing the analogy with a corporate plan, the head of a business division first lists the outstanding items of his information base which are relevant to his area of activity. They are of a more domestic nature and affect his operations more directly than those at corporate level. They are drawn from:

4.3.3   Forecasts of industrial and market trends
4.3.4   Divisional resources
4.3.5   Forecasts of technological trends specific to his interests
4.3.6   Key factors for success in his area of operations
4.3.7   Strengths and weaknesses within his division
4.3.8   Analyses of his direct competitors.

The second part of this part of the plan of a business division contains a reference to the specific corporate assumptions which were received in a planning letter. It also contains divisional assumptions as of level 2, which are put forward by the head of the division in coordination with his staff and the heads of the functions in his divisions (Sections 4.3.10 and 4.3.11).

Opportunities, objectives and strategies

In this case two approaches are required:

1   An approach based on objectives which have specifically been communicated to the head of a division by the chief executive in his planning letter and which have their origin in opportunities at level 1. The unified concept in the corporate plan is regarded as an opportunity for the divisional head on the basis of which he proceeds to develop his divisional objectives in detail and the strategies which he in turn will adopt for their attainment.
2   An approach arising when important opportunities have arisen at the divisional level of working, that is from a study of the division's own information base as it directly affects the division. Such possibilities usually arise from more direct divisional interests rather than those which arise at corporate level. Often they are of the operational kind described in scheme 2 of Figure 4.26 in Section 4.4.3. If they are of sufficient importance, and have been approved through the stage of a preliminary plan, they are quoted in the corporate plan of the chief executive as described in part 3 of the corporate plan (Section 5.3.1).

The presentation in this part of a business division's plan, the sequence of opportunities and so on, would be on the following lines based on the example given in Section 5.3.1.

Opportunity, objective and strategy 1.1 of the corporate plan. Objective 1 of division A is to gain a 20 per cent share of the new market of veterinary chemicals with an ROI of 20 per cent on the capital used.

Several strategies are available and are considered in detail by the head of the division. Possibilities are:

1   To acquire rights to market the veterinary products of another company, preferably a foreign company.

2   To acquire by purchase a company already successfully engaged in the business of veterinary products.

3   To adapt its already existing pharmaceutical products for use in the veterinary field.

Whatever strategies are selected are listed briefly in this part of the business division plan.

Strategy 1.2 of the corporate objectives quoted in part 3 of the corporate plan and directed to the R & D function would be taken up as an objective in R & D planning.

Opportunity, objective and strategy 2 of the corporate plan. Analogous procedures would be followed by division B whose head would consider various strategies to achieve the objective received from the chief executive. Possibilities include the following:

1   Increase of marketing effort (number of salesmen, new promotion).

2   Extension of marketing to new regions or countries (own sales personnel or use of appointed agents).

3   Revision of product range to concentrate marketing effort on lines which give the optimum profit combination of market growth, profit margins, contribution to fixed charges etc.

4   Acquisition of know-how or licences for new products which can be made in existing plants and sold by the division.

Again, whatever strategy or strategies were chosen would be listed briefly in this part of division B's business plan.

Examples of opportunities arising from the second sort of approach—that is those which arise within the business division itself—would be concerned with measurable activities of a domestic nature. Possibilities arise from:

1   Key business ratios applied to the internal working of the division such as stocks/sales, marketing expenses/sales, reduction of debtors.

2   Market planning to accelerate one or more of the features shown in the model of Figure 4.25, such as growth of markets and of market shares, revision of product range concentrating on those of higher profitability, phasing out of decaying products to provide productive capacity for more attractive lines.

The most important of these items would be listed in this part of division B's plan as objectives and strategies.

Action programmes

Following the examples of objectives and strategies in the preceding part, several action programmes will arise. They are presented in this part using the standard form P-9 but only when they involve the head of the division personally or members of his staff. In addition, a list is given of the action programmes which arise on behalf of the heads of the sub-units of the division, for example, the heads of marketing, production, R & D etc., according to the way the unit is organized. Action programmes for the sub-units will arise in the examples mentioned whenever the strategy of the head of the division is to pass this as an objective to the next lower levels mentioned.

Resource requirement

Fixed assets. The major projects for capital expenditure throughout the division, which have arisen in consequence of the strategies chosen, are summarized on similar lines to those in a corporate plan. However, the descriptions in this case will be more specific and the level of expenditure for minor projects will be lower than at corporate level, according to corporate policy in respect of investment decisions and their control. Form P-4 is used to summarize new project expenditure.

Personnel—quantitative. The standard form for personnel (P-8) is used to show the total personnel requirements with the appropriate breakdown of the classes of personnel according to the nature of the organization of the division. The classes for marketing (sales, sales administration, promotion, technical service etc) are especially important. If necessary, classes of personnel are shown in respect of production, R & D, etc. Comments on key positions and personnel are therefore given in this section.

Personnel—organization. The two charts of organization described in Section 5.2.5 are included here.

Finance. Capital investments in fixed assets are given earlier in this part and it remains only to show what finance is required for the conduct of current business throughout the planning period.

Both are shown by the use of form P-3 of the nature of that used in showing the summary of assets in the corporate plan.

Unless a business division is highly self-accounting, no treatment of funds (sources and use of funds) is called for in divisional planning. The divisional head assumes that his requirements for finance for the purpose of planned developments will be available from the central resources of the company. The availability of funds is indicated by the approval of the preliminary plan by the chief executive prior to which the financial plan of the firm as a whole will have been considered and notionally approved during the practical phases of planning on the lines of Figure 4.33.

Budgets

Again, the budgets included in the plan of a business division will depend on its structure and whether it is purely a marketing division or whether it has responsibility for its own functional units.

The essential budgets in the first case are:

B-1 operating statement (profit and loss). The overall divisional statement would give a breakdown for sub-business or marketing units, and any other functions within the division, such as R & D.
B-2 sales planning. In this case the budgets are broken down into sub-businesses or marketing units, possibly also to product groups or even to single products when these are important. The sales planning form B-2 is also rendered in terms not only of sales by value and volume but of profitability and of market shares.
B-2-1/5 sales planning by sub-markets; also rendered in terms of sales, profitability and market shares.
B-3 fixed and current assets shown separately as B-3-FA and B-3-CA.
B-4 planned capital expenditure.
B-7 use of production capacity (in cases when manufacture is a divisional responsibility).

As in the case of the budget in a corporate plan, personnel budgets and action programmes already appear in the corresponding parts of the plan. And lastly, the corresponding B-Q forms are included in final plans to give the breakdown into quarterly budgets, in turn used as a basis for the quarterly control report forms C.

5.3.3 Function plans

Production plans

The responsibility of the head of a production unit in the planning process concerns the provision of the manufactured products which are sold by the marketing units of the business divisions of the company. The provision of the products is planned to harmonize with the sales budgets over the five-year period of the plan in respect of the output and the amount which is held in stock at a given time to meet a specified standard of delivery service, taking into account any variation in seasonal demand. The responsibility extends to the provision of the goods at the lowest cost, to an approved specification of quality and in an approved form of packing. Within these objectives, the production plan shows efforts to make the best use of the existing resources, especially capital investments in fixed assets, and the experience and know-how of its personnel. According to the basic policy of the firm, a further responsibility is to design and erect any further manufacturing installations which are called for by the plans for volume growth of sales when these exceed the level provided by the existing manufacturing resources. Alternatively, the responsibility is to design and negotiate for the erection of further installations by outside parties.

Such is the background against which the plans of the head of production units are prepared.

Distinctions may however need to be drawn between the procedures governing functional plans for production, according to the organization of the firm:

1   *In the simplest case, the manufacturing unit of the company is of the type of Figure 3.5* and the head is directly responsible to the chief executive from whom he receives the appropriate planning letter. The plans in this case are developed in harmony with the sales plans of the marketing unit, coordination being ensured by the corporate planner. The chief executive of the company plays the role of arbiter when problems arise. In this case, the plans become the production plans, at level 2 of the company as a whole.

2   In other cases, *when the production unit is part of a business division* and the head of it is responsible to the head of division, the same sort of coordination takes place through the corporate planner, or the divisional planner, if such an appointment exists. The head of the business division plays a similar role to that of the chief executive in the first case. The plans which arise become the production plans of the particular business division but are level 3 plans.

   In this case, the planning letter may contain items relating broadly to production on the lines described in Section 5.4.

3   In cases where several business divisions exist and each has its own separate manufacturing unit, and there is a *central headquarters appointment of a functional head of production,* the functional head has no direct responsibility for production, but he is an adviser and coordinator of manufacturing resources, methods and policy, acting on behalf of the chief executive to ensure that basic corporate policy is followed and that the firm's resources are exploited equally by all the manufacturing

units in various business divisions. The functional head of production cooperates in the preparation of the plans of production units in order to fulfil these responsibilities, the key items of general applicability being transmitted to him by the chief executive in an appropriate planning letter. Such functional heads are also required to produce appropriate plans at level 2.

From the foregoing remarks, it will be seen that two sorts of plans can arise in the whole area of manufacture:

1   Plans by the operating head of any production unit, whether this be one at level 2 in the firm or one of several, each being part of a business division, and hence of level 3.
2   Plans made by the executive for manufacture at the corporate headquarters which reflect his functional relationship to the operating heads of production units and which show his general company-wide responsibilities in this area.

Summary. As in the case of other unit plans, the head of a production unit here gives his personal views on the resource-demand relationships in his area of responsibility and on the development of the works as an efficient user of the valuable corporate resources it employs in its fixed assets. The inclusion in this chapter of forms of the P-7-type, which analyse the past and future capacity and demand situation, epitomizes the planned use of each of the major installations under his control.

The summary is addressed to the next higher authority, that is, in the case of the simplest organization, to the chief executive, or to the head of the business division in the other cases described.

Key information and assumptions. After noting the volume demand of the sales unit of the concern with which he is associated, the other key items of information will be drawn by the author of the plan from:

4.3.2   Cost indicators, especially for labour and bought-in services.
4.3.4   Resources of the manufacturing unit.
4.3.5   Technology forecasts which relate to his area of working, for example in engineering (mechanical, electrical or civil engineering) in chemical, textile or other processes, in automation, etc.
4.3.6   Key factors for success in manufacture.
4.3.7   Strengths and weaknesses in his organization and resources.

Operating ratios and other measurements of manufacturing performance will rank high in these considerations, many of them giving rise to opportunities and objectives of an economic nature and which are taken up in the following part of the plan.

Assumptions which are noted in this part are those of level 1 for the company as a whole and of level 2 for the business division when the production unit is part of a division. In addition, the head of the manufacturing unit sets down more domestic assumptions, level 3, which directly bear on his affairs. These relate to factors outside his control but upon which a stand is taken and on the basis of which plans are drawn up and on which cost budgets are based. The following are examples of items on which assumptions for the unit are made:

1   Raw materials, availability and cost trends.
2   Energy and other services bought in by the unit.

3 Cost of labour and its availability.
4 Labour agreements through trade unions.
5 Legal controls on safety, environmental pollution etc.
6 Compliance of outside contractors to timetables and performance of new plants to be erected.

Opportunities, objectives and strategies. As suggested in part 2 of the plan, the principal opportunity is the sales demand for products, while the objectives which follow in consequence are the provision of the goods in the correct quantity, at the best cost, in an approved quality and in approved packing. The strategy is to deploy the existing resources efficiently and measurably, and to organize procedures for the provision of new resources if called for during the planning period.

Out of this primary sequence of opportunities there will be strategies for specific sectors within the works units and which arise from the information bases, especially the items drawn from the items listed in Figure 4.17. Thus, objectives are given by the head of the production unit to the key members of his works organization concerning, for example,

1 Plant or process developments
2 Cost reduction projects
3 Personnel training
4 Environmental problems.

Action programmes. The standard procedure already described when discussing Section 4 of both corporate and business division plans is again followed by the head of the production unit, using form P-9.

Action programmes arise from the strategies listed at the end of the preceding part of the plan and, at the level involved in planning, call for working parties or study groups to be set up with well-defined leaders and terms of reference of which the action programme is a summary.

Resource requirements: fixed assets. Apart from the presentation of the capacity analysis given on form P-7 in the summary of the plan, a summary is given for each new major project involving an increase in fixed assets through capital expenditure, of its purpose, timing and economic justification.

Form P-4 for capital expenditure projects is used to summarize these data.

Since the manufacturing unit of a company is often the main user of the capital of the company, this section carries more detail than the corresponding sections of corporate or business plans. Nevertheless, projects included in the plan and given a notional approval, will still need a more intensive scrutiny as to their specification and economic justification before top management can give their final authorization. The precise machinery for this procedure depends on the basic corporate policy respecting capital investment approvals.

Minor projects for capital expenditure may, when their total falls within the monetary limits for such expenditure by the company policy, be simply listed.

Resource requirements: personnel—quantitative. The standard form for personnel (P-8) is used to present the total personnel requirements broken down according to the main classes in the production unit:

1 Personnel directly engaged in production, by major production groups.
2 Personnel engaged in auxiliary sectors such as warehousing, maintenance, laboratories and inspection.
3 Personnel for works administration, social and welfare activities.

Resource requirements: personnel—organization. Two organization charts are included, showing the organization of productive and auxiliary units, with their leaders and numbers of personnel, for the first and last of the five planning years. Suitable notes are applied to indicate intermediate developments between the first and last years.

Finance. As in previous cases, capital investments in fixed assets are shown at the beginning of this part of Section 5 and it only remains to show what finance is required for the expenditures incurred in production costs. There is no income in the case of manufacturing units when production is transferred to marketing units at an ex-works cost.

The standard form P-3, showing fixed and current assets, suffices to show the increasing requirements of funds to meet growing productive expenditure, of which inventories will play a large part.

Budgets. The budget forms comprising part of the plan for the production unit comprise detailed presentations of:

B-1 rendered in terms of the expenditure in materials, labour and services etc. for the principal production units or in product groups whichever is the more meaningful.
B-3 fixed and current assets shown separately as B-3-FA and B-3-CA.
B-4 planned capital expenditure
B-7 use of production capacity. In the case of the production function, these will be rendered in terms of the principal units or product groups, whichever is the more meaningful. The unit costs shown in the vertical columns of form B-7 relate to the standard costs used in the planning process and in total correspond to the line 2.0 in operating statements (B-1) named cost of goods.

As in other cases, personnel budgets and action programmes are included in the appropriate parts of the plan. The corresponding quarterly budgets (B-Q forms) are prepared as a basis for quarterly control reports C, for inclusion in final plans.

Research and development plans

For the purpose of the workbook, research and development (R & D) activities are taken together as the responsibility of a single person although in many cases, especially in large undertakings, the two may be separate. In other cases, there may even be subdivisions on the following lines:

1 Basic research, carried out with no immediate commercial object in view. Such research arises as a consequence of basic corporate policy and is usually carried out centrally in a firm.
2 Research carried out as a function within the company at level 2 or within a business division at level 3.

3 Development carried out centrally, in a business division or within the area of responsibility of such a function as manufacture. Development may also be divided into the development of products for a given use, or finding uses for given products, for processes of manufacture or of plant used in production processes.
4 Product design and engineering, in some sorts of organizations, may be the equivalent activity to R & D in others.

Nevertheless, the plans prepared for all these kinds of activities have much in common, so that this section on the preparation of plans for an R & D unit may be taken as a general model, to be modified as circumstances in a particular organization may demand.

Research planning differs from most others in that it is based on goals or targets (the achievement of a product or a process which has a desired performance) but the objective may not be attained; in fact in some cases the total effort in a project is completely abortive.

There are many factors in R & D planning which cannot be based on forecasts and the elements of assumptions and probabilities (simple chance in some cases) play a greater part than in most other planning activities. A positive and beneficial outcome to a research project cannot always be relied upon.

On this account the planning of R & D is different and the best efforts of those involved are naturally demanded. In fact there is, *a priori,* more need to follow the practical phases of planning than in most other areas. Additionally, on account of the larger number of unknown or unquantifiable factors, good R & D planning is based on a step-wise attainment of the objectives which involve a decision-tree approach to the identification and choice of strategies. The procedure is characterized by its analysis into a progressive series of stages, each of which calls for an assessment of the position, and the nature and choice of the possible stages which follow.

Accordingly, although R & D is more difficult to plan, it is for this very reason that it is necessary to plan and to plan efficiently. This especially applies at the working level of R & D, that is, by those involved at the stage of action programmes.

Summary. As in the case of other heads of planning units, the head of R & D here summarizes the plans of his unit and gives his general comments on the projects which have been selected. It is useful if the head provides a list or table, which shows the features of his planned operations listing the chosen projects, and describing the degree of effort (measured by planned expenditure), the estimated value to the firm in sales and profits, and the probability of achievement in a given time.

The table arises from a cooperative effort between the head of the R & D unit and the head of the marketing unit with which he is associated in the particular project. The form is also the basis of data presented by the head of the business or marketing unit when depicting the sales and profits of new products. The cooperative effort takes place during the practical phases of planning as shown by the network of Figure 4.33, boxes 5, 9, 13 and so on.

Any other special features which the head of R & D wishes to present to the next higher authority to whom his plan is addressed are included in the summary. For example, the broad reasoning for the choice of project priorities, the further resources in personnel, working space and special equipment, which are necessary to meet the demands of the company or the business division concerned, the policy towards basic research, and so on.

Key information and assumptions. The key items of information which influence the choice of projects in the plan are quoted. They arise from many parts of the information base, for example:

4.3.2 Sociological and industrial events and trends; legal constraints concerning pollution, health, etc.

4.3.3 Product and process development in external industry, especially in the firm's markets.

4.3.4 Departmental resources and the possibilities of using special skills, know-how and equipment in the R & D unit.

4.3.5 Technology—the many sources of information in this part of the information base provide an immense number of items which call for scrutiny and analysis in the identification of opportunities. Technology forecasting (as described in Appendix II) when organized as a part of the practical phases of planning, is an essential procedure once the first cycle of planning is over and the discipline is understood by the R & D staff and the corporate planner. Corporate development studies on TF can be organized as part of the information base.

4.3.6 Key factors for success in the conduct of R & D in the fields of interest to the firm. For example, special forms of field testing, use of operational research in the planning of experiments, early economic appraisals of process costs, decisions as to the point at which patent applications are best made, and the use of highly trained scientists at bench level may be key factors in one or other area of research.

4.3.7 Strengths and weaknesses of the R & D resources.

4.3.8 Analysis of reports on, and products from competitors.

This part of the plan goes on to refer to the specific corporate assumptions or those of the business unit with which it is associated. It also contains any assumptions which relate purely to the R & D plan and which concern factors outside the control of the head of the unit. Such level 3 assumptions may concern legal matters and patents procedures, cooperation with third parties such as university centres of research or industrial testing stations, and regulations concerning pollution and health matters.

Opportunities, objectives and strategies. The range of opportunities available to any R & D unit is usually considerable, so that their appraisal and the setting of objectives are correspondingly more complicated.

In the first place, R & D opportunities arise from the analysis of various information bases in several ways:

1 Those received in the planning letter from the chief executive and which form part of the corporate opportunities. Strategy 1.2, quoted in the example of a corporate plan on p. 181 (opportunity 1) is an example of this type.

2 Opportunities identified by business and marketing units during their analysis of information bases and relayed to the R & D unit.

3 Opportunities which are identified by the R & D unit itself.

4 Opportunities which emerge from the conduct of company-wide exercises in technological forecasting (TF) and which may have included, on a confidential basis, such third parties as customers and consultants.

Except in the case of basic research work, the determination of objectives and especially the priority of their claims for resource allocation is rarely a simple task. For this reason, efforts must be made to quantify the opportunities so that management can more clearly decide which provides the most important objectives and hence how to deploy the available resources. The critical factor in corporate planning as a whole is not the exploitation of opportunities in known fields, but the actual *creation of opportunities* for the firm itself.

The R & D unit has the chief responsibility in this direction since products and processes which are completely innovative afford the maximum opportunity for corporate growth.

The allocation of resources in these cases is a matter of basic corporate policy having regard to the existing position of the firm. The choice of other objectives which may extend a market range, or which enable old products to enter new markets, depends upon the measurement of their likely economic advantages. Such factors as the cost of research and development, expected share of markets, sales values and profitability are balanced against the feasibility and the probability of success, and weighted accordingly in the decision-making process.

One key project of a highly innovative character, brought to a successful conclusion, can transform the fortunes of a company.

The part of the plan dealing with opportunities briefly reviews the extent of the opportunities which have been revealed but concentrates on the key items which have been selected in view of the considerations already mentioned in this section. Again, the number of key items should be limited and though much naturally depends on the scale of the R & D activities in relation to those of the company as a whole (allocation of low or high amounts of financial resources), four to six major projects are normally the most which can be capably managed.

The presentation of each project should briefly refer to its origin, the planned effort in terms of money, time and people concerned, its probability and estimated impact on profitability, these data being the basis of the list in the summary of the R & D plan. In view of the greater degree of 'unknowns' in R & D planning, the strategy in each case is preferably elaborated on the lines of a decision tree which in turn becomes the basis of the action programmes which are described in the following part of the plan. In other words the step-wise approach, involving an intensive review of the literature, the mapping out of the preliminary experimental work, its progressive review and the choice of subsequent strategies at later stages of work, should all be set down. Equally clearly, difficult technological stages ('gaps' in knowledge or confidence) should be identified as far as possible. Decision points may be needed in practice, at which a project is wound up after an agreed limit of expenditure is reached, *or* at which a consideration of progress justifies continued allocation of resources but on a modified basis.

Action programmes. The standard form for the presentation of action programmes (P-9) is used in association with a decision tree of the type suggested in the previous paragraph.

One action programme for each key R & D objective should be set up to show the planned activities during the first of the five planning years. Projects which are limited in terms of resource and time allocation (the time being one year maximum) are outlined in the action programme according to the stages which are foreseen in the practical part of the R & D work. Those of a major nature and which, on account of timing, are of a continuing nature intended to occupy more than one year's effort, are outlined in detail as far as the preliminary year's activities are foreseen. Reference to the associated decision tree indicates the overall view. The associated decision tree for each project enables steps to be taken during the currency of the work to ensure adequate preparation for reviewing the work done, and to enable subsequent decisions to be taken on the further stages of strategy.

In most cases, since there are normally only four to six key projects in hand, the head of the department is personally involved in the programmes, but in larger organizations, his principal assistants (section leaders or managers) are named on his behalf. In this case they report to the head of the unit.

Resource requirements: fixed assets. Any major increase in the resources for R & D work are described as capital projects. Minor items are taken together. In the first case, projects will concern buildings for laboratories and for related services, semi-scale or pilot plants, workshops for prototype machines and the like. Other cases, according to the responsibilities of the head of the unit, will be library and patent facilities, accommodation for special equipment such as computers, photographic resources, special equipment such as electron microscopes and engineering apparatus. The equipment in these cases is also regarded as capital expenditure. Form P-4, with suitable titles, is used here.

Resource requirements: personnel—quantitative. The standard form for personnel (P-8) is used to show the total requirements, with a breakdown on the lines of the organization of the R & D unit, showing classes and costs of personnel with their areas of occupation.

Resource requirements: personnel—organization. As in other cases, the chart shows the principal sub-units of the department and their leaders, on the lines of:

1 The head of the department and any immediate staff.
2 Any special units within the department (library, patents, analytical and evaluation units).
3 The number of sections which are regarded as the 'R & D task forces', described according to the major projects upon which they are engaged.

Any extended development of the R & D unit is given on a second organization chart which shows the structure of the department for the fifth planning year, together with notes on the timing and nature of intermediate stages.

Resource requirements: finance. After the needs for finance in capital investment, there is only the need for expenditure of a current nature. It is shown in detail in the corresponding budget item (part 7) so that only the total is shown in this section. Finance may however be required for expenditures outside the firm, for example, the cost of contract R & D conducted in universities and other centres on its behalf, for the field testing of products or machines by independent testing centres, and so on. These are included in the finance section of the plan, reference being made briefly to their reason, cost and expected benefit. Important outside work is mentioned in one or other of the action programmes, if they act as supporting parties.

Budgets. The budget chapter of the R & D plan contains the following:

B-1 rendered in terms of expenditure in materials, salaries, services, etc in relation to the principal projects described in Sections 4.2 and 4.4.
B-3 fixed and current assets shown separately as B-3-FA and B-3-CA.
B-4 planned capital expenditure.

As in previous cases, personnel budgets and action programmes are included in the appropriate chapters of the plan and it remains to recall that the corresponding quarterly budgets (B-Q forms) are prepared as a basis for quarterly control reports C, for inclusion in final plans.

Personnel plans

The plans of the personnel unit take shape during the practical phases of planning (Section 4.8) when the personnel requirements of each of the units of the firm become known. The individual resource requirements in personnel of all units, including those of the corporate headquarters, are coordinated jointly by the corporate planner and the head of the personnel function, and lead to the synthesis of the overall company requirements shown on the standard form P-8. It is at this point that the explanations concerning definitions and the types of personnel involved, dealt with in Section 4.3.4 on personnel resources, become relevant. The corporate total presents trends on the numbers and costs of personnel shown in respect of:

1 The major units of the firm (business divisions and functions at level 2).
2 Personnel classified on the agreed lines.The number of classes shown may be as low as three (senior staff, staff and other workers) but is best limited to five or six, according to the main classes employed by the company.

The planning activities of the head of personnel do not start on the receipt of the individual requirements of the units in the firm. The head of the unit identifies opportunities and makes forecasts during the phase of building up the corresponding information base, so that he is prepared in advance to set up specific objectives and select appropriate strategies.

Depending upon the policy of a particular concern, the head of personnel is responsible also for the higher facets of personnel planning, that is for the planning of management (executive) succession, recruitment and training. The alternative procedure, dictated by the need for confidentiality and for the highly personal involvement of the chief executive, is the separation of the responsibility for executive development from that of personnel in general. In such a case a further planning unit of the firm (management development) is called for.

In all cases however, on account of the highly functional nature of the personnel unit, coordination in many directions is called for. The corporate planner himself is involved and so especially is the head of the functional headquarters unit for production, for he has an overall interest in the firm's personnel engaged in manufacture; production units are often the largest employers of personnel in a company.

Summary. The head of the personnel unit first gives here the highlights of the development of personnel during the currency of the five planning years. His remarks are based on the form P-8 for the company as a whole and for each of the component units. They deal generally with the growth of different classes, their costs, the application of corporate policy and the problems which he foresees, out of which his own opportunities arise. He may refer also to some of the key ratios concerning personnel numbers and costs in relation to the capital used, the sales income and so on, as an indication of the general performance of the company and its units in comparison with known standards of other concerns operating in similar fields of business.

Key information and assumptions. After the requirements of the firm have been noted, the other key items of information relating to personnel will be drawn from the information base as follows:

4.3.2   Sociological and political indicators such as school leaving age, hours of working, annual numbers of graduates, training levies, wage and salary trends, costs of social services, national health and pensions.

4.3.4   Corporate and divisional resources in personnel, availability of specialized staff for use on computers, laboratories etc.

4.3.5   Technological developments and automation which affect personal and sociological behaviour.

4.3.6   The key factors for success such as job satisfaction, motivation and monetary reward.

4.3.7   The strengths and weaknesses of the firm's personnel and how they stack up against the key factors for success.

This part of the plan goes on to refer to the specific corporate assumptions, to which the head may already have contributed in respect of those involving personnel. It also contains any specific assumptions of a more departmental nature and on which no sound forecasts can be made.

Opportunities, objectives and strategies. The first source of opportunities and objectives is the personnel requirements of the firm, which in principle are given to the head of the personnel unit in the planning letter from the chief executive. They become quantified during the phases of planning when they become known by number, class and time of employment during the planning period. Other objectives may be received from the chief executive such as those dealing more specifically with the senior management (see the remarks on executive development in this section).

Other sources of opportunities and objectives arise from the scrutiny of the key items of information by the head of the function himself. These will concern such topics as:

1   Projects and procedures for the engagement of special kinds of staff such as professional people, production workers, academically trained staff, etc.

2   Training of all classes at all levels.

3   Welfare and personnel benefits, pensions, insurance etc.

4   Communication of company information to the staff and workers by house journals and notices.

5   Personnel engineering, for example, optimum employment, compensation and motivation.

6   Relations with personnel associations and trade unions.

Depending upon the inclusion of executive development within the personnel function, opportunities and objectives are presented on the basis of the key positions shown in the one- and five-year organization charts of the company and its units shown in part 5 of each plan. They become available to the head of personnel during the phases of planning and, as already mentioned, are referred to in the planning letter of the chief executive.

The analysis of the development of the units of the company in respect of senior appointments (managers, executives and so on) will reveal the objectives to be attained. The strategies to meet them will call for a review of data and decisions concerning:

1 The expected vacancies arising during the planning period due to organizational development, retirements, transfers etc.
2 The nomination of successors, and candidates for succession.
3 The nomination of 'emergency' candidates, pending the nomination and possible further training of other candidates.
4 Assessment of all personnel in executive positions and of possible nominees for succession.
5 Training and recruitment schemes.

The strategies for the achievement of the objectives in personnel are chosen in line with basic corporate policy, plus the knowledge of external and internal personnel resources, and trends displayed by the head of the unit himself. Nevertheless, he is assisted in no small degree by the corporate planner and, in the case of executive development, by the chief executive himself.

Whether the personnel unit is small or large, efforts should again be made to identify the key opportunities (four to six in number) and the objectives and strategies which arise. These are all directed to the prime objective of ensuring that the personnel requirements of the company are met in terms of numbers, qualifications, cost and timing. In this sense they contribute to the basic corporate objective of profitability.

Other key objectives, in addition to the aforementioned, arise when management development also forms part of the responsibility of the personnel unit.

Each concept is briefly described in this part of the plan and forms the basis of a corresponding action programme as outlined in the following paragraphs.

Action programmes. The standard form for action programmes (P-9) is again used to outline the practical steps called for in the implementation of the projects which arise from the chosen strategies. Each involves the head of the unit except that according to the resources of the department, the assistants of the head man are named on his behalf, for example officers specifically appointed in the unit for training, recruitment or management development.

Coordination of personnel activities has already been stressed in earlier parts of this treatment of the unit plan for personnel. Consequently the following may be mentioned in the action programmes as supporting parties:

1 The head of the headquarters function for production, or failing whom, the head of a production unit, in respect of trade union negotiations.
2 The head of R & D for the recruitment and training of scientists.
3 The head of finance (or his functional equivalent) for professionally trained persons such as accountants, controllers, and legal staff.

Resource requirements: fixed assets. It is unlikely that there will be a demand for capital investment in fixed assets purely for the personnel function but if there is, most organizations will take this jointly with the office and administration requirements of similar units.

Resource requirements: personnel—quantitative. In this chapter of the plan only the personnel requirements of the unit itself are given. Form P-8 is used.

Resource requirements: personnel—organization. According to the structure and staffing of the unit, so the organizational chart shows sub-units, on the lines of:

1 Head of the unit and his immediate staff:
2 Heads of sub-units for recruitment, training, welfare, social services, management development, etc.

Any planned development of the organization is shown on a second chart showing the five-year position, with notes on any intermediate developments.

Resource requirements: finance. The principal need for finance is for the expenditure of the department as such, shown in detail in the budget of the plan, but special items of expense should be mentioned with the reason or purpose, and expected benefits. Such cases are:

1 external recruitment costs
2 special training exercises
3 provision of scholarships at universities and other educational centres
4 costs of personnel in 'sandwich schemes' for training and education
5 hire of outside assistance for staff lectures
6 motivational and communications costs, for example house journals
7 level and cost of government training levies and their recovery.

Budgets. This part of the plan of the personnel unit will contain:

B-1 Rendered in terms of expenditure in salaries, etc broken down to show the principal sub-units of the function.
B-3 Fixed and current assets shown separately as B-3-FA and B-3-CA.
B-4 Planned capital expenditure.

The budget of the personnel function should also contain a complete set of the personnel forms (P-8) for all the corporate units.

As in other cases, action programmes are included in the appropriate part of the plan.

Finally, the corresponding quarterly budgets (B-Q forms) are prepared as a basis for quarterly control reports C, for inclusion in final plans.

Finance plans

There are two aspects of the planning responsibilities of the head of the finance function at level 2 in a company:

1 The plans of the unit itself as a functional department of the firm.
2 That part of the corporate plan which deals with the finance planning of the company as a whole, at level 1.

The first embraces its internal departmental activities in the provision of services concerning finance, to all the units of the company, involving for example:

1 Cooperation with other units in the preparation of their financial budgets.
2 Corporate procedures for accounting and reporting services. In this area comes the question of the costing of production. This in turn will depend on corporate policy as to whether standard costs with the consequential procedures to show planned

variances due to the non-use of resources are used, as distinct from other methods such as direct costing.

3 Services for the handling of income (sales, cash etc) and expenditure (salaries and wages, raw materials, services bought and capital investment payments etc)

The second aspect includes:

1 The preparation of the financial plan of the company which is presented in the budget of the corporate plan of the chief executive.
2 Proposals for the disposal and generation of funds, which are discussed in brief by the chief executive in part 1 of his plan.
3 Financial matters controlled by law, such as annual corporate statements and reports, and balance sheets; foreign exchange controls etc.
4 Fiscal matters, such as depreciation, dividend and income taxes etc.
5 Internal auditing, pensions, insurances etc.

According to the structure and the policy of the firm, the head of the finance function is often responsible for other corporate activities and services such as data processing, organization and methods (O & M), other management services, and possibly general administration. In these events his organization has several sub-units, which if important are called upon to produce their own plans at level 3 in the company.

The treatment of the finance planning unit in this section of the workbook is slanted largely to the finance function as such, but it can also be taken as a model for a controller's function within a business division or within a company, when this is part of a larger group, and when both justify a finance function themselves. The plan may also be taken as a model to be followed by its own sub-units such as those already mentioned, as well as in cases of smaller concerns in which the company secretary is also responsible for finance and general administration.

Summary. The standard contents of this part give the personal views of the head of the unit on the activities and opportunities of the unit as a whole and of its sub-units. Comments are also given supporting those of the chief executive on the structure and use of the financial assets of the firm and its trend towards higher profitability. These do not usurp those of the chief executive but deal more with those in which the head of the unit is personally involved and for which he has identified his own opportunities for action.

Key information and assumptions. The prime source of information to the head of the finance unit are the financial records of the firm and the proposals of its units in the currency of the five-year planning period as they emerge during the practical stages of planning (preliminary and final plans), and as the trend towards more profitable use of the firm's financial resources can be seen. Other sources will be from the information base, especially:

4.3.2 Economic, fiscal, monetary and political indicators, at both national and international levels.
Cost indicators for personnel, materials and services.
4.3.3 Corporate performance in respect of sales, costs and profits as applied to the company's product and product groups.
4.3.4 Financial resources as suggested by the list of Figure 4.14.
4.3.6 Key factors for success; the principal business ratios.

4.3.7 Strengths and weaknesses; the performance of the company and its units in relation to the items in 4.3.6 and in comparison with those of its competitors.

Part 2 of the plan goes on to note the specific corporate assumptions to which the head of the unit himself has already contributed in cooperation with the corporate planner and the chief executive. In addition he may propose assumptions at his level 2, especially those on which the activities of his own unit depend.

Opportunities, objectives and strategies. The principal opportunities and objectives are given in the planning letter of the chief executive to the head of finance. They are based on the adequate and efficient provision of financial services to the company and its units, which become quantified as progress is made towards the formulation of the preliminary and final plans for each forthcoming five-year planning period.

Other opportunities and objectives may be given by the chief executive dealing with items at corporate level, for example, the introduction or extension of data processing facilities, specific projects for the increase in financial resources, their gearing and developments in the organization of the unit itself.

Further opportunities and objectives are sought by the head of the unit himself and, when formulated, lead to action programmes. These may arise in several ways:

1 Within the department itself respecting its own expenditures and performance.
2 Those dealing with corporate items such as insurance, borrowing terms, sale and leaseback projects.
3 In respect of any sub-units which are part of the department.

The key opportunities, objectives and the strategies for their achievement are briefly described, four to six being the number of major objectives which should be listed in the plan. The detailed action arising from the chosen strategies is shown in the action programmes of part 4.

Action programmes. The standard form for action programmes (P-9) is used to outline the practical steps and benefits of the key concepts of the head of the unit. As in other cases, they are only produced in respect of action called for in the first of the five-year planning period. They will be of two types:

1 Those which arise at corporate level and in which the head of the unit acts as the deputy of the chief executive, usually with the support of the corporate planner as part of the headquarters staff of the firm.
2 Those which arise within the department and its own sub-units.

Resource requirements: fixed assets. As in the case of the other functional units already mentioned in this section of the workbook, it is unlikely that the unit will have need for capital investments on its own behalf. If further office facilities are needed, these are joined with those of other units. An exception will arise in cases of high cost items such as data processing equipment, when a choice must be made between buying and hiring.

Resource requirements: personnel—quantitative. The standard form for personnel is used (P-8) and shows the requirements by cost, numbers and classes broken down into the main sub-units of the finance function as a whole.

Resource requirements: personnel—organization. A chart of the organization as in year 1 of the plan is provided showing:

1 The head of the unit and his immediate staff.
2 The sub-units and their leaders (treasurer, controller and cost accountant; managers for data processing, management information services, pensions, insurance etc).

Resource requirements: finance. This section deals only with the expenditure· of the finance unit itself and gives briefly any comments on new features, since the working details are given in the statement in the budget which follows.

Budgets. Formally, there are two separate sections for the budget part of the finance unit's plan, the first being its own domestic budget and the second assembling those for the firm as a whole. The first section comprises:

B-1 Rendered in terms of functional costs such as salaries, services etc., shown, when necesary, in respect of any sub-units belonging to the responsibility of the head of finance.
B-3 Fixed and current assets shown separately as B-3-FA and B-3-CA.
B-4 Planned capital expenditure. In this case, it is often practical to collect the items of capital expenditure on such items as offices and administrative services for various functions, including the company headquarters, in view of their multi-purpose nature.

Again, personnel budgets and action programmes are included in the appropriate parts of the plan and quarterly versions of the financial budgets are prepared on forms B-Q, as the basis for quarterly control reports C, and for inclusion in the final plan.

Purchasing plans

By purchasing is meant the procurement of the raw materials required for the production of the goods sold by the company, though according to the precise responsibility of the head of purchasing prescribed by the basic corporate policy, this may also include the purchase of bought-in services such as power, fuels, water and transport.

The procurement of raw materials is planned to harmonize with the requirements of the planned production budgets, that is, it takes into account the rate of use and the need for minimum stocks.

Whether a purchasing unit is at level 2 in the case of an organization of the type of Figure 3.5 or is a functional activity at level 2 in a more complex organization, or is attached as a purchasing unit to a production centre or a business division, depends upon corporate policy about the sort of organization it wishes to have.

Such policies depend also on whether the bought-in materials are a large element in the cost of the materials produced by the company (material-intensive products such as heavy chemicals), whether they are bought in for further processing (chemicals, textile fibres and so on) or simply for assembly, as often occurs with many engineering products, or even whether one basic product forms the bulk of the procurements of the concern such as in wool textiles.

For the purpose of the workbook it is assumed that a firm takes in a wide variety of materials which represent a significant part of the total cost build-up of the manufactured products, and hence a purchasing unit as such is justified. Under these conditions it may be set up at level 2 or, in the case of large organizations, there may be a central purchasing unit at level 2 operating as a functional unit in relation to purchasing sub-units attached to either manufacturing units or to business divisions.

198

The format and presentation of the purchasing plan is the same in the case of each of these types of operating purchasing units.

Summary. Following the standard approach, the summary is based on the personal comments of the head of the unit and concerns the overall planned purchases, divided into product groups and key products by both volume (tons, gallons or other units) and by value; any special features concerning the origin of major items is also mentioned. Generally the comments relate to trends in procurements, their pricing and security of supply, and are addressed to the next higher authority. It would be useful to include a chart showing the scale of the overall procurement budget in terms of volume and value.

Key information and assumptions. Key items will be drawn from public, trade and business sources and interpreted in the light of:

4.3.2 Concerning price trends, especially for commodities and for materials or components in difficult supply.
4.3.5 Developments in technology which affect quality, price and security of supply.
4.3.6 Key factors for success in purchasing.
4.3.7 Strengths and weakness of the firm and its purchasing power.

Corporate and business division assumptions are noted in this part and others are proposed which the head of the unit feels relevant to the supply position and on which budgets, especially material price budgets, are based.

Opportunities, objectives and strategies. Again the sequence of opportunity is derived from the planned requirements of raw materials for the production of the goods demanded by the sales budgets of the organization.

The planned requirements of materials emerge during the practical phases of planning when sales budgets are transcribed to production budgets which in turn call for information from the purchasing unit concerning materials availability and prices. The corporate planner has a role to ensure that coordination between sales and production is effected through the network or timetable of the practical phases of planning (Figure 4.33 in Section 4.8).

As suggested in the summary, the quantified objectives concern the provision of materials at the lowest prices compatible with:

1 agreed delivery schedules (quantities and times)
2 maintenance of specified qualities and security of supply
3 acceptable packaging
4 acceptable financial (credit) terms.

Apart from the prime objectives received during the practical phases of planning, other opportunities and objectives arise from the study of the appropriate information base by the purchasing unit itself. Thus, special supply and price problems often arise in connection with world commodities which in turn present special opportunities for favourable long-term purchasing agreements; supply contracts for similar materials used by different production units within the company as a whole improve buying power, while special assistance to suppliers on the design (or production processes) for special products, unique to the company and which call for particularly advanced

ACTION PLANNING TEST LIST 25   Section 5.3

QUESTIONS	RESPONSE BY	TIMING OF ACTION ARISING
1 To whom respectively, should plans of levels 1, 2 and 3 be addressed, and who should use them as working documents?	All management	
2 What are the points in support of self-contained or 'mini-businesses'?	Corporate planner and chief executive	
3 How do the budget forms for a business division or a function differ from those used by the company? How do the budget forms for a function differ from those for a business or the company? How do the budget forms for a sub-unit differ from those used by its next higher level? What do they all have in common?	Corporate planner and head of finance	
4 Why do R & D plans cater for a stepwise approach to the attainment of objectives?	Corporate planner and head of R & D	
5 How is the ultimate business value of an R & D objective measured?	Corporate planner, heads of R & D and business divisions	
6 Why should exercises in technological forecasting not be restricted to R & D staff?	Corporate planner and head of R & D	
7 Why should emphasis on innovation be placed on R & D objectives?	Chief executive	
8 What special components are there in the budget part of the plan of the finance function?	Corporate planner, head of finance and chief executive	
9 What special duties has the head of finance in respect of the budgets for: (a) his own functional area (b) other units (c) the company as a whole?	Corporate planner, head of finance and chief executive	

specifications of quality, may prove to be an opportunity. According to corporate policy, investment opportunities may be seen and taken for the forward buying of key materials which call for special allocation of funds. Opportunities sometimes arise from the information base which suggest that the company may benefit from its own manufacture of key products (backwards diversification) or that products which it already makes may be advantageously bought from outside sources. Security of supplies may be achieved by the strategy of a priority list of suppliers.

Action programmes. Action programmes, set up on the standard forms P-9, are called for in the event of any special purchasing objectives and strategies of the kind mentioned in the previous chapter. Often such cases will call for supporting action involving technical or financial help from appropriate departments of the company.

Resource requirements: fixed assets. Although investment projects rarely arise, any which emerge are dealt with on the lines of the previous examples involving capital investments.

Resource requirements: personnel—quantitative. The standard form P-8 for personnel data is used and, according to the size and responsibility of the purchasing unit, shows sub-divisions according to buyers for various product groups, services, packages etc. (Figure 4.13).

Resource requirements: personnel—organization. Two charts are included. They follow the style of charts that have been described when discussing this part of other unit plans.

Finance. In practically all cases the only financial requirement of a purchasing unit is for its departmental costs. Finance required for the procurement of materials, packages and services is attributed to the user unit, usually that of manufacture. Form B-3-CA is used if any return is called for.

Budgets. Apart from the budget of departmental expenditure, rendered on a type of B-1 form, the principal budgets are those for the procurement of materials and services. These are shown on appropriate formats in terms of price and volume, both for unit quantities and for the total amounts required. They show the detail which is the basis of the summary charts in Section 1. Again quarterly versions of all budget forms are prepared for year 1, using the appropriate B-Q forms.

5.4 COORDINATION OF UNIT PLANS AND APPROVALS

5.4.1 Coordination

The coordination of the planning activities of the various units of the firm is a primary task of the corporate planner, particularly so in the early years of planning and less so in later years when the working aspects of the system are familiar to the participants; then, a 'bank of information' is available and experience has been gained from previous years.

Coordination is effected in the first instance through the preparation by the corporate planner of standard planning forms to be used equally by all planning units in the company whenever the subject is equally common. Check lists and questionnaires as illustrated in Section 4 for the assembly of various information bases are prepared in cooperation with the appropriate functional executives or business heads, as the case may be. Approval of suitable versions of the planning forms suggested in Appendix I is given by the chief executive. They are issued by the corporate planner or are issued with the administrative instructions of the planning letter. The budget forms for finance are drafted in cooperation with the head of the finance function.

Understanding of the purpose and requirements of the planning papers is ensured by direct discussion with the heads of planning units. The corporate planner also assists with advice at the meetings which heads of units conduct with their departmental heads, after the planning letters are received and when tasks are allocated within the staff of the unit.

Coordination is further effected by the corporate planner, who ensures that communication and dialogues take place between units which are associated in the development of the plans of each other. The network scheme of Figure 4.33 is important here in showing the recycling nature of the planning process.

In this regard, the following examples illustrate further the procedure of communication and dialogue which follow the receipt of planning letters and which precede the production of the preliminary plans at boxes 14 and 15 of the network:

1   Sales budgets, in line with the objectives, and information on selling prices and past profit margins, are conveyed to the head of the production unit.
2   Resource requirements in raw materials are notified to the purchasing unit by the production unit, the former responding in the light of its information base.
3   Resource requirements in personnel are notified to the personnel unit by the production unit, the former responding in the light of its information base.
4   Estimates of the cost of production are given to the business heads by the production unit.
5   Spare capacity in manufacturing resources is notified to the business head, who may in consequence raise the question of higher sales objectives with his marketing executive.
6   Requirements for additional manufacturing resources become the subject of a provisional project for capital investment, involving coordination between the heads of production, business divisions, finance and corporate planning.
7   Revision of stages 1 to 4 take place in the light of the project raised.
8   The heads of the planning units so far involved prepare drafts of the budget chapters of their plans which are integrated by the corporate planner with the cooperation of the head of finance. If compliance with the original profit objectives is apparent, the heads of units prepare their preliminary plans.
9   The preliminary plans, channelled to the corporate planner on behalf of the chief executive, are integrated and preliminary corporate plans are prepared. The head of finance again cooperates in the preparation of the financial budgets which show the corporate cash flow over the planning period, the use of the financial resources of the company and the trend in growth of profitability.
10   The preliminary plans of the units and of the company are presented to the chief executive for review and approval.

These broad outlines of the coordination procedures represent an over-simplified model which in practice is completed by many other inputs, and which are incorporated in planning network schemes, for example:

1   From marketing to research on the need for new products, and the response from research.

2   The inclusion of foreseen new products from R & D in the production budget of the manufacturing unit.

3   Development of personnel resources by other units such as marketing, for the purpose of achieving higher sales.

4   Investment possibilities revealed by the head of finance in reviewing the cash flow shown by the plan, the valuation of the company's assets and the likelihood of raising further funds.

5.4.2 Approvals

The first important stage in the annual planning cycle is reached when the preliminary plans are presented to the chief executive for review. This corresponds to boxes 22 and 25 of the network scheme of Figure 4.33.

The review is carried out in the light of:

1   The basic objectives and policy of the company.

2   The specific objectives given to each of the planning units according to the contribution required of them toward the corporate objective of profitability.

3   The preliminary plans and proposals of the individual planning units, which when integrated with those of the corporate headquarters, form the corporate plan as a whole.

If the preliminary plans show general compliance with the original objectives of the company, approval is given by the chief executive using the vehicle of a second planning letter which is briefer and simpler than the first letter. This occurs at the 'repeat' stages numbered 23 to 29 in the network scheme.

In this, the simplest case, the approval authorizes the preparation of the appropriate final plans. The work which is then called for, again involving the corporate planner when and where necessary, consists of the refining of preliminary plans, producing action programmes and more detailed budgets which show such things as planned variances in production, quarterly budgets as the basis for control during the first year of the plan, and the development of projects which involve outside agencies. These are the items which were either not called for, nor justified, at the stage of preliminary planning and until approval in principle has been received.

If the response in the preliminary plans is at variance with the objectives set in the planning letter or shows gaps in the use of the existing resources, several courses are open:

1   Where the objective has been met and corporate resources for example in manufacture, are not fully utilized, a higher objective level is proposed for sales, and a request is made that this be reflected in the final plan.

2   When the objective has not been met and it is clear that the planning effort is inadequate, further consideration is asked for. In this case the chief executive may suggest other strategies he believes would be worthwhile, the use of which should be incorporated in the final plan.

3   When the objective cannot be met, in which case the chief executive may accept a plan, but request that special studies of projects be started concerning the problems and constraints, in order that future planning decisions can be made beneficially.

ACTION PLANNING TEST LIST 26

QUESTIONS	RESPONSE BY	TIMING OF ACTION ARISING
1 How, and at which stage, are preliminary plans coordinated: (*a*) informally (*b*) formally?	Corporate planner	
2 What questions are to be answered when preliminary plans are formally integrated?	Corporate planner	
3 Under what conditions are preliminary plans approved and what is the procedure if they are not acceptable?	Corporate planner and chief executive	

The procedure of the preparation of final plans continues on the annual schedule of planning and is again coordinated by the corporate planner. Eventually their integration leads to the production of a final corporate plan which meets the objectives in the planning period or, in grave cases, leads to a revision of the basic objectives and policy of the firm.

The final plans are officially approved by the chief executive in the light of the foregoing comments though he always reserves the right to examine problem areas more closely on a personal basis.

The stages at which coordination and approvals are called for, suggested by the foregoing, are in keeping with illustrations in Figures 4.32 and 4.33 in Section 4.8 dealing with the annual schedules for planning and the network scheme giving the interactions and timetables for associated planning units in the firm.

SECTION 6

Monitoring and Control

6.1   General remarks   209
6.2   Format of control reports   210
6.3   Preparation and presentation of control reports   212
6.4   Variances   213
6.5   Frequency of reporting   214

SECTION 6

Monitoring and Control

6.1 GENERAL REMARKS

No purpose would be served by compliance with the procedures of the practical phases of planning in the absence of an equally well-organized procedure for the reporting of results in a manner which affords a direct comparison of performance with the intended effort. In practical terms, *we need to see how we are doing.* Consequently a formal check on actual results against planned results is an essential feature of the overall process of corporate planning as a way of management.

It is for this reason that the planned activities are formally recorded in a series of quantified and measurable budgets. Most of the budgets in the last chapter of each plan are in financial terms, some are in terms of personnel data or volume of sales, while others are in ratios or percentages. All of them are in terms which enable the actual progress of business to be measured during the control period using exactly the same yardsticks. The insistence on the use of highly standardized forms in the presentation of plans is precisely for this purpose. The sections dealing with standard forms and budgets in Section 5 foreshadows this principle in that the breakdown of the budget data into quarters for the first year of planning continues into the quarterly control forms on a line-by-line basis. Action programmes also written only for one year contain timetables and other numerical features which are the basis of the periodic measurements of the planned activities of their author and his staff.

Sections 6.2 and those following deal more specifically with the format and presentation of control reports.

Although the recording and reporting of business results is required for other purposes than the control of planned operations, such as the ordinary accounting of the firm for invoicing and payments, for legal and tax purposes, the control data on actual performance has a further value in that it contributes each year to the enrichment of the information base on which future planning is more accurately and realistically based. In addition to data on the firm's own performance, the continuous inflow of up-to-date news on external events is particularly useful and is added to the information base of the planning unit concerned.

It is rare that actual results conform exactly to those of the plan. Deviations, referred to as *variances,* arise in practice much more often than compliance, but it is a key feature of corporate planning that their cause is identified as early as possible, regardless of whether the variance is plus or minus.

Remedial action in the case of negative variances is taken so that the original objectives are achieved, while objectives are reconsidered in the event of positive variances indicating new opportunities.

6.2 FORMAT OF CONTROL REPORTS

The collective contents of control reports for each planning unit are arranged to present the following elements:

1 Statistics of the actual performance of the unit against the budget in its plan.
2 Reasons for any variances which may have arisen.
3 Reasons for any variances in the action programmes.
4 New information, its impact and the corrective action called for.

Standard control forms of the type C illustrated in Appendix I are prepared to correspond to each of the budgets in the original plan. The results are shown for the first, second, third or fourth quarter (as the case may be) of the first planning year, together with the variance from the planned budget of the corresponding quarter, expressed in absolute terms and as a percentage of the original whenever possible. The basis of the data used is that shown in the budget form which divides the year into quarterly working periods, that is, the form B-Q which is a part of the budget chapter in each plan.

The control form C also contains a column headed 'Year 1 Revisions' in which is shown the effect of the quarterly variances on the planned results for the year as a whole. Such revisions call for confirmation by the chief executive, according to the explanations provided and discussed at the control meetings, described later in this part of the workbook.

In all cases the control report form C showing the actual results is directly related, on a line-for-line basis, to the second and third classes of standard planning forms for annual and quarterly budgets, that is, forms B and B-Q shown in the table of Appendix I.

Accounting for the variances in performance shown on C forms and for variances in the progress of action programmes is effected through the personal explanations of the author of the plan given on a summary sheet. Any impact on the planned results is stated, especially if this affects the end of the year results. Since action programmes are common to all planning units, accounts of progress on them are given in all control reports.

Enquiries into the reasons for all types of variances are conducted by the next higher authority with the person responsible, on the lines proposed in Section 6.4, dealing with variances. Before the control reports are presented the author is required to review the statistics of his actual performance in order to propose counter-action to deal with any variances which have arisen.

SUMMARY CONTROL REPORT	COMPANY BUSINESS DIVISION FUNCTION		YEAR QUARTER or, or,	SIGNATURE OF AUTHOR OF REPORT
Item and reference	Account of variance		New action proposed, by whom and when	Impact on further quarters and year end results
	Inside control	Outside control		
Budgets B—1—Q B—2—Q B—3—Q etc				
Action programmes —1 —2 —3 etc				
Developments in information base —1 —2 —3 etc				

Figure 6.1 Summary control report (covering quarterly reports and new information)

211

New information, including any being reported as the cause of variances and likely to be recurring in its impact, is listed briefly on the summary sheet. The specific impact in outstanding cases is shown as well as the action which is proposed either to counter an adverse effect, or to exploit new opportunities which are revealed.

The overall impact is shown in revision of the year-end estimates, especially in operating statements and financial objectives. Where new information will influence the practical phases of planning in the next annual cycle of work, new information is also noted by the corporate planner to ensure its inclusion in the information base of the unit concerned.

The style of summary sheet which is recommended is that of Figure 6.1 which provides a standard format for the personal account of the variances, their causes and effect. This form, together with the corresponding C forms, is the basis of the collective contents of each quarterly control report.

It goes without saying, that the review of the full year's activity, is afforded by the report for the fourth quarter. This review forms one of the most important starting points for the ensuing cycle of planning.

6.3 PREPARATION AND PRESENTATION OF CONTROL REPORTS

The preparation of reports is a task of the corporate planner using the organized accounting data in the company for financial reports, sales and personnel data from the corresponding units, collective information in the case of capital investment projects and as a result of personal discussion with the responsible individuals in the case of action programmes. In many of these cases data processing services are the ideal source of management information provided the corporate planner has ensured harmony between the programmes for routine information services and those required for planning and control purposes. The principle is repeatedly emphasized in the workbook that, as experience in planning is gained, many older types of information services give way to fewer systems for both planning and routine accounting purposes.

In the case of larger organizations, control reports are prepared by the divisional planner or whoever has been deputed in the first instance, to be the chief aide of the divisional head in the preparation of the original plan.

The chief assistance given by the planner is in the assembly of data on performance, and although he may draft the explanations for the variances and collect the items of new information and its impact, *this is done on behalf of the author of the plan.* The complete report is finally edited by the head of the unit who appends his signature, thus taking responsibility for the actual results and accounting for the variances. The procedure is similar to that used in the preparation of preliminary and final plans, as outlined in Section 5.1.1.

The collective control report is either discussed on a person-to-person basis with the chief executive or the head of level 2 in the case of lower-level plans, the corporate planner standing in for support and reference, or circulated in advance of a divisional meeting, which is attended by members of the divisional staff (heads of sub-units). The meeting is also attended by the corporate planner and possibly also by the head of the corporate finance function. The chief executive, following the role described on his behalf in Section 2.3, attends divisional meetings and, if he wishes, takes the chair. For him it is a further opportunity to demonstrate his support of corporate planning as his chosen way of management. In practice it affords him a regular opportunity to meet the senior members of the unit, and to appraise them as well as their operations. There are considerable motivational benefits to be gained by this procedure.

Review meetings of either sort, when properly prepared, need take little more than an hour or so, unless serious issues have been raised concerning actual results against plans. In the extreme case of compliance with plans, there may indeed be no cause for a review meeting, on the basis of management by exception only.

An important advantage to the chief executive of review meetings is to enable a discussion to take place of variances and problems that are associated with the plan. On this basis the approval of amendments to the plan involving agreed changes in objectives and strategies, can be carried out without delay.

At the levels of top management and the board of the company, the chief executive presents his corporate report on the overall progress towards the corporate objectives in the same way as the head of a planning unit at level 2. The control report in this case is drafted by the corporate planner (aided when necessary by the head of the finance function), drawing heavily on the control reports of the units at level 2 in the firm as well as on information and results which affect the company as a whole. Both the corporate planner and the head of finance normally attend presentations at board meetings in support of the chief executive. Again, the chief executive edits and finalizes the corporate control report. As in previous cases of actual results complying with plans, little time need be taken in their review.

The scheduling of periodic review meetings depends primarily on the speed with which control information becomes available. With modern procedures, using computer resources, review meetings of units involved in planning should be possible within seven to ten days after the end of the period to be reviewed. The higher level corporate reviews should be possible within five to seven days of the review of units at level 2 in the company.

Reviews of progress at later times than those suggested lose their value and impact, the results become stale, decisions are left open and untoward events will be cumulative in their effect. The lower the operational level of planning in a concern, the quicker are variances perceived and the more quickly they need corrective action (receipt of sales orders, level of debtors, cash-in-hand and so on). Similarly, the chief executive does not await the review of the corporate control report by his board before taking action with his immediate executives at level 2 in the firm.

The preparation of the time schedule for review meetings is the responsibility of the corporate planner. He acts as convenor and records decisions on changes which may arise, ensuring that they are built into the revised budgets of the unit for the outstanding period of the year, and later taken into account during the next cycle of planning. Changes which arise must be reflected in the final profit figures for the unit and the company as a whole.

6.4 VARIANCES

Control reports which show that actual results are substantially in line with plan call for little or no management time, other than to recognize that *progress is on plan*. The time and effort of management are involved when actual results are at variance from the planned objectives as measured by the budgets. This indeed is the principle of management by exception. In practice the involvement of the next level of management is called for only when deviations from plan are sufficient to demand interim action of a corrective nature, or the acceptance of actual results in the light of the explanations that are forthcoming.

The nature of the item in question dictates what sort of variance is tolerable and what sort demands action.

Occasional variances of $\pm 2\text{-}5\%$ are tolerable provided they are not recurring. No action is needed in these cases. Greater variances of 5-10% call for enquiry and explanation, while still greater variances call for grave enquiries and action on all accounts.

Guidelines such as these are set up by the corporate planner in accordance with the basic policy of the firm, the criterion being the extent of their influence on the profit objectives of the firm. Variances of agreed orders of magnitude which call for enquiry should be marked on C control forms.

Variances can be revealed not only in financial terms but through data on volume of sales, personnel and manufacturing performance and in the timetables of projects for capital expenditure and those called for in action programmes.

Management by exception calls for intervention and action on the following lines:

1 Examination if the assumptions were reasonable in the first place.
2 If new and untoward events have occurred which could not possibly have been foreseen (rapid changes in raw material costs, new legislation, the imposition of quotas on exports, etc). In these events new base lines are set up, and no stigma or blame is attached to the head of the planning unit for variances against plan. The variances are outside his control or foresight. The results which are measured and attributed to him are solely those which lie under his own control. Alternatively, the following questions may be asked:
3 Was the information base incorrect, or inadequate?
4 Were the objectives set too high, or too low?
5 Were the best strategies chosen?
6 Were the most appropriate action programmes set up? In these events, lessons are learned and revisions are made, or further questions arise:
7 Was the planning simply carried out badly overall?
8 Was there simply a lack of adherence to the planned action programme, and if so, exactly by whom was there a shortcoming?

In many of these cases, such as 7, there is a reflection upon the chief executive in accepting the plans in the first case, while in the case of 8 the corrective called for by the higher management is clear.

From the lines of approach described it is clear that control is not simply effected by the comparison of financial or other statistics, but by the examination of the *management action that was involved,* both in the initial preparation of the plans and in the execution of the planned activities. Furthermore, control is not effected by comparison against the results of the previous year but solely by the progress which is being made towards the planned objectives of the first year of the planning period. Finally, control is measured in respect of the performance against the controllable items within the area of responsibility of the head of the planning unit.

6.5 FREQUENCY OF REPORTING

The frequency of reporting for control purposes depends not only on the sort of activity in which the firm is engaged but also upon the level at which the information is produced.

At lower operating levels where all the details of all the daily transactions of the firm are handled, much routine management information is available on either a daily or a weekly basis (number and value of orders received and executed, delivery performance schedules, cash receipts and payments, bank balances, debtors, production and stock data and so on). Other information needs reporting only at wider intervals (such things as capital expenditure, personnel data, sales by major industries and product groups).

From the various types of information which arise, control reports which bear directly on unit and corporate plans are prepared for presentation, usually on a quarterly basis, though monthly reporting against the items of the budgets in the plans is necessary in some sorts of businesses. Concerns engaged in highly seasonal sales programmes (agricultural chemicals, tourism, garden tools, Christmas gifts) or involving the purchase of agricultural products which arise on a seasonal basis, or have peak periods of the use of personnel for outdoor work or holiday hotel catering, justify a different basis of reporting.

Notwithstanding the corporate policy to have a formal monthly or quarterly basis of reporting upon progress against plans, an early signal noted at any operating level of the company and which is indicative of a wide variance becomes the basis of immediate enquiry. Management action in exceptional cases is taken without waiting for the next formal review meeting. The planning system is not the master of the management but the opposite. Good planning is intended to minimize the impact of irregularities by the anticipation of foreseeable events, whether beneficial or adverse, but it is both logical and necessary to react to trends and significant variations as soon as they are discerned.

ACTION PLANNING TEST LIST 27   **Section 6**

QUESTIONS	RESPONSE BY	TIMING OF ACTION REQUIRED
1 What is the purpose of control reports, and why are they designed analogously to the budget and quarterly budgets in part 6 of each plan?	All management	
2 How are variances from performance highlighted and accounted for, and by whom?	All management	
3 Who prepares control reports, and who signs them? Who accounts for them and to whom?	All management	
4 What is the effect of new information and who reacts to it?	Corporate planner and all management	
5 What is the response to developments outside the control of the author of a plan?	Corporate planner and all management	
6 Has a precise time schedule been set up for: (a) the preparation (b) the presentation and (c) the accounting of performance with respect to control reports?	Corporate planner	
7 What signals of performance are available prior to the preparation of control reports, and how are they acted upon?	All management	

APPENDIX I

Standard Forms for Planning and Control Purposes

The appendix contains illustrations of the key forms concerned and a table which classifies them according to their use in one or other parts of plans or in the control system which operates during the first planning year. The following notes should clarify the system of standard forms and its use.

PURPOSE

The purpose of the use of standard planning forms is two-fold:

1 To enable the same format to be used by more than one, and preferably by all, planning units. To this end, most of the forms contain a box which carries the name of the particular unit using it. In practice, this is either the company, a business or a function. In some cases, sales planning forms are used to show sales, profits or market shares, by a similar arrangement of box headings.
2 To facilitate the hierarchical accumulation of data, on a line-by-line basis, from lower levels to the next higher level, until at the company level a comprehensive total is shown for the whole organization. In addition this is done over similar planning periods, be they years or quarters.

CLASSES OF FORMS

Apart from the use of standard forms for the information base in the practical phases of planning which have already been described in Section 4, four other classes of standard forms are used in the overall process of integrated management planning. These are shown in Appendix I as:

CORPORATE PLANNING LEVEL — Subject form and number	COMPANY LEVEL 1				BUSINESS DIVISIONS LEVEL 2				FUNCTIONS LEVEL 2 OR FUNCTIONS LEVEL 3			
Part of plan or control → Period covered →	Parts 1–5	Part 6 budgets		Control	Parts 1–5	Part 6 budgets		Control	Parts 1–5	Part 6 budgets		Control
	–5 to 5 years	–2 to 5 years	Quarters in year 1	Each quarter year 1	–5 to 5 years	–2 to 5 years	Quarters in year 1	Each quarter year 1	–5 to 5 years	–2 to 5 years	Quarters in year 1	Each quarter year 1
1 Operating statement (P and L, ratios, etc)	P–1	B–1 for company, B–1 for each business division	B–1–Q	C–1 for company, C–1 for each business division	P–1	B–1 for business division, B–1 for sub-business	B–1–Q for business division, B–1–Q for sub-business	C–1 for business division, C–1 for sub-business	No standard form	Shown on corresponding form for company or business division		
2 Sales planning (Sales by value, volume, profit and markets)	P–2	B–2	B–2–Q	C–2	P–2	B–2 for business division and sub-business, B–2–1/5 for sub-markets	B–2–Q for business division and sub-business and sub-markets	C–2 for business division and sub-business and sub-markets	X	X	X	X
3 Assets — Fixed assets, Current assets	P–3	B–3–FA, B–3–CA	(B–3–Q)	(C–3)	P–3	B–3–FA, B–3–CA	(B–3–Q)	(C–3)	If appropriate, use forms shown for company and business divisions			
4 Capital expenditure (Investment projects)	P–4	B–4	B–4–Q	C–4	P–4	B–4	B–4–Q	C–4	P–4	B–4	B–4–Q	C–4
5 Sources and use of funds (Cash flow and allocations etc)	P–5	(B–5)	(B–5–Q)	(C–5)	As for company level 1 if appropriate				X	X	X	X

6 *Financial statement* (Balance sheet)	P–6	(B–6)	(B–6–Q)	(C–6)	X	X	X	X	X	X	X	X
7 *Use of production capacity* (Planned use of manufacturing resources)	P–7	B–7	(B–7–Q)	(C–7)	P–7	B–7	(B–7–Q)	(C–7)	P–7	B–7	(B–7–Q)	(C–7)
8 *Personnel* (Numbers, categories, costs and ratios etc)	(P–8) based on Figure 4.13	X	(B–8–Q)	(C–8)	(P–8) based on Figure 4.13	X	(B–8–Q)	(C–8)	(P–8) based on Figure 4.13	X	(B–8–Q)	(C–8)
9 *Action programmes*	(P–9) based on Figure 4.29	X	X	See variance control report Figure 6.1	(P–9) based on Figure 4.29	X	X	See variance control report Figure 6.1	(P–9) based on Figure 4.29	X	X	See variance control report Figure 6.1

Notes:

P forms are summaries, used in parts 1–5 of a plan
B forms are only used in the budget, part 6, of a plan
B–Q forms are only used in the budget, part 6, of final plans
C forms are used in the quarterly control report procedure in year 1 of the five year planning period and are summarised on the form of Figure 6.1
X indicates that the item is not called for
The level of use of a standard planning form is shown by the choice of the appropriate form heading
Form numbers in brackets indicate that no illustration is provided, but that guidance is given in the accompanying text for the design of a suitable version

Table of standard forms for planning and control purposes

P forms, which are summaries of key data used in parts 1 to 5 of each plan in order to provide a quick appreciation of the features of each plan. They are always based on the corresponding budget forms.

B forms, which give the detailed budgets for each of the five planning years and are contained in part 6 of each plan.

B-Q forms, which show the quarterly breakdown of the budget data for the first planning year. They are only included in part 6 of final plans.

C forms, prepared quarterly during the first year of the plan and which show the actual results against the planned results in the B-Q forms.

OPERATING STATEMENTS

Operating statements are used at the company and business division levels. The vertical line code (1-20) relates to more detailed statements (usually expenditure) prepared by the subunits in support of the senior unit named at the head of the form.

By the choice of the alternative series of box headings shown on form B-1, it is used to show planning data for a named unit in respect of the totals for each of the five planning years or to show the breakdown of the data for a given year in respect of the subunits concerned.

In the event of the use of the form by a business division, lines 8.0, 9.0, 10.0, 11.0, 15.0 and 16.0 remain unused, unless there is a corporate accounting system of allocating these items.

The first two columns of the operating statement B-1, showing historical data, come into use only when the form shows a total for the first of the five planning years (total year—X). Similarly, the column headed 'total year—X' is used only when the form displays the breakdown of the data of a senior unit to its components in a given year.

FORMS NOT ILLUSTRATED

In the table of the appendix, certain form numbers are enclosed in brackets. These forms are not the subject of illustration, but in practice are easily prepared by the corporate planner using the vertical headings of the corresponding B or B-Q forms and using other forms of which illustrations are provided (for example C forms) as models.

In the case of forms which have a relation to the legal and tax obligations of the company, the preparation of the appropriate forms should be carried out jointly with the head of finance in order that the correct harmonization is achieved. Such cases are the profit and loss statements, the balance sheet, and, also desirable, the cash flow data.

FORMS COMPLETED WITH ILLUSTRATIVE PLANNING DATA

In certain cases, chiefly the summaries of financial items, capital expenditure projects and the use of production capacity, the forms have been completed by *the use of simplified data indicating the style of use*. In addition, the data used demonstrate the growth of benefits to the shareholders resulting from various planning objectives. The growth in profits is shown to rise, both in absolute terms and in relation to the assets used, first, through the increase of sales and margins and also through the use of reserves in production capacity and the improvement of key working ratios.

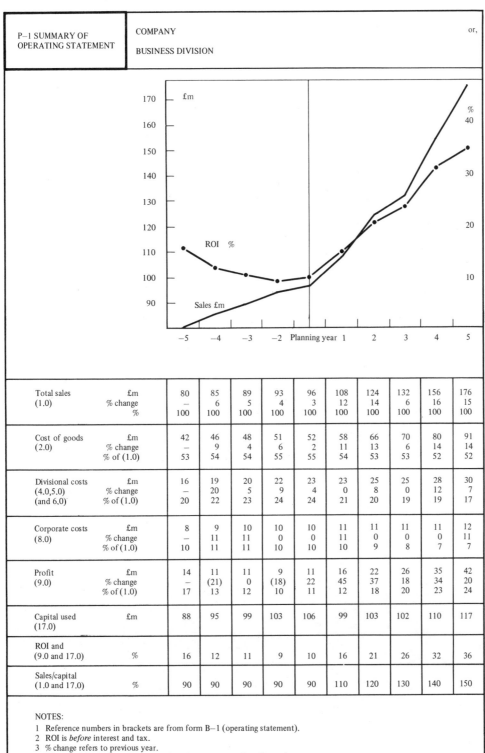

P–1 SUMMARY OF OPERATING STATEMENT	COMPANY BUSINESS DIVISION									or,
		−5	−4	−3	−2	Planning year 1	2	3	4	5
Total sales (1.0)	£m % change %	80 — 100	85 6 100	89 5 100	93 4 100	96 3 100	108 12 100	124 14 100	132 6 100	156 16 100	176 15 100
Cost of goods (2.0)	£m % change % of (1.0)	42 — 53	46 9 54	48 4 54	51 6 55	52 2 55	58 11 54	66 13 53	70 6 53	80 14 52	91 14 52
Divisional costs (4.0,5.0) (and 6.0)	£m % change % of (1.0)	16 — 20	19 20 22	20 5 23	22 9 24	23 4 24	23 0 21	25 8 20	25 0 19	28 12 19	30 7 17
Corporate costs (8.0)	£m % change % of (1.0)	8 — 10	9 11 11	10 11 11	10 0 10	10 0 10	11 11 10	11 0 9	11 0 8	11 0 7	12 11 7
Profit (9.0)	£m % change % of (1.0)	14 — 17	11 (21) 13	11 0 12	9 (18) 10	11 22 11	16 45 12	22 37 18	26 18 20	35 34 23	42 20 24
Capital used (17.0)	£m	88	95	99	103	106	99	103	102	110	117
ROI and (9.0 and 17.0)	%	16	12	11	9	10	16	21	26	32	36
Sales/capital (1.0 and 17.0)	%	90	90	90	90	90	110	120	130	140	150

NOTES:
1 Reference numbers in brackets are from form B–1 (operating statement).
2 ROI is *before* interest and tax.
3 % change refers to previous year.
4 When used for business division, omit corporate costs, unless allocated

Planning form P-1: summary of operating statement

B–1 OPERATING STATEMENT					COMPANY or, BUSINESS DIVISION or, SUB-BUSINESS

Company, Business division or Sub-business				Value: £'000 Volume: units	
Year 2		Planning year			
	%		%	0	
					Home sales (volume) Export sales (volume)
	100		100		Total sales volume
				1.1	Home sales (gross)
				1.2	Export sales (gross)
	100		100	1.0	Total sales value
				2.0	Cost of goods
				3.0	Gross profit (1-2)
				4.1	Sales administration
				4.2	Promotion
				4.3	Service
				4.4	Distribution
				4.0	Total selling expenses
				5.0	Division research and development costs
				6.1	Division headquarters
				6.2	Function M
				6.3	Function N etc
				6.0	Divisional headquarters and functional costs
				7.0	Profit divisional
				8.1	Company headquarters
				8.2	Purchasing function
				8.3	Central R & D function
				8.4	Personnel function
				8.5	Finance function etc
				8.0	Company headquarters and functional costs
				9.0	Company profit (before interest and taxes)
				10.0	Interest
				11.0	Taxes
				12.0	Net profit (after interest and taxes)
				13.0	Depreciation (2, 4, 5, 6 and 8)
				14.0	Cash flow (12 and 13)
				15.0	Dividends
				16.0	Cash flow after dividends
				17.0	Capital used: Fixed Current Total
				18.0	% ROI (9 : 17)
				19.0	% Sales/capital (1 : 17)
				20.0	% Market share

Planning form B-1: operating statement

NOTE:	This form has several uses:

1. Showing the company total divided into business divisions in a single planning year (X)
2. Showing a business division total divided into sub-businesses in a single planning year
3. Showing company, business division or sub-business totals for the past two, and for each of the future five planning years.

According to its use, so the appropriate lines (0–20) are involved.

Company or business division total year X		Business division A or sub-business P		Business division B, or sub-business Q		Business division C, or sub-business R		Business division D, or sub-business S		Business division E, or sub-business T	
		Company, business division, or sub-business									
		Year 1		Year 2		Year 3		Year 4		Year 5	
	%		%		%		%		%		%
	100		100		100		100		100		100
	100		100		100		100		100		100

COMPANY
BUSINESS DIVISION or,
SUB-BUSINESS or,

NOTE: Each form B–1 calls for the use of the corresponding B–1–Q form. According to its use, so the appropriate lines (0–20) are involved.

B–1–Q OPERATING STATEMENT		Q1	%	Q2	%	Q3	%	Q4	%	Total Year 1	%
	Value: £'000 Volume: units										
0											
	Home sales (volume)										
	Export sales (volume)										
	Total sales volume		100		100		100		100		100
1.1	Home sales (gross)										
1.2	Export sales (gross)										
1.0	Total sales value		100		100		100		100		100
2.0	Cost of goods										
3.0	Gross profit (1–2)										
4.1	Sales administration										
4.2	Promotion										
4.3	Service										
4.4	Distribution										
4.0	Total selling expenses										
5.0	Division research and development costs										
6.1	Division headquarters										
6.2	Function M										
6.3	Function N etc										
6.0	Divisional headquarters and functional costs										

7.0	Profit divisional				
8.1	Company headquarters				
8.2	Purchasing function				
8.3	Central R & D function				
8.4	Personnel function				
8.5	Finance function etc				
8.0	Company headquarters and functional costs				
9.0	Company profit (before interest and taxes)				
10.0	Interest				
11.0	Taxes				
12.0	Net profit (after interest and taxes)				
13.0	Depreciation (2, 4, 5, 6 and 8)				
14.0	Cash flow (12 and 13)				
15.0	Dividends				
16.0	Cash flow after dividends				
17.0	Capital used: Fixed / Current / Total				
18.0	% ROI (9 : 17)				
19.0	% Sales/capital (1 : 17)				
20.0	% Market share				

Planning form B-1-Q: operating statement for quarters in year 1

C–1 OPERATING STATEMENT	COMPANY BUSINESS DIVISION SUB-BUSINESS	or, or,	NOTE: Each form C–1 calls for the use of a corresponding C–1–Q form. According to its use, so the appropriate lines (0–20) are involved

Value: £'000 Volume: units			Quarter				Year 1	
			Actual		Variance from budget		Revisions	
0				%		%		%
	Home sales (volume) Export sales (volume)							
	Total sales volume			100		100		100
1.1	Home sales (gross)							
1.2	Export sales (gross)							
1.0	Total sales value			100		100		100
2.0	Cost of goods							
3.0	Gross profit (1–2)							
4.1	Sales administration							
4.2	Promotion							
4.3	Service							
4.4	Distribution							
4.0	Total selling expenses							
5.0	Division R & D costs							
6.1	Division headquarters							
6.2	Function M							
6.3	Function L etc							
6.0	Divisional headquarters and functional costs							
7.0	Profit divisional							
8.1	Company headquarters							
8.2	Purchasing function							
8.3	Central R & D function							
8.4	Personnel function							
8.5	Finance function etc							
8.0	Company headquarters and functional costs							
9.0	Profit (before interest and taxes)							
10.0	Interest							
11.0	Taxes							
12.0	Net profit (after interest and taxes)							
13.0	Depreciation (2, 4, 5, 6 and 8)							
14.0	Cash flow (12 and 13)							
15.0	Dividends							
16.0	Cash flow after dividends							
17.0	Capital used: Fixed Current							
	Total							
18.0	% ROI (9 : 17)							
19.0	% Sales/capital (1 : 17)							
20.0	% Market share							

Control form C-1: operating statement

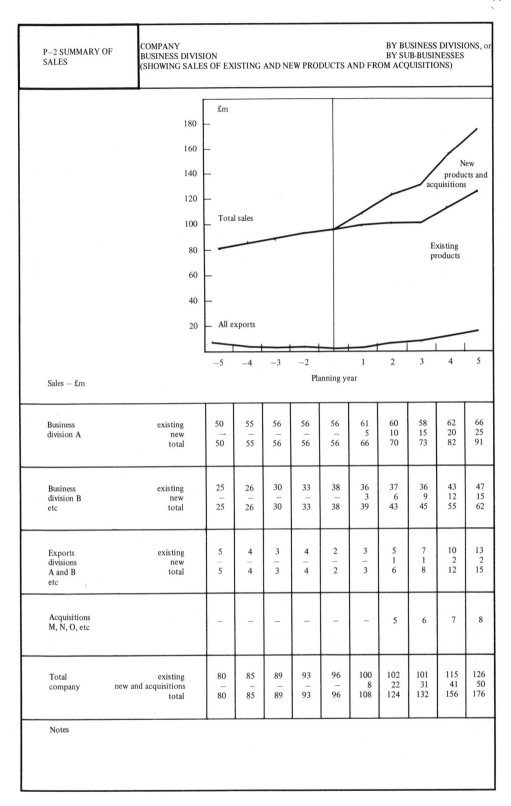

| P–2 SUMMARY OF SALES | COMPANY
BUSINESS DIVISION
(SHOWING SALES OF EXISTING AND NEW PRODUCTS AND FROM ACQUISITIONS) | BY BUSINESS DIVISIONS, or
BY SUB-BUSINESSES |

Sales – £m

		−5	−4	−3	−2	−1	1	2	3	4	5
Business division A	existing new total	50 — 50	55 — 55	56 — 56	56 — 56	56 — 56	61 5 66	60 10 70	58 15 73	62 20 82	66 25 91
Business division B etc	existing new total	25 — 25	26 — 26	30 — 30	33 — 33	38 — 38	36 3 39	37 6 43	36 9 45	43 12 55	47 15 62
Exports divisions A and B etc	existing new total	5 — 5	4 — 4	3 — 3	4 — 4	2 — 2	3 — 3	5 1 6	7 1 8	10 2 12	13 2 15
Acquisitions M, N, O, etc		—	—	—	—	—	—	5	6	7	8
Total company	existing new and acquisitions total	80 — 80	85 — 85	89 — 89	93 — 93	96 — 96	100 8 108	102 22 124	101 31 132	115 41 156	126 50 176

Notes

Planning form P-2: summary of sales

COMPANY
BUSINESS DIVISION
SUB-BUSINESS
BUDGET OF SALES or PROFITS, or MARKET SIZES or MARKET SHARES

BY BUSINESS DIVISIONS, or
BY SUB-BUSINESSES, or
BY PRODUCT GROUPS

NOTES:
1 Value in £000
2 Volume in units
3 Existing and new products

B–2 SALES PLANNING ANNUAL TOTALS YEARS 1 TO 5		Year – 1		Year – 2		Year – 3		Year – 4		Year – 5	
Total sales or profits etc by divisions, or sub-businesses, or product groups		Value	Volume	Value	Volume	Value	Volume	Value	%	% Value	% Volume
A	Existing New Total										
B	Existing New Total										
C	Existing New Total										
D	Existing New Total										
E etc	Existing New Total										
Export	Existing New Total										
Total	Existing New										
Totals											

This form is used to show the following, with the appropriate sub-headings above:

Planned sales by value and volume or market sizes by value and volume

Planned profit by value and % on sales value

Market shares by % value and % volume

Planning form B-2: sales planning

B-2-1/5 SALES PLANNING SUB-MARKETS YEARS – 1/2/3 4 OR 5	COMPANY BUSINESS DIVISION SUB-BUSINESS BUDGET OF SALES or PROFITS, or MARKET SIZES or MARKET SHARES								BY SUB-BUSINESSES, or BY PRODUCT GROUPS			NOTES 1 Value in £'000 2 Volume in units 3 Existing and new products

Planning form B-2-1/5: sales planning for sub-markets

229

B-2-Q SALES PLANNING QUARTERS IN YEAR 1	COMPANY BUSINESS DIVISION SUB-BUSINESS BUDGET OF SALES or PROFITS, or MARKET SIZES or MARKET SHARES									BY DIVISIONS, or, BY SUB-BUSINESSES, or BY PRODUCT GROUPS			NOTES: 1 Value in £'000 2 Volume in units 3 Existing and new products
Sales or profits etc by divisions or sub-business, or product groups	Quarter 1		Quarter 2		Quarter 3		Quarter 4			Total year 1			
	Value	Volume	Value	Volume	Value	Volume	Value	%		% Value	% Volume		
A — Existing / New / Total													
B — Existing / New / Total			This form is used to show the following, with the appropriate sub-headings above: Planned sales by value and volume or Market sizes by value and volume				Planned profit by value and % on sales value			Market shares by % value and % volume			
C — Existing / New / Total													
D — Existing / New / Total													
E etc — Existing / New / Total													
Export — Existing / New / Total													
Total — Existing / New													
Totals													

Planning form B-2-Q: sales planning for quarters in year 1

C-2 SALES CONTROL REPORT FOR QUARTER

COMPANY
BUSINESS DIVISION
SUB-BUSINESS
CONTROL REPORT ON SALES and PROFITS WITH REVISIONS FOR
END OF THE YEAR TOTAL

BY DIVISIONS, or
SUB-BUSINESSES, or
PRODUCT GROUPS

NOTES:
1 Value in £'000
2 Volume in units
3 Existing and new products

Sales and profits by divisions, or sub-businesses, or product groups	Sales — Actual		Sales — Variances		Profits — Actual		Profits — Variances		Sales — Year 1 revisions		Profits — Year 1 revisions
	Value	Volume	Value	Volume	Value	%	Value	%	Value	Volume	%
A — Existing / New / Total											
B — Existing / New / Total											
C — Existing / New / Total											
D etc — Existing / New / Total											
Export — Existing / New / Total											
Total — Existing / New											
Totals											

Control form C-2: sales

Appendix I

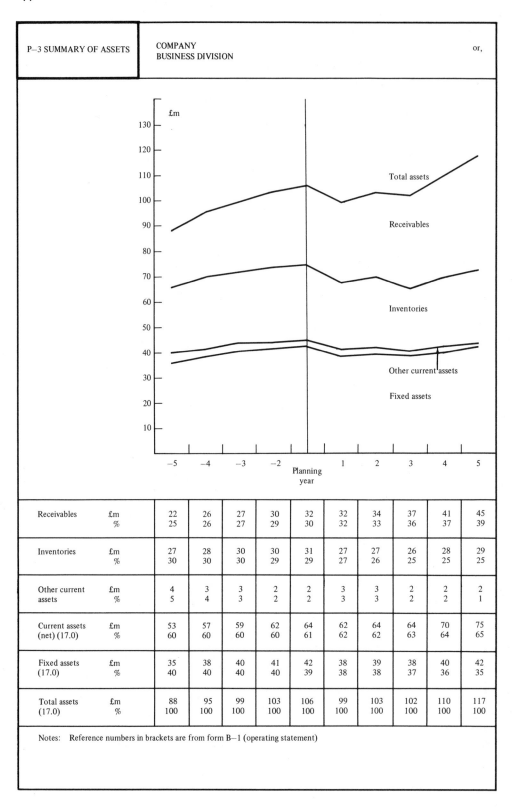

P–3 SUMMARY OF ASSETS	COMPANY BUSINESS DIVISION									or,

Receivables	£m	22	26	27	30	32	32	34	37	41	45
	%	25	26	27	29	30	32	33	36	37	39
Inventories	£m	27	28	30	30	31	27	27	26	28	29
	%	30	30	30	29	29	27	26	25	25	25
Other current assets	£m	4	3	3	2	2	3	3	2	2	2
	%	5	4	3	2	2	3	3	2	2	1
Current assets (net) (17.0)	£m	53	57	59	62	64	62	64	64	70	75
	%	60	60	60	60	61	62	62	63	64	65
Fixed assets (17.0)	£m	35	38	40	41	42	38	39	38	40	42
	%	40	40	40	40	39	38	38	37	36	35
Total assets (17.0)	£m	88	95	99	103	106	99	103	102	110	117
	%	100	100	100	100	100	100	100	100	100	100

Notes: Reference numbers in brackets are from form B–1 (operating statement)

Planning form P-3: summary of assets

B—3—FA BUDGET FIXED ASSETS	COMPANY BUSINESS DIVISION FUNCTION COMPANY HQ and others	BY BUSINESS DIVISIONS & FUNCTIONS or BY SUB-BUSINESSES, etc				All values in £'000

Divisions, functions, etc	−2	Planning year	1	2	3	4	5
Business division A Land Buildings Equipment Others Total							
Business division B (etc) Land Buildings Equipment Others Total							
Function A Land Buildings Equipment Others Total							
Function B (etc) Land Buildings Equipment Others Total							
Company headquarters etc Land Buildings Equipment Others Total							
Company totals Land Buildings Equipment Others Total							

Notes: 1 Shared resources are apportioned
2 Unallocatable assets are shown under company headquarters (others)
3 Annual totals correspond with the fixed assets in P—3 (summary of assets)

Planning form B-3-FA: fixed assets

| B—3—CA BUDGET CURRENT ASSETS | COMPANY BUSINESS DIVISION FUNCTION COMPANY HQ and others | BY BUSINESS DIVISIONS & FUNCTIONS or, BY SUB-BUSINESSES, etc | | | | All values in £'000 Weeks shown as (X) etc |

Divisions, functions, etc	−2	Planning year	1	2	3	4	5
Business division A 　Receivables 　Raw material stocks 　Finished goods 　Others 　　　Total	50 (x) 20 (y) 25 (z) 5 100						
Business division B (etc) 　Receivables 　Raw material stocks 　Finished goods 　Others 　　　Total							
Function A 　Receivables 　Raw material stocks 　Finished goods 　Others 　　　Total							
Function B (etc) 　Receivables 　Raw material stocks 　Finished goods 　Others 　　　Total							
Company headquarters etc 　Receivables 　Raw material stocks 　Finished goods 　Others 　　　Total							
Company totals 　Receivables 　Raw material stocks 　Finished goods 　Others 　　　Total							

Notes:　1　Functions may not need this summary
　　　　2　Annual totals correspond with the current assets in P—3 (summary of assets)
　　　　3　The number of weeks covered is shown in brackets and is included wherever applicable

Planning form B-3-CA: current assets

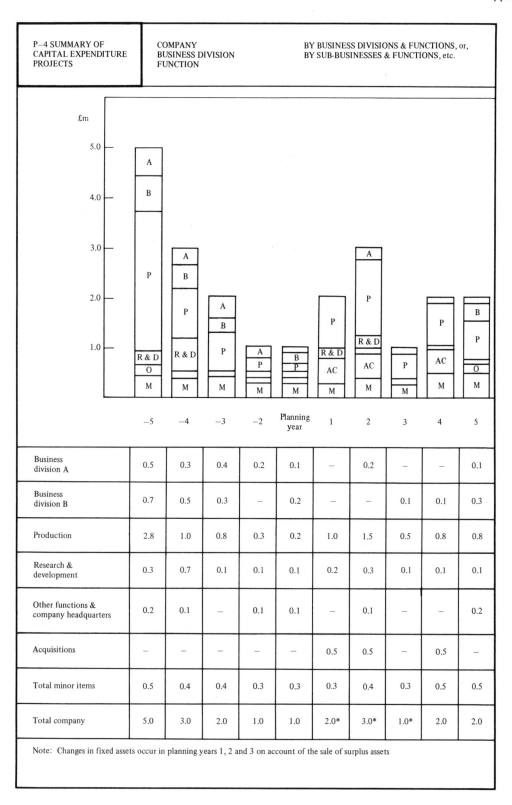

P-4 SUMMARY OF CAPITAL EXPENDITURE PROJECTS	COMPANY BUSINESS DIVISION FUNCTION				BY BUSINESS DIVISIONS & FUNCTIONS, or, BY SUB-BUSINESSES & FUNCTIONS, etc.					

	−5	−4	−3	−2	Planning year	1	2	3	4	5
Business division A	0.5	0.3	0.4	0.2	0.1	−	0.2	−	−	0.1
Business division B	0.7	0.5	0.3	−	0.2	−	−	0.1	0.1	0.3
Production	2.8	1.0	0.8	0.3	0.2	1.0	1.5	0.5	0.8	0.8
Research & development	0.3	0.7	0.1	0.1	0.1	0.2	0.3	0.1	0.1	0.1
Other functions & company headquarters	0.2	0.1	−	0.1	0.1	−	0.1	−	−	0.2
Acquisitions	−	−	−	−	−	0.5	0.5	−	0.5	−
Total minor items	0.5	0.4	0.4	0.3	0.3	0.3	0.4	0.3	0.5	0.5
Total company	5.0	3.0	2.0	1.0	1.0	2.0*	3.0*	1.0*	2.0	2.0

Note: Changes in fixed assets occur in planning years 1, 2 and 3 on account of the sale of surplus assets

Planning form P-4: summary of capital expenditure projects

COMPANY
BUSINESS DIVISION
FUNCTION

NOTES: 1 All values in £m
2 Bar lines show schedules

Ref-erence	Project description and location, objective etc	Planning year and schedule					Project total	Analysis of total			
B-4 CAPITAL EXPENDITURE PROJECTS		1	2	3	4	5		Land	Buildings	Plant etc	Miscel-laneous
1	Plant installation in existing building on site B. Increase of capacity by 500 units per annum Objective no. 2 hydraulic transmission		0.3	0.1			0.4	–	–	0.4	–
2	Building and plant installation on site B. Increase of capacity by 500 units per annum. Objective no. 3 hydraulic transmission				0.4	0.1	0.5	–	0.1	0.4	–
3	Acquisition of ABC Co. Ltd, London. Capacity of 1000 pneumatic transmission units per annum Market value £5m Objective no. 4		2.0				2.0	0.3	0.3	0.9	0.5
4, 5, etc											
M	Minor capital projects	0.1	0.2	0.1	0.2	0.1	0.7	–	–	–	0.7
T	Totals	0.1	2.5	0.2	0.6	0.2	3.6	0.3	0.4	1.7	1.2

Planning form B-4: capital expenditure projects

B-4-Q CAPITAL EXPENDITURE PROJECTS QUARTERLY BUDGETS

COMPANY
BUSINESS DIVISION
FUNCTION

YEAR 1

NOTE: All values in £'000

Reference	Project description etc	Total costs	Overall schedule Quarter – Year Start	Overall schedule Quarter – Year Finish	Expenditure by quarters 1	2	3	4	Total in year 1
1									
2									
3									
4, 5, etc	Minor projects								
M									
T	Totals								

Planning form B-4-Q: capital expenditure projects for quarters in year 1

C–4 CAPITAL EXPENDITURE PROJECTS CONTROL REPORT	COMPANY BUSINESS DIVISION FUNCTION		or, or,	QUARTER YEAR 1			NOTE: All values in £'000	
Project description, total cost and overall schedule	Approved for this quarter	Actual this quarter	Account for variances — give revisions and new completion date	State revised schedule and expenditures				
				Quarters	Year 1			Year 2
Ref-erence				1	2	3	4	1, etc
1								
2								
3								
4, 5 etc								
M — Minor projects								
T — Totals								

Control form C-4: capital expenditure projects

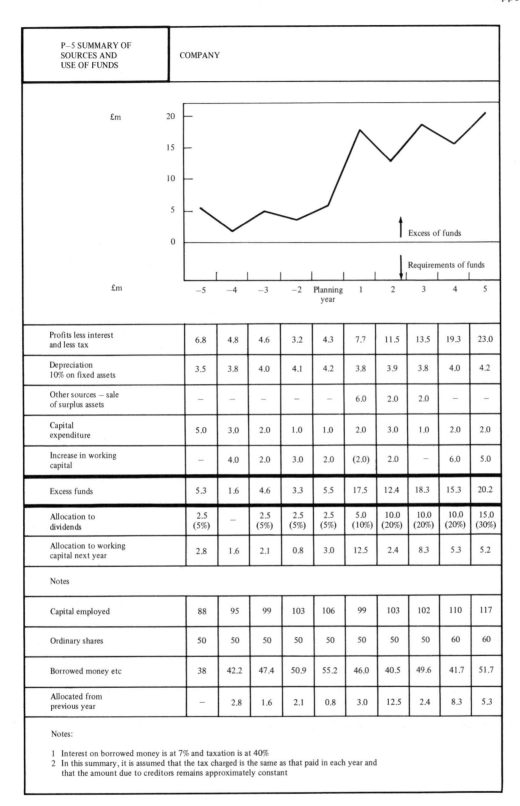

P–5 SUMMARY OF SOURCES AND USE OF FUNDS	COMPANY									
	−5	−4	−3	−2	Planning year	1	2	3	4	5
Profits less interest and less tax	6.8	4.8	4.6	3.2	4.3	7.7	11.5	13.5	19.3	23.0
Depreciation 10% on fixed assets	3.5	3.8	4.0	4.1	4.2	3.8	3.9	3.8	4.0	4.2
Other sources – sale of surplus assets	–	–	–	–	–	6.0	2.0	2.0	–	–
Capital expenditure	5.0	3.0	2.0	1.0	1.0	2.0	3.0	1.0	2.0	2.0
Increase in working capital	–	4.0	2.0	3.0	2.0	(2.0)	2.0	–	6.0	5.0
Excess funds	5.3	1.6	4.6	3.3	5.5	17.5	12.4	18.3	15.3	20.2
Allocation to dividends	2.5 (5%)	–	2.5 (5%)	2.5 (5%)	2.5 (5%)	5.0 (10%)	10.0 (20%)	10.0 (20%)	10.0 (20%)	15.0 (30%)
Allocation to working capital next year	2.8	1.6	2.1	0.8	3.0	12.5	2.4	8.3	5.3	5.2
Notes										
Capital employed	88	95	99	103	106	99	103	102	110	117
Ordinary shares	50	50	50	50	50	50	50	50	60	60
Borrowed money etc	38	42.2	47.4	50.9	55.2	46.0	40.5	49.6	41.7	51.7
Allocated from previous year	–	2.8	1.6	2.1	0.8	3.0	12.5	2.4	8.3	5.3

Notes:

1 Interest on borrowed money is at 7% and taxation is at 40%
2 In this summary, it is assumed that the tax charged is the same as that paid in each year and that the amount due to creditors remains approximately constant

Planning form P-5: summary of sources and use of funds

P–6 SUMMARY OF BALANCE SHEET	COMPANY								NOTE: All values in £m

Balance sheet items	−5	−4	−3	−2	Planning year	1	2	3	4	5
Assets:										
Receivables	22	26	27	30	32	32	34	37	41	45
Inventories	27	28	30	30	31	27	27	26	28	29
Other current assets	4	3	3	2	2	3	3	2	2	2
Total current assets	53	57	59	62	64	62	64	64	70	75
Fixed assets	35	38	40	41	42	38	39	38	40	42
Others										
Total long term assets	35	38	40	41	42	38	39	38	40	42
Total assets	88	95	99	103	106	99	103	102	110	117
Liabilities:										
Banks										
Others										
Total current liabilities	38.0	42.2	47.4	50.9	55.2	46.0	40.5	49.6	41.7	51.7
Share capital	50	50	50	50	50	50	50	50	60	60
Reserves and retentions	–	2.8	1.6	2.1	0.8	3.0	12.5	2.4	8.3	5.3
Total liabilities	88	95	99	103	106	99	103	102	110	117

Note: Items are after allocations to dividends shown in P–5 (sources and use of funds)

Planning form P-6: summary of balance sheet

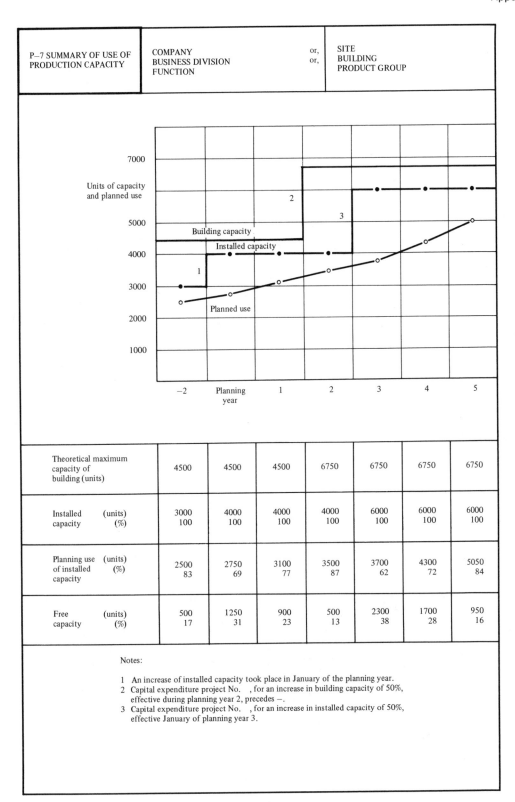

P–7 SUMMARY OF USE OF PRODUCTION CAPACITY	COMPANY BUSINESS DIVISION FUNCTION	or, or,	SITE BUILDING PRODUCT GROUP			

	−2	Planning year	1	2	3	4	5
Theoretical maximum capacity of building (units)	4500	4500	4500	6750	6750	6750	6750
Installed (units) capacity (%)	3000 100	4000 100	4000 100	4000 100	6000 100	6000 100	6000 100
Planning use (units) of installed (%) capacity	2500 83	2750 69	3100 77	3500 87	3700 62	4300 72	5050 84
Free (units) capacity (%)	500 17	1250 31	900 23	500 13	2300 38	1700 28	950 16

Notes:

1 An increase of installed capacity took place in January of the planning year.
2 Capital expenditure project No.   , for an increase in building capacity of 50%, effective during planning year 2, precedes −.
3 Capital expenditure project No.   , for an increase in installed capacity of 50%, effective January of planning year 3.

Planning form P-7: summary of use of production capacity

B—7 PRODUCTION PLANNING	COMPANY PRODUCTION FUNCTION or, BUSINESS DIVISION PRODUCTION FUNCTION				PRODUCTION BY SITE, or SITE BY BUILDING, or BUILDING BY PRODUCT GROUP				NOTES: 1 Volume in units. 2 Cost per unit in £	
Production by — site, or, building, or, product group	Year 1		Year 2		Year 3		Year 4		Year 5	
	Number of units	Unit cost	Number of units	Unit cost	Number of units	Unit cost	Number of units	Unit cost	Number of units	Unit cost
A										
B										
C										
D										
E										
F										
G										
H										
I										
J etc										
Totals		TC		TC		TC		TC		TC

Note: Depending on the product assortments, unit costs may be meaningless in the line of 'totals' hence, give total cost of units produced (TC)

Planning form B-7: production planning

B–8 PERSONNEL NUMBERS, COSTS AND RATIOS	COMPANY BUSINESS DIVISIONS FUNCTIONS	BY BUSINESS DIVISIONS & FUNCTIONS, or BY SUB-BUSINESSES & FUNCTIONS, or etc	NOTES: Total costs, sales, and assets are in £'000 Average costs per person per year in £

	−2	Planning year	1	2	3	4	5
Divisions and functions: 1 Business division A 2 Business division B etc 3 Function A 4 Function B etc							
Categories: 1 Senior management 2 General management 3 Supervisory 4 Operatives							
Total number of personnel							
Total cost of personnel							
Average cost per person per year							
% change in average cost on year before							
Sales per employee							
Assets per employee							

Notes: 1
2

Planning form B-8: personnel

APPENDIX II

Technological Forecasting

In the workbook, technological forecasting (TF) has been discussed briefly in connection with the information base on technology (Section 4.3.5) and in the unit plan for the R & D department of a firm (Section 5.3.3). In view of the considerable importance of developments in technology and information on them as an input to corporate planning, especially to corporate development through the planning of R & D programmes, and even more on account of the lack of information on its organized use in planning, Appendix II is provided and consists of:

1 An extensive list of TF methods which are classified in order to show how they contribute to a comprehensive forecast in terms of the qualitative, quantitative, time and probability elements of a forecast.
2 A procedure to be followed for the initial deployment of TF in a company as part of the process of corporate planning once this has passed its first cycle of use.
3 Further procedures and tasks to be followed-up by the corporate planner in cooperation with R & D for the continuous updating of technological forecasts.

For a first approach to the many methods and terminology used in TF the corporate planner is referred to *Technological Forecasting*, by Gordon Wills, *et al.*, published in the Pelican Library of Business and Management. Those planners and R & D personnel already familiar with TF methodology are referred to the regular issues of *Futures*, published bimonthly by the IPC Science and Technology Press Ltd, UK, and of *Technological Forecasting And Social Change*, published quarterly by the American Elsevier Publishing Co. Inc., of New York, for more advanced papers on the subject.

1   Qualitative methods (yield narrative descriptions of forecast events ie scenarios without dimensions)
     1.1   Intuitive thinking of any kind, brain-storming, synectics and the study of hypothetical situations
     1.2   Analogies — historical, biological and geographic
     1.3   Time independent contextual mapping and modelling
     1.4   Relevance tree approach
     1.5   Morphological analyses and reconstructions
     1.6   Gap analysis — Mendeleyev type
     1.7   Signals of technological change and science fiction, etc.

2. Quantitative methods and/or   } applied to a given qualitative forecast to
                                           } give performance level and/or

3. Time methods   } time imminence in years
3.1   Time series analyses and projections of simple physical dimensions, functional capabilities, economic, demographic and sociological dimensions against time
3.2   Development of time series curves to yield 'S' curves, and finally, envelope curves
3.3   Learning curves
3.4   Relationships between two non-time dimensions
3.5   Input and output and relevance matrices, or substitution models, on a time basis
3.6   Quantitative models
3.7   Quantified analogies as in 1.2
3.8   Delphi methods when systematic methods are not available on account of the lack of numerical data, etc

4   Probability assessments
     4.1   Delphi
     4.2   Cross impact
     4.3   Gaming methods, etc

Notes: 1   Many methods in 2 and 3, yield quantitative and time forecasts simultaneously
            2   Delphi methods used for 2 or for 3 singly, should prescribe the scenario, 3 or 2 as the case may be, and also an assumed probability
                  Likewise, when used for probability, the first three elements should be prescribed

The four elements of a comprehensive technological forecast and the methods which contribute to them

1   Catalogue of scenarios

Corporate planning and R & D departments to invite contributions of scenarios, old or new, which will be *largely intuitive in origin*, from a wide range of corporate personnel such as planning, R & D, marketing, market research and services, etc. Provided the confidentiality of the scheme can be preserved consultants, friendly customers and suppliers may also be invited to contribute.
The two first mentioned departments also to contribute scenarios using *systematic methods* of generating qualitative forecasts, for example morphology, relevance approaches and others in class 1 of the table of methods in the appendix.

The scenarios from any source (usually dimensionless at this stage) should have a bearing, even though indirect, on the business of the firm. To preserve anonymity, a code number only should be used to identify the contributor.

2   Screening of scenarios

The scenarios are screened by an 'expert panel' drawn from senior members of planning, R & D, and marketing departments, their assessments being in terms of the meaning of the scenario, its newness and feasibility, whether large technological gaps are evident and whether the concept represents an opportunity or a threat to the firm.

3   Delphi exercise applied to surviving scenarios

A one-round, or preferably two-round, exercise, as to 'time' based on selected scenarios, and making assumptions as to the quantitative levels and a probability of 'very likely', that is, 75% plus.

4   Analysis and presentation

Surviving scenarios with an imminence of not more than 10 years are analysed by the planning and R & D executives for decisions as to opportunities for the company. These are presented to top management for corporate planning decisions as to objectives and strategy.

Procedure for the initial deployment of technological forecasting in a firm

1   R & D and planning personnel to review the work of the initial cycle of TF activity and refine any outstanding forecasts.

2   Market research staff to study any available data by time series methods to determine trends in economic and technical levels of known activities to help suggest quantitative and time elements in forecasts with a view to prescribing objectives for R & D.

3   R & D to study complex or higher-level forecasts to identify components which may be meaningful to the firm. Relevance tree analysis is called for in this case.

4   Planning and R & D staff to apply TF methods within the planning of R & D programmes themselves.

5   Business divisions, with the cooperation of the corporate planner, to organize a wider Delphi exercise applied to important scenarios which continue to emerge, or even upon important and publicly known issues. Key customers and consultants may participate provided that confidentiality can be assured.
     In some cases, such exercises may be applied to debatable corporate issues. Thus, major technological developments foreseen in any business or manufacturing area deserve such a formal treatment.

6   Corporate planning staff to keep abreast of new methods of TF and to prepare a manual of simple guidelines for future cycles of TF thus building it into the annual corporate planning programme.

7   The custodian of the catalogue of scenarios to institute a system of receiving, from any source, items of technological news which may have an impact and lead to new scenarios. 'Signals of technological change' are the keywords in this connection.

Further procedures for the updating of technological forecasting in corporate planning

APPENDIX III

Relationship between Annual Rate of Increase and Cumulative Increase over a Number of Years

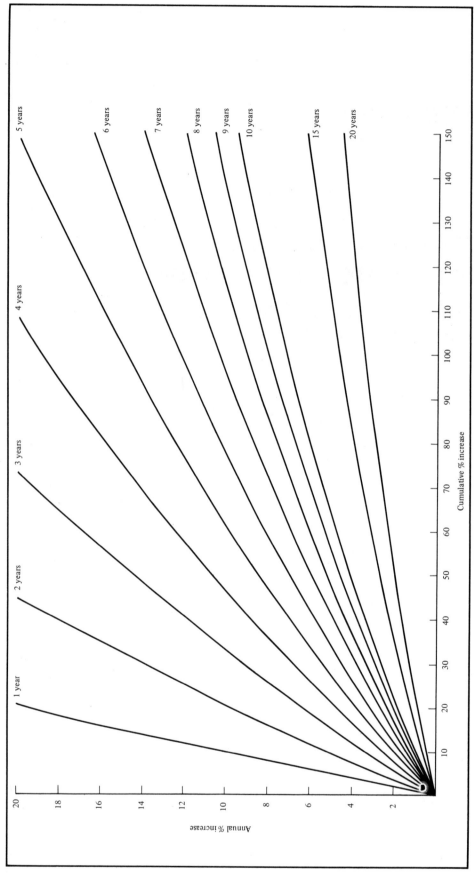

Appendix III   Relationship between annual rate of increase and cumulative increase over a number of years

Bibliography

Today there is an immense amount of literature on the subject of corporate planning and its component disciplines. Some books are of a general nature, some are anthologies of presentations on separate aspects and others concentrate on developing the detail of single subjects. Over and above these are journals, published at monthly or quarterly intervals, which provide for the regular updating of knowledge on most aspects of the subject.

Those mentioned below form only a starting point on the practice of corporate planning. The working practitioner would do well to extend his library, first by the judicious inclusion of appropriate anthologies—and possibly one or two other general treatises —but then by subscription to one of the journals mentioned. Afterwards would follow an interest in the publications and journals of each individual discipline and the reviews and notices of new books which are published in these journals.

GENERAL PUBLICATIONS ON PLANNING

Corporate Planning—a Practical Guide, by John Argenti, George Allen & Unwin, London, (1968), 271 pp.
Although one of the earliest treatises, this book still has a factual and down-to-earth style, laying great stress on the basic stages of planning for profitability.
Introducing Corporate Planning, by David E. Hussey, Pergamon Press, Oxford, (1971), 210 pp.
A very readable book which might well be read after the present volume and which contains many practical tips from the author's wide experience.
Top Management Planning, by George A. Steiner, Macmillan, London (1969), 795 pp.
Without doubt this is the most comprehensive textbook on the subject and contains numerous case studies and quotations from American practice.

ANTHOLOGIES ON PLANNING

Business Planning for the Board, edited by Hugh Buckner, Gower Press, London, (1971), 216 pp.

Corporate Planning, Selected Concepts, edited by Basil W. Denning, McGraw-Hill, London, (1971), 373 pp.

Handbook of Strategic Planning, edited by Bernard Taylor and Kevin Hawkins, Longman, London, (1972), 456 pp.

Planning Series, I, II, and III, Reprints from the *Harvard Business Review,* over recent years, Boston, USA, 555 pp total.

SPECIAL TREATISES ON ASPECTS OF PLANNING

Decisions, Strategies and New Ventures, by W. G. Byrnes and B. K. Chesterton, George Allen & Unwin, London, (1973).

Planning for Products and Markets, by Douglas Foster, Longman, London, (1972).

Technological Forecasting, by Gordon M. Wills *et al.,* Penguin, London, (1972), 281 pp.

Corporate Planning and the Management Accountant, edited by Philip Sadler and Alan Robson. A joint publication from the Society for Long Range Planning and the Institute of Cost and Management Accountants, London, (1973).

Case Studies in Corporate Planning, edited by Peter Baynes for the Society for Long Range Planning, Pitman, London, (1973).

JOURNALS

Long Range Planning (the journal of the Society for Long Range Planning), published quarterly by Pergamon Press, Oxford. First issued September 1968.

European Bibliography of Corporate Planning, 1961–71, issued as a supplement to *Long Range Planning,* in June 1972, 21 pp.

Managerial Planning, a bimonthly publication, PO Box 70, Oxford, Ohio, 45056, USA.

Technological Forecasting and Social Change, published quarterly by the American Elsevier Co., New York. First issued June 1969.

Futures, published bimonthly by IPC Science and Technology Press UK in cooperation with the Institute for the Future USA. First issued September 1968.

After these references to an extended bibliography, there would come an interest in more highly specific subsectors of planning such as are provided by publications on manpower, finance, operations research, corporate policy, R & D management, and the like and which would only be met by reference to those catering for the specialist worker or professional executive with such functional responsibilities.

Index

Accountants 173
Accounting system 111–12, 173
Acquisitions 84, 86, 104
Action planning test lists 6, 17, 29, 34, 37,
    40, 43, 48, 52, 55, 65, 73, 76, 82, 85, 87,
    90, 92, 106, 110, 114, 116, 120, 166, 174,
    200, 204, 216
Action programmes 4, 13, 26, 35–6, 38, 57,
    88, 94, 103–6 *passim,* 109–11, 119,
    163–5 *passim,* 169–72 *passim,* 203,
    209–12 *passim,* 214
  contents of 109
  format of 109–11, 154
  supervisory responsibility for 111
  in unit plans 175, 178–9, 182, 186, 190–1,
    194, 197, 201
Administration 30–1
Annual planning schedule 105, 117–19,
    158–9, 204
Approvals 118, 202, 203–4
Assumptions 24–5, 35, 53, 57–63 *passim,*
    71, 88–91, 130, 168–9, 214
  corporate 89, 91, 93, 115, 189
  and their levels 89–91, 118, 169
  in unit plans 177, 181, 184, 188–9, 193,
    196–7, 199

'Backwards' diversification 86, 201
Balance of payments 62

Balance sheets 27, 179, 196, 218
Banking 30, 175
Bank lendings 59, 72
Board of company 176, 213
Borrowing 72, 179, 197
'Bottom upwards' methods 64, 98, 102, 117
Brand name 80
Budgets 4, 13, 26–7, 35, 38, 71, 104, 105,
    111–15, 163–4, 168–71 *passim,* 172–6,
    201–3 *passim,* 209, 210
  annual 113
  divisional 113
  format of 59, 112, 167, 175, 202
  quarterly 95, 113, 119, 179, 195, 201,
    203, 209
  in unit plans 174, 179, 183–4, 187, 191–2,
    195, 198
Buildings 67, 69, 133, 191 *see also* fixed
  assets
Business
  definition of 53–6, 150
  function of 53–4, 96
Business portraits 86–8, 145
Business ratios 78–9, 101, 112, 167, 182,
  196, 209

Capital 66, 71, 72, 112
  key uses of 69
  reserves of 72

Capital expenditure projects   27, 170, 172, 202, 212, 214, 218
  in unit plans   179, 183, 186–7, 191, 198
Capital investment, *see* investment
Case studies and examples   35–6, 57, 63, 64, 68, 75, 79–80, 89, 96, 99, 177–8, 181–2, 202
Cash flow   72, 172, 179, 202, 218
Central Statistical Office   60, 95
Centre for Interfirm Comparison (London) 79
Charts   30, 66
Chief executive   9, 16, 31–2, 58, 83, 101–2, 179, 192, 194, 202, 212–13 *passim*
  and approvals   203–4, 210
  and planning letters   6, 15, 37, 71, 89, 94, 115, 117, 193, 203
  responsibilities of   11, 14, 41, 53, 172, 175, 202
  role of   11–13
  and workbook   5
Company, analysis of   91
Company manual   6, 13, 16, 41
Company seminar   14
Company services, *see* management services
Competitor analysis   64, 83–6, 143, 177, 189
Computers   57, 108, 165, 191, 193
  capacity   70
Consultants   14–15, 27, 64, 189
Contingency plans   30, 35
Contractors   186
Contract R & D   191
Contributions   112, 114
Control   13, 21, 26–7, 109, 112–13, 164, 170, 209 ff.
Control reports   112, 164, 173, 215
  forms   59, 167, 179, 184, 210–12, 214
  frequency of   214–15
  quarterly   173, 210, 212
  preparation and presentation of   212–13
Cooperation   26, 66, 84, 93, 171, 188, 189, 202
Coordination   66, 94, 165, 184, 192, 199, 201–3, 204
Corporate development   10, 11, 16, 27–30, 35, 38, 41, 44, 47, 86, 97, 118
Corporate image   80
Corporate plan   31, 38, 88, 118, 175–9, 181, 203–4
Corporate planner   16, 38, 84, 192
  advice and assistance of   13, 165, 176, 184, 194, 197
  appointment of   14, 41

Corporate planner *continued*
  and budgets   112–13
  job specification of   11, 41, 44–7
  office location of   10–11, 32
  and resources   66, 68, 70–2
  role and responsibilities of   10, 13–14, 30, 53, 60–1, 62, 66, 80, 83, 88, 93, 101–2, 109, 117, 175, 199, 201–4, 212–14 *passim*, 218
  and technology   56, 57
  and workbook   5–6, 13
Corporate planning
  basic model of   21ff
  definition of   3–4
  development of   10–11, 15–16
  introduction of   14
  as management tool   9–10
Cost centres   70, 112
Cost control   95
Costs
  allocatable   64
  corporate   64, 71, 113
  of planning operation   26
Credit   62, 66, 199
Credit and debit accounts   27, 72
Critical path network   118
Current assets   171, 172, 179, 183, 177, 198
Customer calls   100
Customer contacts   84, 189

Data processing   197, 212
Debentures   72
Decision-making   21, 26, 108, 190
Decision tree   103, 104, 188, 190
Delegation of responsibility   9, 37–8, 164
Department of Trade and Industry   60
  Business Monitors   64
Depreciation   62, 69, 72, 98, 196
Development areas   62
Distribution   30
Diversification   97
  see also Backwards diversification
Dividends   172, 196
Divisional management committee   180
Divisional planners   10
Dunn and Bradstreet Reports on Key Business Ratios   79, 99
Duty list   91

Economic indicators   58, 88
Economist Intelligence Unit (London)   69
Engineering design   97, 188

Environmental problems 186, 189
Equipment and machinery 67–9, 94, 191
Exchange rates 62, 88
Executive committee 176
Expenditure
  divisional 164
  statements of 173
Exports 59, 61, 64
External events 56, 58–63, 88, 89, 127–9,
  168

Feed-back 25, 32, 35, 51, 56, 57, 69, 71,
  165
Final plans 35, 94, 102, 105, 111, 165, 171,
  173, 184, 203–4
Finance 41, 66, 71–2, 94, 137
  requirements in 171, 178–9, 183, 187,
  191, 195, 198, 201
Finance department 4, 26, 30–1, 72
  head of 111, 172, 175–6, 179, 202–3,
  312–13
  plans of, 195–8
Financial Times Actuaries Share Index
  lists 99
Fiscal indicators 58, 61
Five year unit plans 118, 173, 179, 195
Fixed assets 66, 67-70, 72, 74, 98, 170–1
  requirements in unit plans 178, 179, 183,
  184, 186–7, 191, 194, 197–8, 201
Forecasts, forecasting 3, 5, 16, 25, 51,
  56–63 *passim*, 88, 89–91, 93, 98, 102–3,
  118, 168, 177, 192
Fortune's survey of industry 99
Funds, allocation and generation of 172,
  179, 196
'Futures planning' 16

'Gap' 100
'Go it alone' 14
Goodwill 66
Gross domestic product (GDP) 57, 59,
  60–1, 63, 130
Growth 10, 54, 84, 93, 96, 97
  annual 108
  rates of 25, 26
  targets of 98
  see also profits; profitability
Guidelines 22–4, 54–6, 66, 121

Hire purchase 30
House journals 193, 195

Imports 59, 64
Increase, annual and cumulative 249–50
Independent interviewers 80, 84
Index of Industrial Production 63
Indicators, indices 58–63, 99–100, 123–30,
  195
  cost 60, 62, 71, 125
  depreciation 69
  international 59, 88, 89, 123, 168, 176
  major industries and business 60–1, 64,
  126
  national 59–60, 88, 89, 124, 168, 176
  other 61–2
  volume 64
Industrial development 189
Industrial outputs 64
Inflation 64, 88, 99, 100
Information 5, 193, 212
Information base 15, 16, 24–5, 27, 30,
  51–3, 56ff, 95, 97, 99–104 *passim*, 118,
  133–48, 164, 170, 212, 217
  analysis of 93, 96, 189
  compilation of 91, 146
  in unit plans 181, 186, 199
Innovation 97
Input-output matrices 95
Insurance 30, 175, 193, 196, 197
Integrated management planning 10, 11,
  16, 27–30, 41, 44, 46, 113, 118, 217
Interest rates 62
Interfirm comparisons 71, 95, 99, 101, 144
Internal events 56
Investment 69, 72, 172, 203
Investment department 30
Investment grants 62
Investment policy 171, 186

Job specifications 44–8

Key customers 61
Key factors for success 15, 16, 77–81, 83,
  177, 185, 189, 193, 196, 199
  examples 79–80
  measurable 78–9
  other 79–80
Key information 168, 169, 177, 181, 185,
  188–9, 193, 196, 199
Know-how 67, 72, 172, 182, 184, 189

Labour 60, 186
Labour turnover 70, 100

Land 67, 69, 133
Legal controls 186, 189
Leisure 62
Licensing 26, 72, 77, 97, 104, 182
London Graduate School of Business
  Studies 60
Long range planning 4, 10, 30, 33–5, 38
Long term loans 72
Long term trends 27
Looping process, *see* feed-back

Macro-indicators 59–60, 62, 63, 168
Management by crisis 9
Management development 192, 194
Management by exception 27, 213–14
Management information personnel 66
Management by objectives 4, 10, 26, 109
Management services 30, 60, 95, 96, 113,
  196
Management style 54
Management training 15, 16, 192
Manufacturing, *see* production
Market demand 74
Marketing 30–1, 84, 86, 95, 142, 179, 180,
  182
  definition of 87
Marketing department 69, 70, 74, 83, 112,
  189, 203
  head of 91, 175, 188, 202
  plans of 179–80
Marketing strategy 61, 105–6
Market leaders 75
Market research 30, 41, 64, 66, 74, 84
Markets 25, 63, 84
  examples 63
Market shares 61, 63, 64, 95, 100, 102,
  108, 178, 182, 190
Medium range plans 33–5, 38
Meetings 14–15, 16, 212–13
Memorandum and articles 53
Mergers 84, 86, 97
Monetary indicators 58, 61–2
Monitoring 13, 41, 112, 164, 170, 209ff
Mono-divisional organization 31
Motivation 16, 70, 93, 193
Multi-divisional firms 30, 31–3, 88, 117
Multi-market company 59
Multi-national organizations 31, 175
Multi-regional organizations 31, 33, 175

National Health Service 71, 79

National Institute for Economic and Social
  Research 60
Nationalized industries 99
Network schemes 94, 118–19, 159, 202–3,
  204
Notices 193

Objectives 25–6, 57, 71, 81, 93–4, 97–102,
  103, 108, 163–4, 169, 210
  basic approach to 61, 98, 99–101, 151
  basic corporate 3, 5, 13, 22–4, 26, 35, 38,
    51, 53–6, 77–8, 94, 98, 101–2, 115, 121,
    176, 203
  and competition 86
  divisional 3, 13, 36, 102, 115, 117, 203
  in first planning cycle 101–2
  functional approach to 53–4, 96
  minimum 63, 100
  normative 100–1
  revision of 25, 89, 204, 213
  in unit plans 177, 181–2, 186, 189, 192–4,
    197, 199
Obsolescence, 74
Operating statements 173, 179, 180, 183,
  218
Operational research 41
Opportunities 4, 25–6, 30, 56–7, 59, 61, 66,
  67, 74, 77–8, 93–7, 111, 148, 163–4, 169
  and competition 83, 86
  corporate 36, 78, 95, 181
  creation of 98, 190
  examples 96
  identification of 25, 96
  levels of 35, 61
  origin of 168
  quantified 25
  in unit plans 177, 181–2, 186, 189, 192–4,
    197, 199
  in use of resources 69, 71, 72
Optimization 108
Orders 100
Organizational defects 15–16
Organization for Economic Cooperation
  and Development 60

Packaging 97, 184, 186, 199
Pareto's Law 78
Patents 66, 74, 97, 100, 172, 189, 191
Pensions 62, 71, 193, 196
Performance data 56, 63–6, 101, 167, 212,
  214
Performance levels 81

Perrin   21
Personal income   59
Personnel   66, 70–1, 84, 136
   budgets   175, 209
   development and training of   97, 171,
      193, 203
   new   94
   requirements   171, 178, 183, 186–7, 191,
      192, 194–5, 197–8, 201, 202
   special   193
Personnel associations   193
Personnel costs   60, 70–1
Personnel department   30, 70–1, 171, 202
   plans of   192–5
Personnel engineering   193
Personnel planning form   71, 136
Personnel recruitment   26, 193–5
Pharmaceuticals   35–6, 79–80, 178, 182
Planning cycles   41, 97–8, 115, 168, 212
   first   15, 27, 53, 54–6, 57–8, 61, 68,
      80–3 passim, 92, 95, 100, 109, 117, 152,
      173
   second   80, 83
Planning department   26, 27, 41–4
Planning letters   6, 15, 37, 62, 71, 89, 94,
      115–17, 118–19, 169, 202
   contents of   117, 155
   No. 1   13, 156
   No. 2   105, 115, 165, 203
   in unit plans   177, 181, 184–5, 189, 193,
      197
Planning levels   35–8, 89
Planning officers   41
Planning periods   33–4, 38–40
Planning phases   15, 21–2, 51ff, 163
Plans
   format and presentation of   163–7
   kinds of   30–5
   length of   167
   parts of   167ff
Planning schedules, see annual planning
      schedule
Planning studies   16
Planning system   13
Plant capacity, see production capacity
Policy, policies   22–4, 54–6, 66, 94, 115,
      121, 172, 180, 194, 195, 204, 215
Political indicators   58, 62, 193
Population growth   59
Preliminary plans   35, 94, 104, 111, 113,
      115, 118, 165, 169, 171, 173, 183, 202,
      203
Price competition   69
Price trends   64, 199

Product assortment   61, 64, 68, 108, 182
Product costs   95
Product delivery service   95, 184, 199
Product groups   63, 95, 131–2
Production   67, 140, 179
Production capacity   68–9, 94, 108, 133,
      135, 178–82 passim, 184, 187, 218
   spare   108, 202
Production costs   69, 79, 195, 202
Production department   27, 30–1, 69, 70,
      75, 79, 117, 180, 202
   budgets of   175
   head of   175, 184–5, 202
   plans of   184–7, 198, 203
Product life   141
Products, new   61, 203
Profile questionnaire   86
Profitability   36, 54, 61, 63, 64, 72, 77–8,
      95, 102, 104, 108, 113, 168, 176, 182,
      190, 196
   diminutions of   98
   'flooring' of   99
   growth of   77, 94, 97, 98–9, 202
   ratios   112
Profit centres   31–2
Profit growth   10, 63, 97, 104, 218
Profit levels   25
Profit and loss statements   218
Profit objectives   152
Profit ratios   99
Promotion, promotional activities   30, 72,
      79–80, 94, 95, 97
Purchasing department   30, 86, 202
   plans of   198–201

Questionnaires   74, 83, 86, 96, 103–4, 202

Raw materials   60, 86, 100, 102, 185, 198–9,
      202
Regression analysis   57
Relevance trees   77
Remuneration   70, 71, 193
Research and development (R & D)   96,
      139, 179, 182
   expenditure   72, 95, 190
   results   27, 75
Research and development department   26,
      30–1, 70, 77, 98, 102, 104, 112, 117,
      165, 178, 180, 203
   plans of   187–92
Resource requirements   164, 169, 170–2,
      202

Resource requirements *continued*
   in unit plans 178–9, 183, 186–7, 191,
    194–5, 197–8, 201
Resources 24–6 *passim,* 66ff, 81, 94, 112,
   177, 186, 189–90
   allocation of 94, 190
   catalogues of 72
   cost of 94
   new 67
   unused 173
Retail selling 69, 175
Return on investment (ROI) 99, 113,
   177–8
Revisions 25, 204, 210
Risk element 99

Safety systems 97
Sales 30, 62, 63–4, 84, 94, 98, 102, 112, 180,
   186, 190, 203
Sales budgets 175, 199, 202
Sales income 61, 64, 164
Sales objectives 69
Sales programme 108, 183
Sales volume 26, 209, 214
Scholarships 195
Self criticism 81
Services, technical 30, 61, 95
Share capital 72
Shareholders 54, 71, 98, 172
Short range plans 33–5, 38
Social security contributions 71, 88
Social services 60, 62
Society for Long Range Planning 16
Sociological changes or indicators 58, 62,
   189, 193
Standardized forms 165–7, 201–2, 217ff
   classes of 217–8
   purpose of 217
   table of 219–43
Stock exchange analysts 79
Stocks 27
Strategies 3–4, 16, 25–6, 35–6, 38, 93–4, 97,
   100, 102–8, 153, 163–4, 169
   alternatives 72
   case study in 104–5
   corporate 77–8
   revisions in 145, 213
   systematic approach to 103–4
   in unit plans 181–2, 186, 189, 192–4, 197,
    199
   see also marketing strategy

Strengths and weaknesses 15, 78, 80, 81–3,
   96, 100, 138–42, 177, 185, 197, 199
   of competitors 86
   in resources 66, 189, 193
Summary 168, 173, 176–7, 180, 185, 188,
   192, 196, 199
Summary sheet 212
Suppliers 84, 86, 199, 201

Takeover 77
Taxes, taxation 58, 62, 88, 98, 196, 218
Technological change, signals of 77
Technological forecasting (TF) 41, 74–5,
   77, 177, 184, 189, 245–8
Technology 74–7, 189, 193, 199
Testing centres 191
Threshold objectives 100
Times survey of industry 99
Timetable network, *see* network schemes
Timetables 35, 109, 115, 117–19, 204, 209,
   213, 214
'Top-downwards' methods 64, 98, 102
Trade associations 64, 79
Trade controls 62
Trade unions 91, 186, 193
Training levies 62
Training programmes 27, 193–4, 195
Transferability of currencies 62

Unit plans 175ff
University of Cambridge, Department of
   Economics 60
Up-dating 21, 41

Variances 88, 210, 212, 213–14, 215
Volume growth 63
Volume indices 64

Wage rates 102
Welfare, welfare units 70, 71, 193
Workbook
   objectives of 4–5
   use of 6
   who should read 5–6
Working capital 171, 172, 179
Works infrastructure 68–9
World commodities 199